The Accompaniment

The Accompaniment

Assembling the Contemporary

PAUL RABINOW

The University of Chicago Press ❋ *Chicago and London*

PAUL RABINOW
is professor of
anthropology at the
University of
California, Berkeley.

The University of Chicago Press, Chicago 60637
The University of Chicago Press, Ltd., London
© 2011 by The University of Chicago
All rights reserved. Published 2011
Printed in the United States of America
20 19 18 17 16 15 14 13 12 11   1 2 3 4 5
ISBN-13: 978-0-226-70169-1 (cloth)
ISBN-13: 978-0-226-70170-7 (paper)
ISBN-10: 0-226-70169-7 (cloth)
ISBN-10: 0-226-70170-0 (paper)

Library of Congress Cataloging-in-Publication Data
Rabinow, Paul.
    The accompaniment : assembling the contemporary /
Paul Rabinow.
        p.   cm.
    Includes bibliographical references and index.
    ISBN-13: 978-0-226-70169-1 (cloth : alk. paper)
    ISBN-10: 0-226-70169-7 (cloth : alk. paper)
    ISBN-13: 978-0-226-70170-7 (pbk : alk. paper)
    ISBN-10: 0-226-70170-0 (pbk : alk. paper)
        1. Anthropology. 2. Interdisciplinary research.
3. Anthropology—United States. 4. Interdisciplinary
research—United States. 5. Geertz, Clifford. 6. Hyman,
Paul.   I. Foucault, Michel, 1926–1984.   II. Title.
    GN33.R25 2011
    301—dc22   2010045281

Contents

Introduction: Think About It

"We can't go on talking to each other," said Mr. K. to a man. "Why not?" asked the latter, taken aback. "In your presence I am incapable of saying anything intelligent," complained Mr. K. "But I really don't mind," the other comforted him. "That I can believe," said Mr. K. angrily, "but I mind."

«BERTOLT BRECHT[1]»

"He who bears knowledge has only one virtue: that he bears knowledge," said Mr. Keuner.

«BERTOLT BRECHT[2]»

The above are two of Bertolt Brecht's *Geschichten vom Herrn Keuner* (*Stories of Mr. Keuner*), the very, very short stories that Brecht began writing during the 1920s. Herr Keuner is nicknamed "the thinking man." Although Brecht never explained why he had chosen to name Mr. Keuner "the thinking man," Brecht's friend Walter Benjamin attempted to do so on several occasions. In a radio talk, Benjamin first interpreted the name as deriving from the Greek word *keunos*, meaning "concerning or pertaining to everyone." An etymologically related word in Greek, *koine*, means "everyday speech," and *koinon* refers to the political community. In short, these terms point to what is shared or understood by people in common. Such an interpretation is consistent, of course, and in its own distinctive way, with Brecht's Marxism.

Benjamin's second interpretation also involves a Greek reference. He proposed that *Keuner*, which as such has no particular significance, comes from the German *keiner*—no one. "Benjamin connects 'no one' or 'no man' to the reply that Odysseus gives the blinded one-eyed Cyclops, Polyphemus, as he escapes from the giant's cave. That is to say, continues Benjamin, Mr. Keuner . . . is both 'a man of many devices' like Odysseus and equally like Odysseus, is 'much traveled,' and 'much enduring.' Thus the name Keuner, in this interpretation, is itself a ruse, a device, camouflage for the 'no man' undermining the class state from within, seemingly accommodating to force."[3] This interpretation as well seems consistent with a certain style of Marxism.

Both of these interpretations, however, seem not quite right. The thinking man hardly seems to qualify as everyman in any society, and the ruses of the oppressed, weapons of the weak, whatever their other virtues, do not seem to be mainly about thinking. To be generous, I sense that Benjamin is being overly charitable to his friend; this sense is reinforced by Hannah Arendt's muted criticism of the artistic fate of Brecht's work when he returned from exile in the United States (with a Swiss passport at the ready) to head the Berliner Ensemble in East Germany. "Brecht's troubles," Arendt writes, "had started when he became *engagé* (as we would say today, but the concept did not exist then) when he tried to do more than be a voice, which was how he began. A voice of what? Not of himself, to be sure, but of the world and of everything that was real. Yet that was not enough. To be a voice of what he thought was reality had carried him far away from the real."[4] When Brecht starting speaking for everyone in a coded language, purportedly embellished with hidden Joycean meanderings, all the effects of the real, for which he is otherwise known, were dissipated.

Where I am leading us, what is most pertinent in the first of the two very, very short stories is Mr. Keuner's response. He responds with anger to the condescendingly comforting response of "a man." The response is appropriate because Mr. Keuner refuses the indifference that neglects to express care for the stakes of the situation. It is also appropriate because what is at stake is virtue, intellectual virtue, as the second very, very short story recounts. He who bears knowledge has the virtue of bearing it as well as having the obligation to care for the knowledge and the bearing of it. In sum, it is perfectly proper, nay required, for a citizen (of the world) to respond with *thumos,* spirited anger, when that virtue is devalued through indifference or Babbitry.

>>><<<

Ever since the publication of Nietzsche's 1873–75 *Untimely Observations,* philosophers and thinkers have had a new option named for them as one of the possible relations with (and to) the present and the past—the untimely (*inactuel, Unzeitgemasse*). To be untimely is a mode that is interdependent with the manner in which one understands and practices *observations* (or interventions, *betrachtungen*). Consequently, there are two connected but independent terms at play here: the "untimely" and "observations." Both are dependent, it turns out, on the mode of temporality in which, and with which, one positions oneself in the present. For Nietzsche, that time—and its ambiguous temporality—was the contemporary. The German term for the contemporary—*Zeitgenossen (Zeit, time, + Genossen, companions)*—can be inelegantly, if correctly, translated as "those who accompany us in time." Thus, to accompany others in time depends, because "to accompany" is a transitive verb, on where you are, where you are seeking to go, and with whom you want to be accompanied.

For Nietzsche, to be untimely meant not only to see through those things that were taken for granted by those writing during that historical period in Europe but also to diagnose the pathological symptoms and causes of their understandings. Thus, the affect associated with this use of the mode of the untimely is alternately one of *pathos* or *thumos.* For Nietzsche, at that historical moment, the main malady of the obsessions Europeans held that blinded them to their own blindness was their fetishization of history, their overvaluation of history as a privileged mode of understanding and as a privileged site of significance. Nietzsche's strategy for disrupting what he took to be the complacency of those living during his time alongside him was to craft a scathing critique designed to sear through their illusions, their self-satisfactions, as well as what he took to be their other insidious moral and intellectual failings. Of course, part of the scorn that Nietzsche directed toward his contemporaries derived from his sense that he, too, until recently, had shared these same illusions.

The form that Nietzsche gave to his critique was to center on the work of specific individuals—philosophers, artists, and cultural critics (Schopenhauer, Strauss, Wagner, and so forth)—a form he employed throughout his life. He shaped this form to suit an agonistic manner, a genre that often spilled over into the antagonistic. This manner of preceding is one that, once again it is worth remembering, he applied to himself as well as others; Nietzsche moved back and forth from the cut and thrust with specific individuals to diagnosing the *Zeitgeist* ("spirit of the times") with only "culture" (as in "German culture") operating as a mediating term in his scalar gymnastics. Ultimately, one can plausibly argue that these creators Nietzsche discursively sparred with were living at the same historical time as Nietzsche, but, he came to realize, they were not his contemporaries; he could not and would not accompany them either in the direction they were taking or the one he was seeking.

Later on, actually only a decade or so (1887) later, Nietzsche argued that it was the "will to truth" (covered over by the "will to knowledge") that blinded knowledge seekers—above all the would-be philosophers—to what they were actually doing, actually seeking. "We are unknown to ourselves, we men of knowledge—and with good reason. We have never sought ourselves—how could it happen that we could ever find ourselves?"[5]

But whom could he find to accompany him in this quest? To find someone to accompany you, Nietzsche advised, start with yourself. In so doing, it can be hoped, if not assured, that others might join you along the way.

Men of Knowledge in Search of Redemption or Salvation

At a time when the American university system is under attack as irrelevant or worse, I can only say that it has been for me a redemptive gift.
«CLIFFORD GEERTZ[1]»

Salvation ensures an access to the self that is inseparable from the work that one carries out on oneself within the time of one's life and in life itself.
«MICHEL FOUCAULT[2]»

Strangely enough, at the height of their fame and productivity, neither Clifford Geertz nor Michel Foucault was in a position to direct graduate students. This state of affairs resulted from their own choices. Geertz had left the University of Chicago in part because of the upheaval of the times; the Vietnam War and the civil rights movements produced an atmosphere within the University of Chicago that he did not find comfortable. Although he did do some occasional teaching later on, it was purely voluntary and only when it pleased him. He never, to my knowledge, expressed any regret about leaving the training and interactions with graduate students behind.

Coincidentally or not, it can be argued that once Geertz left the University of Chicago for the Institute for Advanced Study at Princeton, his influence gradually waned within anthropology, and although he remained productive, he produced no major groundbreaking work there. The reasons for that state of affairs are various and cannot simply be assigned to the change of venue. In my opinion, however, that circumstance should not be excluded from the mix. In my view, Geertz paid a price for not being more concerned and connected.

At the Collège de France, France's most prestigious institution of higher learning, Michel Foucault was in a position neither to direct doctoral theses nor to endure the joys and annoyances of institutional academic politics. He could have taken up a position in a degree-granting institution (e.g., Ecole des Hautes Etudes en Sciences Sociales) in addition to his position at the Collège de France (as did Pierre Bourdieu and Roland Barthes), but Foucault chose not to pursue that avenue. As described below (chapter 4), Foucault grew increasingly uncomfortable with the gilded cage of the Collège de France. His search for a different and better venue for his work was explicit and pronounced and was one reason that he came to spend as much time as he could at the University of California at Berkeley from 1979 onward.

Redemption

Clifford Geertz, my doctoral advisor, wrote the lines in the epigraph above to close the preface of his collection of highly influential essays, *The Interpretation of Cultures*, at the Institute for Advanced Study at Princeton. In 1970 Geertz had been named as the first social scientist to hold a permanent position at the Institute for Advanced Study, an august, privately funded institution, previously staffed by physicists, mathematicians, and historians of a classical stripe. Geertz left the Department of Anthropology at the University of Chicago partially because the luxurious conditions for unfettered work as well as the incomparable prestige of the position he was being offered at the Institute for Advanced Study were too attractive to refuse and partially because the University of Chicago, and the Department of Anthropology in particular, was, as with many other institutions of higher learning at the time (in the United States as well as many other countries) in upheaval. Geertz, like his esteemed colleagues and friends Edward Shils and Saul Bellow, was deeply anticommunist, supporting the American war effort in Southeast Asia, albeit with deep ambivalence about the manner in which the war was being conducted.

Many students, including myself, opposed the war and made our opinions known, often in an uncivil and at times personal manner. That being said, I did work with (or alongside) Geertz because I found his intelligence challenging and decided to leave his politics and his irritable personality in suspension, eventually as matters of reflection (chapters 1 and 2). My decision was no doubt a mix of intellectual curiosity, youthful naiveté, and personal ambition.

The upheaval, contestation, and challenges of the graduate students, aided by the support of a few faculty members, especially Bernard Cohn and David Schneider, was disruptive of Geertz's highly disciplined work routines as well as his sense of what the life of the mind was supposed to be. The boundaries between science as a vocation and politics as a vocation were, he felt, being blurred. If Max Weber had written a third essay on "Ethics as a Vocation" (following science and politics) on how to manage the heterogeneous and often incompatible imperatives of knowledge seeking and the uses of legitimate violence, there might have been some guidance on how to juggle, if not to reconcile, the unstable and troubling demands of the day.

Geertz was famous for his writerly skills; whatever else he was, Geertz was an author, laboring with great care and attention over his prose. He would work sentence by sentence, not advancing in the text under construction until each sentence had been crafted to his personal standards. In that light, his choice of the term "redemptive" is curious. Which register was Geertz thinking of when he wrote those lines? Was it "absolution for past sins and/or protection from damnation"? In that case, what sins did Geertz think he was being redeemed from? Or, was it on a more fiscal register: "Redemptive value: price of a security before its maturity date"?[3] Regardless, Geertz listened to his personal daemon and left for the Institute for Advanced Study at Princeton. Why leaving a venue that he considered redemptive for one with no pedagogical mission (technically not a part of the American university system at all) was evoked but not explained.

Salvation

As described in chapter 4, Foucault's quest was much more Nietzschean than Geertz's in the sense both of a profound dissatisfaction with the state of things and of a pressing, compelling drive to find a form of knowledge that would lead not only to self-knowledge but to what Foucault in his lectures during the 1980s called *salvation*. By this term, he was explicit that he did not mean anything Christian or otherworldly. Rather, Foucault was in search of a practice of thinking that would not only be critical in the Kantian and post-Kantian sense but also "rebound" back from the world to the thinker in such a way that the thinker, and presumably, on another register, the world, would be changed.

In struggling with the twin challenges of "What Is Enlightenment?" and how to forge a philosophic ethos that would overcome the constraints of modernity, Foucault accepted Kant's formulation of the problem but not his solutions; he distanced himself from Baudelaire's modern attitude, whose domain of transformation was that of art. Instead, he sought to reshape elements of Baudelaire's ethos and to turn certain of its elements into a practice that was located in the world of society and politics while retaining a certain critical adjacency.

But he encountered severe problems. Throughout his life, but especially after the leader of the Socialist Party, Francois Mitterand, was elected president of France in 1981, the demands for Foucault and other intellectuals to play a public role were intense, although what that role was supposed to be remained unclear. The Socialist Party wanted intellectuals to be loyal supporters of a kind, criticizing others and animating debate on the social question but not questioning the government's policies, at least in public. One thing became clear to Foucault; the ready-made slot being made available for him to fill was not one he was comfortable filling.

One part of the problem was political positioning.

> From the beginning, I have been considered an enemy by the Marxists, an enemy by the right wing, an enemy by the people in the center. I think that if my work were essentially political it would end up finding a place somewhere in the long run.
>
> Where?
>
> I don't know.[4]

Partially in consequence of these events and demands, during these years Foucault turned elsewhere. His last three years of lectures at the Collège de France, as well as the second and third volume of the *History of Sexuality* (delivered to Foucault on his death bed), were devoted to practices of care of the self and truth speaking in the ancient world. It was there that Foucault sought a passage that others had charted and whose retracing and rethinking might make it possible to find a better way today to govern the self and others.

Throngs attended Foucault's lectures in Paris and elsewhere, and many read his books; few apparently understood where he wanted to go or why; and very few indeed attempted to accompany him. Some of the last group were in San Francisco and Berkeley during his frequent visits during the 1980s and for whom, at least in part, he wrote "What Is Enlightenment?" and "Friendship as a Way of Life" and other essays on contemporary life. The "Friendship" essay was an exchange in 1981 for the French gay magazine *Gai Pied* with three friends, including the novelist René de Ceccatty. Foucault began the interview by refusing to accept that, because sex had become vastly easier to engage in for a younger generation, focusing on sex as the deepest signifier of our being was what made today different from yesterday. Rather,

Foucault saw new forms of association as posing a more important challenge for those seeking to change things together now that certain sexual and social taboos had been loosened.

> This notion of a mode of life seems important to us. Will it require the introduction of a diversification different from the ones due to social class, differences in profession and culture, a diversification that would also be a form of relationship and would be a "way of life?" A way of life can be shared among different age, status and social activity. It can yield intense relations not resembling those that are institutionalized. It seems to me that a way of life can yield a culture and an ethics.[5]

Those personally closest to Foucault were his small circle of French friends, mainly artists. Fictionalized insights into this moment are found in a number of novels but above all in Hervé Guibert's *À l'ami qui ne m'a pas sauvé la vie.*[6] That friend who did not save his life from AIDS was Foucault—*Fuchs,* the fox, a nickname his intimate circle used, drawn from a poem by René Char.

Perhaps, at that time, the true contemporaries found themselves thrown together not only in the joy of a newfound freedom but equally in the face of disaster. These men in dark times were encompassed by an affect of doom (or its blind denial), a radical change of temporality, and for some the pressing obligation of accompaniment. As René de Ceccatty writes with a frightening clarity in his book *L'accompagnement:* "Without having chosen it myself, caught up in the logic of events and by the will of a friend, I was led to accompany him into death."[7]

Foucault's turn to care, truth speaking, and ethics was cut short by his untimely death. If there ever was someone who did not die, satiated with life, to use Max Weber's famous term, it was Foucault. If there ever was someone attempting to meet the demands of the day, it was Foucault. Because I explore these issues in more depth in chapters 3 and 4, I will leave that discussion in suspense here.

Having had the privilege of knowing and working with these

two men of knowledge, and having had neither the possibility nor the desire to exit from the university system, I have had to engage with different challenges of inventing and managing practice, venue, and form. My recent attempts to do so are described in Part Two of this book. The point of the reflections in Part One on these two different but gifted thinkers is that they posed important problems, they experimented with a wide range of mainly discursive forms (although both were engaged and interested in other media), and they employed a wide repertoire of concepts drawn from multiple sources and thereby expanded the scholarly disciplines and imaginations. Consequently what form they gave to these practices, what venues they worked in or eschewed, provide some orientation to the perils and hard work of thinking. That orientation aided in placing the need squarely on the proverbial table for other practices, forms, and venues as other problems arose. Both Geertz and Foucault struggled with the question of the difference that today makes with regard to yesterday; being attentive to and learning lessons from how they approached that problem will, I hope, help in posing more acutely another question: what difference does today make with regard to tomorrow?

Humanism as Nihilism: The Bracketing of Truth and Seriousness in American Cultural Anthropology

There has never been a document of culture which was not at one and the same time a document of barbarism.

«WALTER BENJAMIN[1]»

Those who fancy themselves free of nihilism perhaps push forward its development most fundamentally.

«MARTIN HEIDEGGER[2]»

Nihilism is a modern term and a modern problem. Its rise as an issue in society and in reflections on society is roughly coincident with the rise of modern social sciences. If, following Nietzsche, we see nihilism as the equating of all beings, the leveling of

Originally published in a slightly different form as "Humanism as Nihilism: The Bracketing of Truth and Seriousness in American Cultural Anthropology," in *Social Sciences as Moral Inquiry*, ed. Norma Haan et al., 52–75 (New York: Columbia University Press, 1983). © 2010 by Columbia University Press. Reprinted with permission of the publisher.

meaningful differentiation, the transvaluation of all values, then it might appear logical that anthropology should have escaped this cultural process. A field whose very foundations rest on the existence of an Other—different ways of being human—ought to be the locus of the preservation of difference. I will argue in this chapter that, despite itself, American cultural anthropology has had the opposite effect.

It has frequently been pointed out that the numerous attempts to treat man as an object or a thing are potentially dangerous, dehumanizing, and insidious. In this chapter I will examine the lineage of anthropological theorists who have developed the concept of "culture" and argue that their attempts to construct a science of culture have also led—despite their intent—to a form of nihilism, a reduction of the Other to the Same.

Schematizing broadly, I argue that modern anthropology has taken two major steps in this direction. The first, associated with Franz Boas, was the articulation of the concept of culture as a replacement for and attack on the racist, hierarchical views of nineteenth-century anthropology. Politically admirable, Boas's attack on racism transformed American anthropology into a science concerned with cultures as wholes, one concerned with diversity and pluralism. The price Boas and his students paid for the construction of cultural relativism was the bracketing of truth. Each culture could not be taken at face value. Earlier anthropologists had ethnocentrically ranked all peoples in relation to the values of the West. For Boas and his students, there were underlying universal boundary conditions of what it meant to be human. All cultures dealt with these in their own way. There was a common human condition with diverse solutions. All Otherness (these diverse solutions) could be understood as really being the Same (the universal boundary conditions).

The second step, located in the Parsonian tradition and its offshoots, seeks to limit the overly broad culture concept by rooting it in underlying but changing biosocial evolutionary processes and in the concept of "symbol," which gives historical specificity to different cultures. The focus is on experience and action as a way of articulating these dimensions. The task of anthropology becomes not just the appreciation of different cultures as "ways of life." Rather, cultures are seen as clusters of symbols. These symbols are analyzed as a group's commentary—its discourse—on experience. The role of the anthropologist is to imaginatively translate their frames of meaning into our frame of meaning. By so doing, the anthropologist enters into a fictive conversation with the other culture. The only price to be paid is the bracketing of the seriousness of the speech acts of the Other. All cultures are brought into the universal conversation of humanity, but what each has to say is only one more text to be translated into Western discourse.

Both moments of American cultural anthropology have major achievements of analysis, cross-cultural description, and convincing intent that are undeniable. I am not questioning motives here, as moralism will get us nowhere. But what is worth examining is how this type of inquiry, by a dogged and at times even heroic championing of anthropology as science, has undermined the deeper intent of its own project, resistance to the iron cage of modernity.

The Bracketing of Truth: Cultural Relativism

The successful reconstitution of anthropology as a nonracist, nonhierarchical, and relativist science of culture is usually associated (quite correctly) with the name of Franz Boas. Boas led the assault within anthropology both on racism (and the centrality of race in general) and on the unified schemes of cultural evolution that had so dominated both right- and left-wing thinkers throughout the nineteenth century. Boas used the science of culture that he was building as the weapon with which to attack the concept of race. The unity of a people was cultural and had nothing to do with biology. The scientific framework of explanation and the ethical framework of differential evaluation were brought under siege by Boas and his students in the name of cultures—in the plural.

The modern anthropological concept of culture turned on a clustering of terms: historicity, plurality, behavioral determinism, integration, and relativism. Each has its own genealogy—Boas was hardly the first to posit any of them—but their confluence in the culture concept was an event of major significance. According to Stocking, "Once the one grand scheme of evolutionism was rejected, the multiplicity of cultures which took the place of the cultural stages of savagery, barbarism and civilization were no more easily brought within one standard of evaluation than they were within one system of explanation."[3]

Boas is best known for his rigorous particularism, his zealous emphasis on the ethnographic specificity of each culture. Culture traits might be found in different milieus, but culture was more than just disparate traits; it was an organized way of life. So Boas's particularism lay on the level of cultural wholes. Boas was a crusading nominalist, reacting vigorously to the damage done to truth and morality by the premature and false schematizations of his immediate predecessors in anthropology. The result of this particularism of cultural wholes was to establish a trend of relativism and antitheoretical description that were to be the twin marks of American cultural anthropology since his time. By knocking down the universal standards of comparison, Boas opened the door for cultural relativism. The shattering of the vertical order of evolutionary schemes left, so to speak, a horizontal plane on which each culture had a place that was as valuable as any other.

Boas from the earliest days of his scientific career opposed both the analysis of separate elements taken out of their historical and cultural context and the universal classification of wholes that predetermined the place of particular facts. Boas commonly used each of these two poles to attack (today we might say deconstruct) the other. He refused to admit, for example, that like causes always had like effects—which horrified Durkheim—because, for Boas, the integrative whole always had a primacy over the place of the parts. Conversely, however, he demanded an almost fanatical and literal attention to the facts—literal transcription of texts was a mode for a while—which ultimately made the classification of the whole almost impossible.

According to Boas, "In ethnology, all is individuality."[4] But that individuality resided on the level of the integration of a particular group—the "genius" of a tribe. Meaning was the concept that mediated relations of elements and wholes. Insofar as it implied a causal direction, the movement was from whole to element: "From a collection of string instruments, or drums of savage tribes and the modern orchestra, we cannot derive any conclusion but that similar means have been applied by all peoples to make music. The character of their music, the only object worth studying, which determines the form of the instruments, cannot be understood from the single instrument, but requires a complete collection from the single tribe."[5]

Thus, the seeds of the distinctively American variant of holistic analysis—the transformation of the German historicists' conception of *Geist* and *Volk*—emerged in a preliminary manner in Boas's work. The main difference from the Germans, however, is that Boas and his students doggedly called this type of activity science. He refused the de rigueur distinction between *Natur-wissenschaften* and *Geisteswissenschaften*. Boas wanted to study culture scientifically with methods that were universal. Seawater and Eskimos, to cite two of Boas's interests, could be brought within the same purview. The advances of cultural science would go hand in hand with those of the physical sciences. In both, the critique of tradition, the progressive liberating power of reason, would be an instrument of humanity in its fight against the realms of unreason. This was Boas's faith.

This position must be situated in the context of its formation: the reaction against universalizing, hierarchical, and racist evolutionary schemes on the one hand, and scientific analysis, in a causal/functional frame of the distribution of traits (meaningless in themselves, Boas thought), on the other. Somewhere uneasily situated between the debris of these two currents, Boas and his followers attempted to construct a hybrid science of culture that has both defined and bedeviled the mainstream of American anthropology throughout the twentieth century.

For Boas, "On the one hand, culture was simply an accidental accretion of individual elements. On the other hand, culture—despite Boas' renunciation of organic growth—was at the same time an integrated spiritual totality that somehow conditions the form of its elements."[6] The "somehow" became a central concern for Boas and particularly for his students. Boas placed the emphasis on an integration that was psychological, one of ideas, so as to avoid resorting to any external condition as the basis of a culture's way of life.

So, in an important sense, the result of the Boasian revolution was to successfully displace the evaluative procedures of earlier modern attempts to comprehend other peoples. Each culture was seen as distinctive, each people had its own genius—there was no way to rank them. One had to respect their individuality and their autonomy and had to promote a general tolerance for human difference. Implicitly, a purification of all ethnocentrism was at the heart of the matter. Paradoxically, perhaps, the natives under study would not be able to do much themselves but "express" the underlying holistic way of life that shaped their smallest movements. This meaningful pattern of culture could only be articulated, grasped, and discussed by the anthropologist. Hence, the seriousness, absurdity, joy, or horror of a particular people's way of life was both given heightened importance and dramatically relativized at the same time. The daily activities of a people were displayed in their full dignity as worthy of respect and tolerance. But only the anthropologists—not the people themselves—could understand, describe, and analyze this cultural whole. They live it, we think it.

The full implications of this cultural relativity and new science of anthropology emerged with Boas's students. By 1926 they controlled all the major departments of anthropology in America.

Perhaps the best place to look for a concise statement of the cultural relativist position that Boas's students developed is in

Melville Herskovits's textbook *Man and His Works,* published shortly after the Second World War.[7] Although other Boasians would put these points in different ways, Herskovits's formulation touches all the crucial bases in a direct and unblushing fashion. Herskovits opens his chapter titled "The Problem of Cultural Relativism" by claiming that it is a human universal to make evaluations of ways of life other than one's own. All groups do it. Scholars and scientists in our culture have laboriously catalogued and organized these judgments into schemata and charts. The initial hope was that we would thereby reveal universals of evaluation, but the result has not been one of consensus. Herskovits says, "It has become increasingly evident, however, that evaluations of this kind stand or fall with the acceptance of the premises from which they derive."[8] Many of these criteria are in conflict, and there is no obvious way to decide between them. Many other human groups understand this and have developed an attitude of tolerance toward diversity. Our civilization, however, has lost its tolerance and feels the need for consistency and uniformity. This has bred intolerance. A central task of anthropology is to combat this attitude.

Herskovits gives the example of marriage. There are many different ways in which people marry, although not an infinite number. They all seem, almost by definition, to perform the basic task of marriage; otherwise these societies would have ceased to exist. So, on a simple functional and utilitarian scale, we have no way to choose between different arrangements. Furthermore, if we examine these various systems from the inside, from the point of view of the people who practice them, not only do these customs work, but they seem desirable: "Evaluations are relative to the cultural background out of which they arise."[9] Utility of a functionalist sort and contextualization of attitude are the first two criteria Herskovits puts forward.

Each of the societies that anthropologists study, Herskovits continues, has an underlying value system. Reality for each group, and ultimately for each individual, is shaped and experienced in terms of this underlying value system. Hence, it follows that reality is variable and plural. In social life "the very definition of what is normal and abnormal is relative to the cultural frame of reference."[10] It is the job of the anthropologists to penetrate these value systems and to make them available to others.

This leads us directly to the question of cultural relativism. We must evaluate value systems in their own frame—otherwise we are being ethnocentric. Ethnocentrism, however, is really only a danger when it is linked with power. For, as Herskovits admits, most groups are not relativists; they evaluate others in generally negative terms. It is a well-known ethnographic truism that many societies call themselves "humans," implying that other groups are something lower and less fully human. But Herskovits argues that this claim has been overread and that discourse has been mistaken for reality. The truth is that these groups denigrate other groups verbally but are tolerant in their actions. "It is when, as in Euro-American culture, ethnocentrism is rationalized and made the basis of programs of action detrimental to the well-being of other peoples that it gives rise to serious problems."[11]

We should learn from other cultures that a recognition of difference and tolerance can go hand in hand. "For cultural relativism is a philosophy which, in recognizing the values set up by every society to guide its own life, lays stress on the dignity inherent in every body of custom and on the need for tolerance of conventions though they may differ from one's own."[12] Such a position, Herskovits argues, should lead us to see "the validity of every set of norms for the people whose lives are guided by them, and the values they represent." He wrote this sentence after the Nazi experience without adding any qualifications.

Herskovits closes his chapter on relativism by claiming triumphantly that cultural relativism is a position that opposes absolutism—the existence of any fixed standard. It is, however, not opposed to universals, "those least common denominators to be extracted, inductively, from comprehension of the range of variation which all phenomena of the natural or cultural world manifest."[13] Universal forms are found as human imperatives in all cultures, but no fixed contents are to be found in any of these forms. "Morality is a universal, and so are enjoyment of beauty, and some standard of truth."[14] Morality is both universal and relative to the particular value system that gives it content. Anthropology will be a tolerant science of particulars founded on the universals of human existence. Respect for difference is its guiding principle, relativism its norm.

Every culture is worthy of respect; from the outside no judgment of the truth or goodness of another culture is possible; function ensures respect; conformity to the group's standards is the imperative of all social life; there are universals of human existence that are empty; contents vary but are all founded in a value system that underlies attitudes and behavior; the scientific function of anthropology is to describe this value system; the political function of anthropology is to fight ethnocentrism and promote tolerance.

Cultural relativism marks a major stage in the reduction of the Other to the Same. All differences are preserved and denied at the same time. All are treated equally. Previously, cultures had been ranked on a Eurocentric scale. But the critical assault of cultural anthropology was successful in exposing the ethnocentric bias implicit in all the hierarchies of evaluation and classification previously constructed. The motto, echoing Husserl, might well be "to the cultures' underlying value systems themselves."

All that is necessary for the cultural relativist to achieve this aim is to bracket the truth claims or beauty claims or morality claims of the culture under consideration. In this act of anthropological purification—ridding ourselves of ethnocentrism—we take *no* culture at its word. We start by bracketing the truth claims or value positions of our own culture, and then we do the same for the culture we are attempting to comprehend.

According to this position, on the one side there are the boundary conditions of what it means to be human, the basic conditions of life that all human beings must make some sense of. On the other side, there is the cultural interpretation of a particular people, which gives one reading of these basic conditions: this is their value system. Because all the value systems that function are equally plausible ways of making sense, none of them can be taken as any truer or better than any other. So, for example, Margaret Mead can take a category such as sexuality as a universal. She can then show that there is a spectrum of possible variation in the ways a culture shapes the sexuality of its people. No one style is the true way to do things. Anthropology shows us the diversity of sexual practices, that's all. Sexuality itself has no content; it is just a human universal.

Of course, each of the cultures that the anthropologist studies thinks that its way of being human is the best way. This is each culture's only mistake. The anthropologist, seeing that any way is only one possibility among others, brackets the truth of each claim. By the bracketing of the literal seriousness of a culture's claims, a kind of truth is preserved in each culture. Each is a plausible way of filling in the general conditions of being human.

By so doing, however, all cultural differences have been both preserved and destroyed. First, difference is emphasized, that is, the uniqueness of each culture; then it is reduced to the Same. They are all doing the same thing. All these value systems are the same insofar as they are worldviews, or echoes; their content differs, but there is no way to choose between them as long as they survive. The role of anthropology is to describe the plurality of these meaningful lifeworlds. Each way of life is worthy of respect because ultimately each is equally untrue. The being of man is all that we can affirm. This is everywhere the same. Ultimately difference (although praised) is suppressed: the Same is triumphant.

The Bracketing of Seriousness: Symbolic Anthropology

The triumph of Boas's students both institutionally, in shaping the profession of anthropology, and intellectually, in establishing the absolute primacy of culture over race, is truly an important turning point in modern thought. Many brilliant monographs appeared (one thinks particularly of Ruth Benedict's work at a distance on the Japanese), but little systematic theory.

A subtle but significant shift began to take place as the students of Boas began to come of age in the profession during the 1950s and 1960s. Dissatisfaction was expressed about the lack of analytic sophistication in the culture concept. A crisis point of sorts was reached with the publication of Kroeber and Kluckhohn's book on culture, which listed the great profusion of fuzzy definitions that were currently in use.[15] To give a complex movement yet another simplifying tag, we can say that "symbolic anthropology" emerged in reaction to what was perceived as an overly broad and analytically weak emphasis on cultures as wholes. The locus of this work was Harvard. Here Talcott Parsons and his colleagues and students sought to build a general theory of action. One of the components of this theory would be a specifying of the place and function of the culture concept.

As with the Boasians, this was no single-minded, coherent school. Disparate interests and approaches abounded even within the Parsonian lair. Much empirical work of distinction emerged, even if the promises of a comprehensive theory today seem somewhat overoptimistic. For the sake of convenience, I will concentrate here on the work of Clifford Geertz. This will be convenient not only because I am most familiar with his work, having studied with him, but also because the scope and depth of Geertz's work encompass most of the main problems to be considered. Furthermore, the second stage of this new problematic, which I want to chronicle briefly, is currently associated with Geertz and his students.

I will argue that just as the cultural relativists reduced Difference to Sameness by bracketing the truth claims of cultural statements, so the symbolic anthropologists have taken a further step in the advancement of nihilism by bracketing the seriousness of cultural statements. Their position argues strenuously against the underlying universal boundary conditions of the relativists. They are seen as vacuous and unspecifiable. In their place a natural evolutionist picture in which culture has an active role in human evolution is juxtaposed with a view of meaning as historically produced and located. These two poles are brought together in the analysis of experience and action. But the bringing together has turned out to be an exceedingly difficult enterprise. Without these common parameters and without any formally statable propositions, culture becomes commentary. This commentary is taken up by the anthropologists and translated back into our own discourse. Ultimately, all seriousness is reduced to a common denominator, our frame of meaning. The proposed "conversation of mankind" takes place not in many tongues but in only one.

Geertz begins by assuming that (at least within anthropology) the battle Boas waged has been won. He begins a reverse cycle in which he claims that the problem is no longer to establish the primacy of culture over race but to begin to whittle down the imperialistic reach of the culture concept. If culture is everything, then it loses its explanatory value. The problem, Geertz argues, is, rather, to arrive at a conception of culture that limits it. What is needed is a more circumscribed and therefore an analytically more powerful formulation.

This limiting, specifying, situating rethinking of the culture concept begins with Geertz's attempt to place the concept of culture within a framework of human evolution. As he puts it in his article "The Growth of Culture and the Evolution of Mind": "Recent research in anthropology suggests that the prevailing view that the mental dispositions of man are genetically prior to culture and that his actual capabilities represent the amplification or extension of these pre-existent dispositions by cultural means is incorrect. The apparent fact that the final stages of the biological evolution of man occurred after the initial stages of the growth of culture implies that 'basic,' 'pure,' or 'unconditioned' human nature, in the sense of the innate constitution of man, is so functionally incomplete as to be unworkable."[16] The evolution of the human body is inseparable from that of human culture. "Rather than culture acting only to supplement, develop, and extend organically based capacities logically and genetically prior to it, it would seem to be ingredient to those capacities themselves. A cultureless human being would probably turn out to be not an intrinsically talented though unfulfilled ape, but a wholly mindless and consequently unworkable monstrosity. Like the cabbage it so much resembles, the *Homo sapiens* brain, having arisen within the framework of human culture, would not be viable outside of it."[17]

By situating culture as an essential internal component of human evolution, Geertz roots it within a biological and evolutionary context. If his argument carries, then it has several important consequences. The first is that there is no way to strip culture away in order to get at a more essential human nature. Culture, in Geertz's view, is in no way epiphenomenal or accidental; it has literally shaped us. But this lesson has been largely ignored in anthropology. The two main ways that the irreducibly important place of culture has been negated are described by Geertz as the rationalist approach and the lowest common denominator approach. Geertz locates the beginnings of the first in the French Enlightenment view that underneath the artificiality of custom and the false pandering and passions of social life can be found natural man. Natural man is either the noble savage living untroubled beyond and before the hypocrisies of social life or the rational and universal man. This view holds, as we have seen, that under the swirling diversity of human custom all are—or at least could be—capable of the same reason, the same full humanity. Not only are all men capable of logic and reason, but reason is everywhere the same.

Geertz labels the second evasion of the irreducibility of the particularities of culture the *consensus gentium*—a consensus of all humankind—approach. He says, "At the level of concrete research and specific analysis this grand strategy comes down, first, to a hunt for universals in culture, for empirical uniformities that, in the face of the diversity of customs around the world and over time, could be found everywhere in about the same form, and, second, to an effort to relate such universals, once found, to the established constants of human biology, psychology, and social organization."[18]

This approach has failed to provide substantial categories and not empty ones, specific groundings and not vague underlying realities, because it can never achieve the ends it proposes for itself. "There is a logical conflict between asserting that, say, 'religion,' 'marriage,' or 'property' are empirical universals and giving them much in the way of specific content, for to say that they are empirical universals is to say that they have the same content, and to say that they have the same content is to fly in the face of the undeniable fact that they do not."[19]

But even if some such universals could be found (and the search both in America and on the Continent goes on), the question remains what one would have if one found them. There has always been a conflict (or at least an implicit tension) within anthropology between the particularities of the peoples we go out to study and the theories we use to describe them. If the theory was not general enough, then the risk of mere descriptivism, naive empiricism, was present. The other side of the coin, however, is that if the theory is general enough, then we tend to get a rather washed-out, thin soup of "behind these seemingly bizarre customs lies John Doe just like you and me." The more general the theory, the less it could do justice to the particulars under consideration. So, culture, for Geertz, is irreducible to underlying universals: it is resolutely particular. There is no culture in general. Culture is not some superorganic realm. It is rooted in the evolution of the species.

Having, at least in principle, reestablished the interconnection of biology and culture that had been deconstructed by Boas, Geertz clearly must go on to specify the characteristics of culture in a way different from his predecessors. The concept that enables him to do this is "symbol." He takes it directly from Suzanne Langer. Just as culture has been used too broadly, Geertz argues, so too has symbol. Its meaning must be restricted if it is to be a useful analytic tool. Symbol "is used for any object, act, event, quality, or relation which serves as a vehicle for a conception—the conception is the symbol's 'meaning,' ... concrete embodiments of ideas, attitudes, judgments, longings, or beliefs."[20] They are not qualities of mind or mysterious entities but public objects like any others.

Culture is a system of these symbols, these embodiments of conceptions. Its generic trait is that these complexes of symbols are "extrinsic sources of information."[21] They give form to processes external to themselves in a public world. Just as the order of bases in DNA forms a coded program, so culture patterns "provide such programs for the institution of the social and psychological processes which shape public behavior." Geertz emphasizes that this is meant not as some strained analogy but is to be taken quite literally. "But, unlike genes and other non-symbolic information sources, which are only models for, not models of, culture patterns have an intrinsic double aspect: they give meaning, that is objective conceptual form, to social and psychological reality both by shaping themselves to it and by shaping it to themselves. . . . The intertransposability of models for and models of which symbolic formulation makes possible is the distinctive characteristic of our mentality."[22]

So the publicly shared and shaped cultural world in which Homo sapiens has been literally formed will be the object of Geertz's analysis. It is here that experience "provides a means of communication between the space of the body and the tune of culture, between the determinations of nature and the weight of history."[23]

Culture is constituted of clusters of symbols. It is public. It is this publicness that renders the meaning embodied in symbols accessible to analysis, both by the natives and by the anthropologists. Culture is public because meaning is. It takes place on the street, in the marketplace, in mosques, in offices, and on battlefields. Our lives take place—to paraphrase Geertz's paraphrase of Weber—in webs of signification we ourselves have spun.

But culture, for Geertz, cannot be analyzed in its own terms. It is neither the somehow holistic expression of a people's way of life (à la Benedict) nor a sealed realm of symbols with internal logical or syntactic interconnections (à la Lévi-Strauss). Geertz has strong words of condemnation for those who attempt to treat culture as a closed domain of signifiers. Rather, Geertz has always set these symbols over against something nonsymbolic. At the deepest level, as we have seen, he situates culture in the frame of those "enduring natural processes that underlie" social lives.[24] But, of equal import, culture is contrasted with society. Culture is the meaningful dimension, and society is the behavioral. Just as Geertz has tried out a string of metaphors for the natural processes (genetic code, computer model, and so forth), so too there are a string of metaphors for the cultural versus the social (the logico-meaningful vs. the causal-functional, meaning vs. behavior, significance vs. structure). But they are all attempts to make the same point. Culture is not sui generis. It is only through social action that culture finds its articulation. As Foucault puts it, this focus on experience seeks to "articulate the possible history of a culture upon the semantic density which is both hidden and revealed in actual experience."[25]

What we are after, then, and this is where "interpretive anthropology" splits off from the more hermetic analyses of "symbolic anthropology," is the informal logic of social life. We seek to describe and interpret the taken-for-granted assumptions of an Other's world that makes what at first seems terribly exotic seem normal, everyday usual to those who are accustomed to living in it. As that life is shaped publicly by embodied conceptions that are linked together into a whole and articulated in experience, we can describe it. There is a fundamental underlying commonality and a fundamental surface of historical and cultural difference. It is that difference we seek to describe.

We do this by trying to understand the actor's point of view—that is to say, by piecing together the symbols and institutions that constitute the social life of the people we study. We cast our interpretations in terms in which we imagine the natives themselves conceive their own experiences, in terms of the symbols that formulate that experience. But this certainly does not mean that we are trying to be native or, more important, that such interpretations are the ones the natives use. After all, we are the anthropologists. The object of study is one thing and the study of it another. Geertz says, "We begin with our own interpretations of what our informants are up to or think they are up to, and then systematize these."[26]

What we do as anthropologists is construct interpretations of what we take to be other peoples' realities. The writing of ethnography is what makes us anthropologists. We create fictions. These ethnographic fictions are constructs of other people's constructs. As Geertz puts it, "Anthropologists have not always been as aware as they might be of this fact: that although culture exists in the trading post, the hill fort, or the sheep run, anthropology exists in the book, the article, the lecture, the museum display, or sometimes nowadays the film. To become aware of it is to realize that the line between mode of representation and substantive content is as undrawable in cultural analysis as it is in painting."[27]

What is the aim of this interpretive anthropological enterprise? Geertz is extremely reserved about the goals of his enterprise. Here he contrasts with the proselytizing stance of the Boasians, who were actively involved in spreading the good word. A leitmotif in his work is a call to science. However, this "science" contains no laws, is not capable of prediction, is not formulizable, is not falsifiable, and contains no generalizations. The tag is important only as a rhetorical device to ennoble the project and to maintain a strict neutrality, not because anything resembling what is commonly accepted as science has been produced.

The aim of interpretive anthropology for Geertz is to bring us "in touch with the lives of strangers . . . [and] in some extended sense of the term to converse with them."[28] That is all. Geertz juxtaposes this intercultural conversation with other, more grandiose ends. "The essential vocation of interpretive anthropology is not to answer our deepest questions but to make available to us answers that others, guarding other sheep, in other valleys, have given and thus to include them in the consultable record of what man has said."[29] This does *not* mean that other people's answers are in some way truer, more penetrating, more moral, more authentic, or more real than ours. We will learn no specific truths from the Balinese or the Moroccans. The task of the anthropologist is to report observations, not to answer questions—the truth does not lie elsewhere any more than it is hidden at home.

The point is to enter into the imaginative universes of others, to construct fictions about these cultures and thereby extend the range of human discourse. The task of anthropology is to go out to other peoples' valleys and watch them watch their sheep, to return home and construct an account, to preserve their culture for the historical record. Ethics, science, and truth all become aesthetic.

In a preface to the book *Language and Art in the Navajo Universe* by Gary Witherspoon, Geertz poses the task of interpretive anthropology in a slightly different way. He sees it as "the comprehension of the frames of meaning in which other people move and the communication of that comprehension to others."[30] In this instance it is the Navajo frame of reference that is being explored. Geertz explains, "Witherspoon approaches his material with the eye of a man seeking to grasp a deep and difficult idea, not that of one trying to describe an exotic project or a curious practice. The effort is to bring Navajo thought within the range of Western discourse, so that we might have some conception of its nature and some appreciation of its power."[31]

Cultures differ in their frames of meaning. These frames can be brought into a common discourse. For the relativists this discourse was nominally the Western discourse of science. But because what was being described was grounded in a common human condition and was cast in a universal language of science, its claims, albeit naive, were nonetheless consistent. But when we move entirely into discourse, the discourse we engage in can only be Western. The claim is that by making the Navajo's frame of reference accessible to us, the "long strangeness between us will finally begin to end."[32]

In this stance, we no longer need to ground discourse in underlying boundary conditions. As we saw in the cultural relativist position, the anthropologist bracketed the truth claims of various cultures as a way of affirming the universal ground that made all cultures equal expressions of an underlying common humanity. There was still a referent. In the interpretive position, there is a second bracketing. The anthropologist not only remains neutral as to the truth claims of a particular culture but now also brackets the seriousness (in the traditional sense of Western philosophy) of the truth claims themselves. Not that there is any failure to understand the statements encountered as being a series of meaningful speech acts; the anthropologist is not bracketing meaning, like a structuralist or behaviorist. Rather, what is bracketed is precisely the claims of serious speech acts to serious meaningfulness. What is suspended is not only the claim to context-free truth but the claim that such a claim is intelligible. The interpretive anthropologist will treat both reference and sense as mere phenomena.

The possibility of pure description of another culture from the outside is now possible. What Geertz once referred to as "a scientific phenomenology of cultural forms" has found its method.[33] We observe what the natives think is true, that is, what they take seriously. We construct an account of their universe, their frames of meaning, and then we converse with it. We bring it into our conversation. The anthropologist thus succeeds in studying what is serious and truthful to Others without it being serious or truthful to him. As we have been told, there are no truths to be brought back from faraway places. There is nothing specific to be learned from other cultures: they have nothing to teach us, any more than presumably we have to teach them.

Ultimately, when this new purified phenomenological anthropology has come of age, we will all understand that culture is discourse, that there are many variants of it, and that a heightened conversation is our goal. We will be able to bring this project to fruition when not only a small number of Westerners have become anthropologists but presumably everyone else as well. When the Navajo comes of age and learns to translate his frame of reference into what can *only* be our frame of reference, then the long strangeness between us will have ended—and so will all difference as well.

Conclusion: Truth and Power

To say that the discipline of anthropology emerged in a highly charged political world, during a century in which most of the peoples whom anthropology has taken as its object of study have been either destroyed or radically transformed by their contact with Western (and other) civilizations, is to restate a truism. All the same, we should not forget that just because something is obvious does not mean its importance is decreased. Several questions still remain: How have anthropologists understood the situation, and, more specifically, how have they sought to situate their own developing understanding of anthropology as an intellectual discipline within their diverse interpretations of the political realities of the time? How has the development of the science of culture been related to the political commitments of its founders?

In order to consider (or simply to pose) these questions, let me briefly suggest a convenient schematization of relations of truth and power. I propose this not because I think it exhausts the possibilities or adequately accounts for a complex and less coherent history or because I wish to moralize about our anthropological ancestors; rather, I see this as a means of opening up a debate about how we might proceed from here.

In the first position, that represented by Boas, the role of the anthropologist as scientist was to speak truth to power. Boas was a profoundly political man: a typically secular, emancipated German-Jewish liberal with a strong faith in the force of reason as a fundamental tool of emancipation and as an absolute value in its own right. The calling of the intellectual, for Boas, consisted of the advancement of reason through science and the conquest of tradition, irrationality, and injustice. Not unlike Freud, Boas had a faith in reason that never wavered, although his faith in human beings withered rather dramatically.

Born in 1858, Boas came of age in a Bismarckian Germany in which the values he held were put in question by the rise of nationalist and anti-Semitic movements. Boas himself embodied a fundamental contradiction that was to characterize American anthropology: confronted with a situation of strong destructive political mobilization around national symbols, Boas reacted (and here he is typical of anthropologists) neither by adopting a strong national identity himself nor by choosing to join a political movement that directly confronted the problem. Rather, he immigrated to America and redoubled his faith in the necessity for a science of anthropology that would do battle with biological racism and cultural chauvinism by undercutting their scientific rationale.

Boas arrived in America in the late 1880s during a period of nationalist fervor, racial prejudice (including anti-Semitism), and anti-immigrant frenzy, which were more than once turned on him. The virulent anti-German propaganda in America and the intense patriotism "even in our Eastern universities" during the First World War forced Boas to recognize the weight of tradition and passion even among the elite. This led Boas to redouble his commitment to anthropology, even if it weakened his faith in the progress of humanity. As Stocking says, "He clearly assumed that the anthropological world view might, if appropriately propagated, override forces of economic or diplomatic self-interest."[34] At the same time, there were moral and political limits for the discipline. Boas became the first—and still the only—person ever to be expelled from the American Anthropological Association (for publicly exposing and denouncing the use of anthropologists as spies during the war). Reinstated after the war, Boas successfully placed his students (Mead, Kroeber, and so forth) in leading departments, which they eventually took over.

In his last years, coincident with the rise of the Nazis, Boas never doubted in his humanist faith that cultural values were primordial and that reason was the guiding beacon to resist fascism and nihilism. For him, tradition, self-interest, and power were the enemies, while rationality remained untainted. Between the authentic local expressions of culture and the ideal of a pure critical reason lay a dangerous and polluted realm of political strife, emotions, social domination, economic exploitation, and myriad forms of petty interest. Although anthropology could not ignore these dimensions of human existence, Boas considered them to be external to anthropology in a fundamental sense. Both the political and the biological were extrinsic to his understanding of reason and culture. The anthropologists' credo remained: speak truth to power, focus truth on prejudice, separate truth from passion.

The dignity and achievements of Boas and his students are not in question—they were centrally responsible for making antiracism an accepted part of the American academic agenda—but neither are their limits and contradictions. The position of speaking truth to power, opposing humanism to nihilism, is still with us; and it is by no means the worst alternative. But ultimately this position has not proved sufficiently hardy, either intellectually or politically, to have spawned a science or a politics that lives up to the standards of coherence and efficacy by which these individuals wished to be judged. Viewed from some distance, the heroic and stubborn insistence on the externality of humanism and nihilism has, despite itself, contributed to the spread of that which it was constructed to oppose. As the truth of anthropology became increasingly empty of content, and as world circumstances changed, the reformist zeal has come to sound increasingly like American moralizing and less like universal reason.

In an important sense, the second position, that represented by Geertz, has no politics at all. The ascetic imperative of Boas or Weber, who sought to separate truth and politics, still entailed an active vigilance lest these two realms fuse. It never occurred to these European intellectuals that political concerns were not central to the life of an intellectual—they saw them as so central that they had to be kept in check. The sacrifice demanded of the scientist was not the loss of political passions but only that the passions be kept clearly distinct from scientific activities qua science. Over the time of two generations, the tension between these two callings, and hence the potential threat they posed for each other's autonomy, was gradually dissipated. In its place an ethics of scientific comportment became a code of civility. As this code took center stage, the more directly political concerns were weakened. In a not entirely self-conscious way, the fundamental commitment to academic civility became a model—text and conversation—for all human activity. Those who refused the dialogue (or were never invited to join), even those who tried to expand its terms, ran the risk of being cast outside the pale of science and humanism.

Of course, there are political implications in a model that poses civility and conversation (between colleagues, between cultures) as the norm. Edward Shils, for example, clearly articulated these issues. He defended the university first against the attacks of Senator McCarthy in the 1950s and later against the critiques and disruptions of student radicals in the 1960s and 1970s. But the defense posed the ideal of a university setting outside the political fray. The bulk of writing about how the larger political contexts affect scholars concerned the disruption of civility within the university and refused to place the breakdown (temporary and partial as it was) within a larger political context of war and massive government intervention in the financing and functioning of the university. This must be seen as a retreat from the breadth of Boas's understanding and commitments. Civility and passionate political commitment were too often posed as being contraries, self-validating contraries, as both critics and defenders of the university too frequently insisted on their mutual incompatibility. As Geertz says in the preface to his collection of essays, *The Interpretation of Cultures,* written in 1973, "At a time when the American university system is under attack as irrelevant or worse, I can only say that it has been for me a redemptive gift."[25]

Once again, politics is bracketed to save science. But, as we have argued, no real science emerged from this bracketing. This humanist effort to avoid what is perceived as the threat of barbarism has retreated to a restrictive civility in which the university becomes the institutional and ethical model for all humanity.

But it is a university not easily recognizable. It is as if the endless petty squabbling, the massive involvement in social and political affairs, and the workaday bureaucratic environment were not noble enough to be included. But these "hard surfaces" are exactly what we were supposed to focus on in our analyses of other cultures, not so as to reduce culture or meaning or reason to them, but as a means of avoiding the "danger that cultural analysis will [turn] into a kind of sociological aestheticism."[36] The university and science are somehow exempted from the hard analysis to which other cultures are subjected. For the life of the mind to be "redemptive," it must be not of this world.

Short of redemption, where do we go from here? I am *not* advocating that we jettison the moral and intellectual achievements of the aggressively antiracist anthropology of Boas, or that we discard what has been constructed and made to function of a civility that allows for dispute within a community of shared discourse. The main conclusion I draw from the analysis presented in this chapter is that it is the dogged separation of truth and power in order to construct a science that has had the most deleterious effects on anthropology; it is the conception of humanist activity that has unwittingly pushed these anthropologists into a kind of nihilism that is the exact opposite of their intent.

So where do we go with this? First, we go to a genealogy of the problem: asking how we have gotten where we are. This chapter itself offers little more than a preface to such a project, which would have to extend further into the past and include a sustained analysis of the institutional arrangements within which anthropology was formed, as well as an analysis of the emergence of other disciplines and the uses to which these disciplines were put. Second, we go to a rethinking of humanism, nihilism, and the relations of truth and power. Although many people are currently working in that direction, it will come as no surprise that I think the work of Michel Foucault offers us the most developed and powerful approach currently available. Obviously this is not the place to rehearse Foucault's entire project. Let me touch only on his analysis of intellectuals.

At least since the Enlightenment (and, in a different form, since the origins of Christianity), the figure of the intellectual has been defined by its relationship to a universal message. The intellectual has been a master of truth and justice. Whether Voltaire or Marx, the intellectual claimed a special right to speak for all of humanity, at least that part of humanity that embodies a universal message, whether of the law, of reason, or of history. The intellectual has been that one who, as Foucault puts it, opposed power, despotism, and injustice in the name of justice and reason. "The universal intellectual derives from the jurist/notable and finds his fullest expression in the writer, the bearer of values and significations in which all can recognize themselves."[37] Because he speaks the truth, the intellectual has always seen himself as outside of power. Foucault calls this the "speaker's benefit."[38] As long as truth is external to power, those who speak the truth are in an enviable position. In fact, Foucault argues that one of the main reasons truth and power have been posed as externals is to guarantee the authority of those who proclaim this separation. "What sustains our eagerness to speak of sex [power] in terms of repression is doubtless this opportunity to speak out against the powers that be, to utter truths and promise bliss, to link enlightenment, liberation, and manifold pleasures; to pronounce a discourse that combines the fervor of knowledge, the determination to change the laws, and the longing for the garden of earthly delights."[39]

The anthropologist as a cultural figure easily adopted this position. Clearly, as we have seen, the role of the anthropologist has been to stake out the claims of all humanity: to speak the truth of science, to show us a more fulfilling life that others have led. We should have little trouble recognizing Boas in this portrait. We need only think of Boas's most famous student, Margaret Mead, and her unabashed crusading, her radically confident pronouncements on everything from sex to war in all available media, to see a modern version of the anthropologist as humanist intellectual.

Because of a complex set of technological and economic changes in Western society (analyzed in a similar fashion with

different conclusions by Habermas), Foucault thinks that the
universal intellectual is disappearing as a cultural figure. Its last
gasp was the figure of the "writer." "All the fevered theorization
of writing which we witnessed during the sixties was no doubt
only a swan song; the writer was desperately struggling for the
maintenance of his historical privilege. But the fact that it should
have been precisely a question of theory, that the writer should
have needed scientific guarantees, based on linguistics, semiol-
ogy, psychoanalysis, . . . all this goes to show that the activity of
the writer was no longer the active center."[40]

Except that in France such intellectuals were de rigueur on
the left, we should have no trouble locating Geertz in this sketch
of the writer. If there exists a more "writerly" anthropologist, he
is not publishing his work. The problem of authority is somewhat different here, however, in that Geertz no longer claims
to be speaking for humanity—which he denies exists—or for
any particular groups, or out of a defined scientific consensus.
Hence, his claim to authority—one that he has certainly well
established—must stem from the authority of his prose. Clearly,
what Foucault calls "writing as the sacralizing mark of the intellectual" is well represented here.[41]

But this turn is not so surprising. Foucault claims that the
universal intellectual has been replaced by the "specific" intellectual: the jurist/notable has been replaced as a cultural figure by
the savant/intellectual. No longer the crusading voice of humanity and justice, the specific intellectual is a scientist (usually in
biology or physics), "the figure who possesses—along with a few
others, and either in the service of the state or against it—certain
abilities, which can favor life or destroy it definitively."[42] Because
these technocrats possess specific and vital information, a certain
quality of generality and urgency is granted to their statements.
It is not that they are in a position to give us universal truths,
but they are in control of information whose implications affect
everyone. In a certain sense they gain power because of their
specific abilities on which our civilization has grown increasingly
dependent.

Perhaps because anthropology does not generate this kind of vital information, only a parody of this figure exists within the discipline. Marvin Harris has unquestionably replaced Margaret Mead as the official media spokesman on all issues about which anthropology presumably has answers to give. Harris is a kind of *Sesame Street* version of the expert who pronounces truths whenever he is asked on the true meaning of all customs. His answers always reveal that behind culture and diversity lies that which is the really real—techno-economic structures (calories and self-interest), as he calls them. Surely this stance (and its wide acceptance) also reflects the desperate claim that anthropology must possess some vital technical specializations that its unemployed doctorates can sell to the hospitals, forestry services, and military departments of the government. After asserting a claim of utilitarian importance, these technocrats always present the ultimate relevance of anthropology as its unique ability to bring a humanist concern to the problem at hand, be it the delivery of health care to minority communities or the ethnic identification of skeletal remains in Vietnam.

As we all know, narratives are supposed to have endings. This chapter does not have one. We have had, in my opinion, too many narrative endings that have deceptively claimed to represent a solution that does not exist except as a literary device. Perhaps it is appropriate, to borrow a phrase from Geertz, to blur our genres. By stopping abruptly, I leave the reader in the same position as the writer—midstream.

2

Chicken or Glass: Between Clifford Geertz and Paul Hyman

He who comes into the world so as to upset nothing merits neither respect nor attention.

«RENÉ CHAR[1]»

The unexpected, born-again renaissance of Paul Hyman's trove of unsettling beauty and idiosyncratically engaged witnessing through the efforts and insights of Susan Slyomovics deserves our most sincere gratitude. Slyomovics's act is one of simple audacity and perceptivity. "Audacity" may seem too grand a word, given the riveting work Slyomovics has done on human rights abuses in Morocco.[2] Not to downplay the significance and power of that work or those long-standing horrific practices in any way, nonetheless by the early twentieth century there exists a genre of narration and performance concerning torture and its horrors, its tragedy, and its disturbing banalities. In fact, Slyomovics's book powerfully documents this state of affairs in its mode of cool chronicle, thereby producing the devastating effects of a clear-

Originally published in a slightly different form as "Chicken or Glass: In the Vicinity of Clifford Geertz and Paul Hyman," in *Clifford Geertz in Morocco*, ed. Susan Slyomovics (New York: Routledge, 2009). Reprinted by permission.

sighted and antimaudlin presentation of a terrible reality long since known and long since submerged. Her organization of a conference that features Hyman's photographs is perceptive because she seized their singularity and audacious vision and because so many others had ignored them. There were things to see, and to say, and to learn, and to discuss, beyond the discursive and the conceptual.

A Critical Disturbance

Slyomovics's simple but decisive act of recognition of Hyman's photographic oeuvre as well as his presence in Morocco functions as a disruptor (to use Gilles Deleuze's term) of the parade of appropriately nostalgic eulogies (are there any other kind?) that have followed Clifford Geertz's death. We can rest assured that the patina of pious affect and unconcealed sentimentality ever-accumulating as Geertz's heritage will not lack for care keepers and guardians. Let us be clear: this state of affairs is perfectly normal. Its unimpeded continuance, however, is also normalizing in the sense that the repetition of one narrative line (with its minor variations) lays out a field of what counts as true and right in this history, and therein lies the rub. The history is more complex, as is what counts as true and right. Any true thinker would feel betrayed by this lack of critique: loyalty worth its salt must include honesty.

Other contributions in this collection attest to the aesthetic power and reflect on the cultural significance of Hyman's photographic contributions per se. However, less attention has been paid to the arrival and brief stay of Paul Hyman in Morocco. This arrival turned out to be a minor disturbance to the scripted flow of things at the time as well as their representations in the future perfect that had been orchestrated by the maestro himself and his supporting cast. Cliff, Hilly (Hildred Geertz), and Larry ("I am Cliff's man in the gray flannel suit") Rosen were nothing if not serious about their project. Although seriousness in one's work, diligence in respecting one's hosts, and commitment to bringing facts and insights to bear in a volatile state of affairs are virtues, as Jean-Paul Sartre often observed the *esprit de sérieux,* the prescriptive attitude of the bourgeoisie to reality and to those different from themselves, their air of self-importance, called for criticism. Today, "criticism" is a charged term that is taken to be (often appropriately) a trope of denunciation. Criticism, however, takes its modern meaning from Kant and his three critiques, where the term means the establishment of legitimate limits. Thus, the *Critique of Pure Reason* is not an attack on reason but an attempt to demonstrate its limits, forms, and powers. Kant had intended to write a fourth critique (in addition to pure reason, judgment, and practical reason), a critique of historical reason. That critique would have addressed the limits of historical conditions, their contingency, and their relative importance. In effect, over the last two hundred years, the modern human sciences, although not dallying in the arrogant and the comic travesties of what they took to be the natural sciences, have done little else. Or, more accurately, when done well they continue to pursue the goal of understanding and practicing the pursuit of historical understanding: the appropriate mode of comprehension of the contingent, the fleeting, the ordinary, the local, and the singular.

Chicken or Glass

The above remarks are no doubt outsized words for the small anecdotes that follow. Yet, anthropologists, the miniature painters of the social sciences, as Geertz put it (borrowing from Claude Lévi-Strauss), are attuned to small events, minor processes, petty breakdowns, and the like as places to pause and inquire as to what is happening in front of us. These are not quite the petty, gray details that the Nietzschean genealogists seek out as the sites of malicious struggles over the real, covered over by grand words, but perhaps they are not so far distant from those sites of contestation over meaning and respect, for the self and for others.

Regardless, here are a few minor incidents and some untimely observations on their significance.

Paul Hyman happens to be extremely gifted at languages. He was a musician (and a mathematician) and had that gift of recognizing and reproducing tone, timbre, and pattern that most of us lack. Hyman had been a French major at Columbia. A professor of French nationality told his French conversation class that he could teach them to speak French quickly but only if they spoke English quickly. Although trivial as an insight, the claim was a critical one. It was a critical one in the sense that it indicated a legitimate limit. Of course, the university world is full of language professors who are not natives and who perform their duties more or less satisfactorily. That being said, for some, and Hyman was one of those souls, taking up a pursuit in which one would feel oneself to be judged as constantly inadequate and about which one could do little to remedy the situation was, when added to a myriad of other obstacles, enough to make him move onto different vocational pursuits, in particular, photography.

One of the essential aspects of speaking Arabic in Morocco in the provincial setting of Sefrou and its hinterlands was the centrality—not the totality—of what Jean Duvignaud in his classic *Change at Shebika: Report from a North African Village* incisively called the "palaver" of daily life.[3] There was almost always, as the American idiom has it, time to kill or, better, to fill: there was ample unemployment and underemployment, there was a culture of indirectness and alert redirecting of questions, there was a vast reservoir of salutations and verbal adornment, and there was a joy in the rather baroque ornamentation of phrase and counterphrase that, in some imaginary quantitative analysis of speech acts at the time, would have had to hold a place of prominence. Certainly, this genre of performance, of palavering, was much practiced and socially esteemed. Not being able to engage in this palaver or simply refusing to do so, whether for reasons of temperament or out of an engrained dispositional *esprit de sérieux,* constituted a critical limitation for those attempting to participate in, to respect, and, ultimately, in subtle but significant ways, even to understand what was going on.

Hyman, who had time to fill, was dispositionally primed to adopt and enjoy this form of Moroccan palaver. The fact that Hyman mastered the skill's basics is striking because it is not actually a skill he excels at in English (or French). One indication of this observation is that with insistence in the years following our time in Morocco, and even today decades later, there is a range of talk that we use our no doubt comical Arabic to enact. Even in e-mail of late these greetings and relationship-affirming seeming non sequiturs serve that purpose. They are a salutary counterbalance to the "hi" of e-mail, not to mention the regressive telegraphy of text messaging. In a word, Hyman quickly learned a certain cut of Arabic just like many Moroccan youths at the time learned a cut of English or Swedish or German that was at one and the same time utterly fluent and distinctively and massively partial. I remember a conversation with a young Moroccan about Jimi Hendrix (about whom he had more superlatives to display than I did), who, when asked about the Moroccan school system, lacked even the most basic vocabulary to continue the discussion. No one had ever asked him such questions before. This was a matter of demand, not ability.

In a like manner, Hyman had nothing to say about parallel cousin marriage (in any language, it is true) but could fill hours over tea bantering about what appeared to be very little. Serious work in Arabic, with its extraordinary beauty and complexity, was not what Paul had come to master: no grammar books, no educated tutors, no formal lessons. Equally noteworthy, that whole range of seriousness, the array of command of language, that could not have failed to be associated with the curt rationality of colonialism was absent from Hyman's linguistic arsenal. Whoever this guy was, he was not a willing representative of dominance. Whatever else this rather exceptional foreigner with his fringed pants possessed, it seemed, with all the time in the world, he was no colonist, technocrat, or even Peace Corps worker there to improve the Moroccans' lot. In sum, Hyman was not in Morocco to till and sow the field of normalization, to capture the culture's deep meaning, or to put the boys in the café on the world map. It was no surprise, therefore, that his Arabic was both fluent and limited, precise and thin: this guy was no threat and, from the start, wittingly and unwittingly, established trust.

In that available light, Clifford Geertz's performative limitations in Arabic are critical. Geertz had all the requisite dictionaries, tutors in Chicago and in Sefrou, a familiarity with the scholarly literature on Arabic, and extensive theoretical reflections on the relations between language and culture. That his accent was horrific was of minimal importance; that he was constitutionally allergic to chatter and impervious to palaver (no doubt in any language) constituted a telling diacritic of who he was and how he was perceived, as well as what he himself was able to perceive. Perception, here as elsewhere, it is worth remembering, is not the same thing as conceptualization or narration, abilities Geertz possessed in abundance.

Early on in Hyman's stay, Geertz wandered down from his villa on the adjacent hillside (formerly the French quarter) to observe some kind of procession that was under way in honor of a saint. He invited Hyman to join him. They caught up with the group meandering on a pathway at the edge of town; Hyman asked Geertz, "What is going on?" Geertz shuffled over to a young boy in the procession and entered into a brief verbal exchange. He returned to Hyman and said in his gruff, rapid-fire delivery, "Chicken or glass." Hyman, nonplussed, responded to the effect of "Oh?" Geertz rapidly glossed his cryptic claim by explaining that the Moroccan words for chicken and glass sounded alike, and he did not know for certain which one was being used. For years later, Hyman and I would introduce the speech act "chicken or glass?" into our conversations, often, no doubt, to the utter consternation of those with whom we happened to be mingling, especially as it was usually accompanied by peals of laughter and a hearty "*eh-way a Sidi?*" The point is not the cheap one that Geertz was not very skilled in Arabic, especially spoken Arabic. Rather, it is that had Geertz been attuned to banter and chatter rather than direct questioning, he would have found out not only whether it was chicken or glass but what was going on and how the participants felt about it, the famous "ethos" of anthropology.

Although this is not the place to enter into a more scholarly discussion of the importance of the anthropologist and command of language, let us just remember that Geertz made fluency a point of controversy, a critical touchstone of how anthropology ought to be practiced. Speaking "the language," Geertz held, was the ethical and epistemological diacritic of the discipline. That being said, Hyman's presence and the insights his minor disruptions occasioned, demonstrated that whatever conclusions learned professors may arrive at on the above matter, one had to acknowledge that language was a practice and that practice was composed of diverse dimensions as a performative art; (relative) mastery was more than grammar, more than vocabulary, more than accent. Finally, Hyman's presence also showed that making no attempt to demonstrate the aforementioned mastery, while hanging out in an attentive manner by a keen urban observer of the human comedy, could show us many things about those observed as well as those authorized to observe them.

Concave or Convex

If grasping the centrality of daily life and its zones of lack of deep meaning can be a problem for the cultivated anthropologist, so too can arenas be held to be overly saturated with significance. One of those arenas is sexuality. It is worth remembering that we are talking about events taking place in 1969. Although Hyman and I at least had been beneficiaries of the sexual energy of the time and of our generation, the scholarly literature on Morocco and/or Islam of the day languished in its own self-imposed discursive prudery. Studies of parallel and cross-cousin marriage, not to mention segmentary lineages, abounded, but the sex and sexuality of the people strategizing in all those diagrams was passed over in silence and perhaps shame.

To his credit, Geertz was interested in sexuality in Morocco. He was, however, too bashful to broach the topic with his informants who had just traipsed up the hill and sat in his study informing him of how things were in the land below. So, he seized the occasion, however awkwardly, of Hyman's presence, the guy was a New York fashion photographer after all, to see whether Paul would be willing to do some informal fieldwork. Geertz assumed that Paul's Arabic was insufficient and furthermore that opening such an inquiry in Sefrou would be risky (*sic*, a Geertzian pun awaits); when he heard that Hyman and I planned a short trip to Tangier, and knowing that we both spoke French, Geertz seized the day, broached the topic, and underscored both its casual interest to him and its potential importance for the ethnographic record. What was the difference, for example, between homosexuality, homoeroticism, and male friendship? Sketchy references to the Greeks were provided. All very serious but not yet freighted with decades of scholarship and political correctness. A naive time.

Off we went to Tangier. Sex was not hard to locate, only to avoid. Sexuality, to accept Foucault's famous distinction some years later, the discourse of the thing, was harder to find. As it turned out, when Hyman and I had lived together in Paris (during 1965–66), he had befriended a cosmopolitan Jewish homosexual. Through George we contacted some of his friends in Tangier; through Hyman's friendship with George some of the customs and habits of that age-set were already familiar. A conversation with one of George's Tangier cohorts cleared things up fairly quickly. What was the difference between homosexuality, homoeroticism, and male friendship? Hyman asked the aging queen. The response was elegant and eloquent: "concave and convex." What counted was who was penetrating and who was penetrated. All the rest was secondary. However, it became clear that there was one further distinction that several young men who made a living from engaging in sex with the older male tourists insisted on: if the penetrator was not a Muslim, there was no shame; who cared what they wanted and what they did, as long as they paid. Any other questions?

Before the politically correct among our contemporaries get all huffy, of course, more research would reveal that this claim, like most such claims, was a bit more complicated. So be it. Remarkable as it may be, nowhere in this discussion did the topic of *nisba* come up.[4] Moroccan identity had more axes than one marketplace could reveal; other arenas of commerce, it turns out, would have provided other lessons.

Patrons and Clients

Fundamentally, Cliff Geertz was an awkward human being who learned to use that awkwardness to his own continuing advantage. What in others would be taken as rudeness or abruptness in social interaction was more frequently than not attributed to the man's genius and forgiven or at least forgotten. In the Morocco fieldwork years, I had no particular gripe with his distance, curtness, and general "away-ness." He was rarely available, infrequently had anything to say when we did meet, yet he continued during that time to write captivating essays, and many of his mumbled offhand remarks proved to be fertile suggestions for things to follow up on. By and large, this arrangement suited me fine because it left me alone to do what I thought needed to be done. When I was sick in Morocco, the Geertzes' maid brought me soup. Not a bad arrangement, all things considered.

In 1969, instead of returning to the University of Chicago to write my thesis, I decided to move back to New York. I rented an apartment on St. Mark's Place, down the block from W. H. Auden, whom I never met. The East Village in those days was inexpensive and full of nourishing Jewish and Ukrainian cafes and restaurants. I wrote my thesis, *A History of Power in a Moroccan Village*. Geertz read a draft and said, "There is a thesis in there somewhere, keep going." I kept going. Spending a good deal of time with Hyman at Max's Kansas City, just off Union Square, a hangout place for part of the fashion world, I rewrote the thesis. I received my degree. I was offered two jobs at different branches of the City University of New York and accepted one at Richmond College, then an experimental upper-division college. The first book I taught was *Village in the Vaucluse,* a book about a French village where small things, and palaver, held great import; it was also a site of wise insights about things French.

With some prodding, Geertz agreed to have me as his assistant at the Institute for Advanced Study during the fateful year of 1972–73. The year was fateful in a number of ways. For me, the fact that Pierre Bourdieu was there and initially did not speak much English was a gift as it meant I got to spend a great deal of time with him in the early months. He hated the Institute for Advanced Study for its smugness and attributed or misattributed a set of spiritualist motives to Geertz. Bourdieu held a clear and well-articulated position that with his appointment as the first social scientist at the Institute for Advanced Study, Geertz had a unique responsibility to the human sciences. Bourdieu thought, and said, that Geertz should take the opportunity to form a program of interpretive social science and, if not establish a school, at least make the vast resources, both symbolic and material, of the Institute for Advanced Study the foundation for a larger project. Geertz would have none of it. "I am not a cruise director," he pronounced on one occasion; of course, no one would ever have considered that he was, nor was that role what Bourdieu was proposing. Exercising the prerogatives of power and privilege that were now securely his, Geertz felt he did not have to answer to anybody and acted accordingly. Bourdieu explained to me on the basis of a detailed sociological analysis of the French academic scene that he would later publish in a different version under the title *Homo Academicus* how he would be nominated for and voted into the Collège de France. He would start a journal, build alliances, and gradually advance his vision of the social sciences. He had elaborate justifications about the impersonality of these strategies. He took things seriously, very seriously.

The year was also a fateful one because the nomination of Robert Bellah as a member of the nascent School of Social Sciences at the Institute for Advanced Study was rejected in a nasty academic manner. Around the time of the decision, the Bellahs lost one of their daughters. Although I did not spend much time with Bellah that year, nor was I privy to the Institute for Advanced Study's politics, three years later I participated in a National Endowment for the Humanities seminar for college teachers at Berkeley during the academic year 1975–76 that Bellah directed. During that year, I met William Sullivan, with whom I edited two books, and Hubert Dreyfus, with whom I became fast friends of a philosophic sort and with whom I would write a book on Michel Foucault several years later.

Bellah, it is a pleasure to add, saved my career. By accepting me in his NEH seminar, I was able to connect with Sullivan and Dreyfus as well as learn from Bellah himself a great deal about an interpretive social science that was morally committed. Although I did not agree with all of his positions, I remain deeply impressed with Bellah's clear sense of right and wrong and his profound loyalty to those he valued. By this point, I had written the manuscript of *Reflections on Fieldwork in Morocco* but was basically ready to abandon it because it had been rejected by four or five presses. The editor at the University of Chicago Press told me to put it in a drawer and take it out when I was famous. Geertz told me it would ruin my career. Bellah tactfully intimated that it might be wise to stop asking Geertz for recommendations. Bellah talked to the University California Press, and now, thirty years later, the book is still in print. It did not ruin my career.

During this period, the Geertz team was giving shape to what eventually became *Meaning and Order in Moroccan Society*. I was invited to contribute a chapter but was told it had to be on a set of specific topics, none of which interested me (irrigation systems and so forth). I wrote what was no doubt an uninteresting and flat essay and sent it to Hildred. I never heard anything about it. When Hyman mentioned that the book was going to press, I inquired about the status of my essay: Cliff told me to talk to Hilly; Hilly said that she had sent me a letter explaining why they were not going to include my essay in the book. Having never received the letter, I asked to see a copy. I never heard from her again. Basically, I was relieved because I did not share their view of fieldwork, anthropology, or this particular book. I do not doubt that my essay was poor. That being said, I was disgusted by the lack of the most minimal courtesy or human consideration. But by this point in my career I was beginning to learn enough about academic life that it was no longer a shock to encounter such inconsideration and assumed lack of accountability. These people took themselves very seriously. I saw very little of the Geertzes in the decades that followed; we exchanged extremely brief greetings at anthropology meetings from time to time. Aside from an extremely uncomfortable Wenner-Gren conference in Fez, where Geertz, Marshall Sahlins, and Edmund Leech exchanged verbal insults and expressed mutual contempt, that was that.

Although I did not fully share Bourdieu's attacks on Geertz or admire the unbridled ambition they both were invested with, I did agree that something more should have been done with the opportunities presented by the Institute for Advanced Study. The contrast with Bellah, who became a committed public intellectual and devoted the next part of his life to his group of young scholars collaboratively attempting to influence the moral direction of the American polity, could not be more striking. One can only wonder whether Geertz's refusal to collaborate with others or articulate and defend a common cause, intellectual or otherwise, was not ultimately his own burden, his own Achilles' heel. In my opinion, his refusal to engage in the "theory" or "Writing Culture" debates and skirmishes of the 1980s and 1990s seems related to the ever more involuted prose, devastatingly reviewed as a soufflé that deflates if you stick a fork in it. Whatever personal demons the man struggled with, his retreat from larger engagement, from challenging collaboration, from accepting the responsibility for the construction of a new venue for the human sciences in America, was a loss for the larger polity of scholars and thinkers.

And, I think it is fair to say, this refusal of collaboration was a loss for Geertz as well. Although being your own patron is a well-known practice, one we all practice to one degree or another, and although being a Big Man carries with it incessant obligations and annoyances—as the villagers used to say, "*les grosses têtes, jamais labes*"—systematically refusing responsibilities and rela-tionships—"I am not a cruise director"—may leave one without debts but also, as Bourdieu has analyzed so keenly, outside of the circle of exchange in which the cycles of gift and countergift are endlessly deferred and never completed so as to solidify and fortify social relations.[5] Said more simply, as the Moroccans put it when describing one of the locals who wandered back and forth without accruing debts or credit, without tying himself to family or locale, "*za et msha*," "he came and went." The phrase is not a compliment, only an observation of someone considered to be more or less mad. The tone was tolerant, even affection-ate, but always tinged with a certain comic pathos. Obviously the analogy is far from exact, but it is not exquisitely imperfect either.

Poses

Before and after his stint in Morocco, Paul Hyman worked as a fashion photographer in New York, having apprenticed in his trade, albeit in an amateur mode, in a similar milieu in Paris. Hence, it was fashion that uneasily defined the orientation, prac-tice, vision, and values of what was seen, taken, captured, or lost. At the typical fashion photographer's studio, the pulsing con-stellation of people and energy centered on the director. Moving closer to the director, practicing the techniques and nuances of his style, and aiding his overall production were among the ne-cessities and challenges of apprenticeship. The promised rewards of money, fame, glamour, sex, drugs, and rock and roll were om-nipresent in their luster while being all too frequently elusive in the quotidian reality. In this world, aging was the great demon, the gates through which only a very few managed to pass (for example, Richard Avedon). Although age and their looks were both the haunting demons and hovering angels for the models, in a less obvious but still compelling way, so too did this inevitable specter haunt the photographers. No one needed to be reminded, having played the role themselves, that in this scene, there were always younger, less marked, more ardent aspirants ready to work, play, and deal more vigorously and decisively than those just a little older. Not surprisingly, in conversations late at night or during midmorning caffeine exchanges, there was a leitmotif, wistful and bitter, of art, vision, and real photography shadowed by the acute awareness of the banality and exploitative character of what was actually on display. Pointing out this contradiction, this structure and its affect, easy for the anthropologist, harder for the friend, occasioned diverse but always riven responses. So much talent, so much bullshit.

Hyman's voyage to Morocco, his mission underspecified and undercompensated, had nonetheless the allure of a moment for him to shoot much more freely. It became a tacit test, an *épreuve*, as the French say, of character and desire. This anthropological photo opportunity would not be anything like the fashion shoot in Marrakech (taking shape even then), but who knew what it would be? It would be a turn into the unknown: definitely not toward the exotic but an unmarked exploration of the talent and imagination of the observer, the photographer. How good was he? Was all that lamenting at Max's Kansas City anything more than the dawn of the days of wine and roses? Who knew? Who knew how to gauge the answer?

≫≫≫≪≪≪

Roland Barthes, in his 1980 *La Chambre Claire, notes sur la photographie*, at least reread today, provides some benchmarks that clarify the question of judging, of gauging these matters. As with all Barthes' work, this book-length essay attempts to balance, often unsuccessfully, and from time to time with stunning clarity, his own hyperrefined subjectivism with his standard device of deploying concepts and principles from would-be sciences (structuralism, discourse theory, semantics, psychoanalysis, and so forth). Barthes used this checks-and-balances approach as a rhetorical check, aiding him to discipline, to counter, to remand his own wayward consciousness to the prison house of the real.

More than halfway through the book, Barthes announces with a declarative joy and relief, apparently having just discovered it, a principle guiding his philosophical meditations (and sporadic psychoanalytical ruminations) concerning the nature of photography: "From the beginning, I had determined on a principle for myself: never to reduce myself-as-subject, confronting certain photographs, to the disincarnated, disaffect *socius* which science is concerned with."[6]

Hyman did not require any elaborate self-policing in order to fix this principle, the principle of refusing to picture anything, above all the Moroccans, as bloodless, immaterial, hygienized things that Barthes declaims as the normative object of a science of the social. In this instance such a temptation had never structured Hyman's subjectivity; so, when the Geertzes proposed that he photograph parallel cousin marriages, or unproductive agricultural fields, Hyman had no trouble refusing the request to capture a social science concept not only on the object side but, of course, on the subject side as well (*ne jamais réduire le sujet que j'étais*).

And yet, Hyman's photos are at an infinity of aesthetic and ethical distance from the orientalist blather that the photo shoots in Marrakech continue to disseminate. Barthes' *Mythologiques* had demolished the semantic underpinnings of this insidious fantasy world long before Edward Said.[7] Hyman's photos show us something specific, particular, and singular. And here, acutely, Barthes provides the means to establish a bridge from fashion photography to Photography, capital P. What underpins the nature of Photography? Barthes writes: "The pose . . . a real thing happened to be immobile in front of the eye. I project the present photograph's immobility upon this past shot, and this is the arrest that which constitutes the prose."[8]

If there is anything that springs out as a persistent leitmotif from Hyman's photographs, it is that they are posed. This posing is often quite formal. I believe that there is a strong ethical component to his poses. With Hyman there is no surreptitious attempt to "capture the moment" à la Henri Cartier-Bresson, who shot his photos with his camera cocked at his waist, just as there is no elaborate studio setup requiring professional lighting equipment, makeup, and hair stylists, as well as the requisite elaborate darkroom work of a Richard Avedon. And yet, Hyman's photos are posed, and they consistently mark that posing for the viewer. As an anthropologist, this form seems ethical to me because Hyman always engaged those he was photographing; he wanted them to be aware of what he was doing. He wanted their attention. He wanted them to pose naturally or perhaps culturally, but in any case, as they saw fit. The pose was not imposed. This claim, of course, does not mean that all the photographer had to do was arrange people and things and then click. Rather, again Barthes seems on the mark when he observes, "The true photograph total, it accomplishes the unheard-of identification of reality (*'that-has-been'*) with truth ('there-she-is!'); it becomes at once evidential and exclamative."[9]

Barthes is making two claims here: the first that for him is central is the capturing of a being's existing at a moment in time—*cela a été*. By itself, however, any snapshot will do that much. The second claim—*c'est ca!*—is a truth claim of a very particular sort. Specifying that particular sort requires Barthes to make several more distinctions. We know that the truth claim will not be of the asepticized kind. We also know they will have strictly nothing directly to do with thick description or deep play. The reason Barthes gives is the alchemy of unexpected confusion of reality and truth that "*la vraie phtographie totale*" yields. But this talk is getting murkier and murkier, far beyond the intentions of Hyman.

The talk of a distinction between reality and truth and then their unexpected confusion through the truth of total photography indicates that Barthes has lost his way. His theory will not enable him to tell us from the object side what is going on in the photographs that move him. As usual, he is surer when it comes to his own feelings. And here we arrive at the distinction for which Barthes has received the most critical attention: between *studium* and *punctum*. *Studium* might be translated as a "study," but that is too academic, too reserved, too reflected. Rather, subjectively, Barthes uses the term to point to a kind of documentary capacity that photography is well suited to produce and by which by now millions of consumers or spectators are well disposed to receive. The *studium*, Barthes writes, returning to the home ground of his own taste and reactions, is "that very wide field of unconcerned desire, of various interest, of inconsequential taste."[10]

The taken-for-granted (because learned and practiced and disseminated) disposes both photographer and audience to the picking out of an image, "*sans acuité particulière*."[11] This is the aspect of seizing some bit of stereotyped reality that Pierre Bourdieu claimed as the defining characteristic of photography in his sociological study of photography, *Un Art moyen*.[12] Clearly, however, Barthes is not doing sociology but rather is searching to understand why certain pictures, especially those of his mother, move him so strongly. And this embrace of his own taste and reactions brings him to the other learned term, the counterpunch to the banality, the ordinariness affectively and substantively, of the *studium*, the *punctum*. The term shares its Latin roots with the term "to punctuate," as in the marking, the underscoring, of something made. Barthes performs a reversal here; in emphasizing punctuation as the diacritic of true photography, it would seem to be the subject who performs the defining act. But for Barthes, the *punctum* is an objective quality; it comes, like an arrow, from the photo, to pierce the viewer's consciousness: "A photograph's *punctum* is that accident which pricks me."[13]

Although it is plausible that some parallel tension between the marking of time, cultural expectation, and this small affective piercing (Barthes calls it a fly bite—*émouchèment*—at one point) may exist in other forms of photography, its particular acuity in Hyman's photos comes, it seems to me, from his transformation of the sociological study into the marking of a singular moment as well as from the deft equipoise with which these scenes of vulnerability, tenderness, and energy in a troubled world have been composed.

3

Foucault's Untimely Struggle: Toward a Form of Spirituality

> If we define spirituality as being the form of practices which postulate that, such as he is, the subject is not capable of the truth, but that, such as it is, the truth can transfigure and save the subject, then we can say that the modern age of the relations between the subject and truth begin when it is postulated that, such as he is, the subject is capable of truth, but that, such as it is, the truth cannot save the subject.
>
> «MICHEL FOUCAULT[1]»

In his series of essays on Kant written during the 1980s, Michel Foucault attempted to discern the difference today made with respect to yesterday. As his essays as well as his lectures (especially at the Collège de France and Berkeley) during the early 1980s demonstrate, he was drawn—and devoted the bulk of his scholarly efforts to a renewed form of genealogical work on themes, venues, practices, and modes of governing the subject and others—to experiments in new forms of friendship, sociability, and transformations of the self and others that he saw taking

Originally published in a slightly different form as "Michel Foucault: An Untimely Struggle," *Theory, Culture and Society* 26, no. 6 (2009): 25–44. Reprinted by permission.

shape or imagined were taking shape around him. This work, which has come to be known unfortunately as the "late Foucault," arose out of deep dissatisfaction with his own life conditions, the larger political climate of the time, and a profound and unexpected rethinking not only of the specific projects he had intended to carry out but of what it meant to think.

This chapter explores some of the elements at play during this deeply (re)formative period of several years, which as they unfolded were in no way intended to constitute a "late Foucault," but instead quite the opposite, even if fate would have it otherwise. The chapter is organized around a "prelude" that introduces the problem of what *mode* is appropriate for giving form to thinking. It proceeds to argue that Foucault engaged in a struggle to redefine the *object* of thinking, that in order to do so he was led to pursue a *venue* in which such thinking could be practiced, and finally to an increasingly articulate and acute quest for a *form* that would constitute a difference between what Foucault diagnosed as an impoverished modern problem space (alluded to in the quote that started this chapter) and a future in which things might be different and better.

Prelude

Friedrich Nietzsche's *Untimely Observations* (*Unzeitgemässe Betrachtungen*, French *Considérations inactuelles*), like almost everything he wrote, was a work in progress, a work on the way. In his notebooks of the period (1872–74), the young Nietzsche outlined plans for an ambitious "philosopher's book" that would transform the discipline as well as the practice of thinking itself. Although he never wrote precisely that book, it could be said that he never stopped working on it. In 1874 Nietzsche published a series of polemic essays; these essays are aggressive; they fit the tone and timbre of his no longer youthful *On the Genealogy of Morals* (1887), whose subtitle is *Eine Streitschrift*, translated as "polemic," but a better translation would be "conflictual" or "contestatory" writing. The term refers to a German eighteenth-century genre of criticism: at its most artful it is a term of agonistic engagement carried out antagonistically.

If Nietzsche's preferred affect was contestatory, the title, *Unzeitgemässe Betrachtungen*, grouping these disparate interventions together, indicates the mode in which he was operating. That mode is a distinctive and significant composite; it can be pursued in a variety of affective registers. Nietzsche's term *Betrachtungen*, which translates into English as "observations" and into French as "considerations," misses the refractory intent of the engaged and active state in which Nietzsche worked. Hence, *Betrachtungen* is better conveyed as something more like the purposively oxymoronic "*vigorous contemplations.*"[2] *Unzeitgemässe* literally does mean "untimely," but the French, "*inactuelles,*" is more precise not only in its inclusion of a general temporal dimension but in its identification of that temporal dimension as the "actual."

Combined, the two terms and their affective stylization yield a mode best captured by the French term "*l'intempestif.*" The semantic range of the term covers not only "untimely" but also "ill-timed," "unreasonable," or "inopportune." The term captures a striving to bring something forth, something that could be actual but does not yet exist. Of course, this claim does not mean that there is something waiting around to come to fruition but only that, taken up in a distinctive way, the things of the actual and existing world can be made into something appropriate and inopportune. Such an event would be appropriate at least retrospectively in that it reconfigures existing things and relations, and it would be inopportune in that it disrupts those existing things and relations and changes their tone, register, and directionality.

The striving for such alteration—close to the present, contesting the present, seeking something that might be becoming in the present—is found everywhere in the *Untimely Observations*. Of the four essays Nietzsche grouped together under that title, the one that is still frequently taken to be pertinent today is the essay titled "On the Utility and Liability of History for Life." He opens that essay by asserting: "In any case, I hate everything that merely instructs me without augmenting or directly invigorating my activity. These words are from Goethe, and they may stand as a sincere [*ceterum censeo* at the] beginning of our meditation on the value of history. For its intention is to show why instruction without invigoration, why knowledge not attended by action, why history as a costly superfluity and luxury, to use Goethe's word, should be seriously hated by us—hated because we still lack even the things we need and the superfluous is the enemy of the necessary."[3]

Gilles Deleuze, in an interview late in his life, "*Contrôle et devenir*," returned to Nietzsche's use of history. He insisted (to his Marxist) interlocutor Tony Negri that historical contextualization can never be more than a partial determination of things; hence, an appeal to a method of historical contextualization, while frequently a necessary preliminary for understanding, was not sufficient. Rather, for Deleuze, an adequate account of an event—its signification, its explanation, its effects, its affects—had to take the critical limitations of the uses and abuses of history into account. Like Nietzsche, although in a different form, Deleuze affirmed the challenge of philosophy as finding a way to produce concepts and affects, ones necessary for our survival and our flourishing. Method alone was not the route to such invention.

Significant events, Deleuze declaims, were always accompanied by "a history-less penumbra (*nuée*)."[4] This state of affairs arose from the fact that emergent things can be understood as a form of experimentation, or what Deleuze calls a "counter-movement" (*contra-effectuation*). Thus, although historical conditions are necessary for there to be experimentation or countermotion because without these conditions there would be only indeterminacy, the historical conditions themselves are not sufficient to explain either events and their eventual effects and countereffects.

Deleuze identified two modes in which one can take up an event. The standard one consisted in methodically delimiting the event in its temporality and scope, its preconditions, its consequences, and its eventual historicality. He contested that method, arguing instead for a second mode in which one is "swimming upstream as it were, in placing oneself within the flow of the event in its becoming, to rejuvenate and to age simultaneously, to pass through each of its elements and each singularity. Becoming (*le devenir*) is not history; history designates only the collection of conditions, as recent as they may be, that need to be overcome in order 'to become,' to create something new. That state of becoming is precisely what Nietzsche called the 'inopportune' (*l'Intempestif*)."[5]

Exactly what Deleuze intended by his idiosyncratic tropes is not easy to grasp, but at the very least, they direct us to the critical task of the *thinker*: to seize an event in its becoming while the work of the *historian* is to insist on the importance of historical elements as conditioning whatever takes place. The latter method, of course, produces valid knowledge of a specific sort; the former, the "inopportune"—*l'intempestif*—operates adjacently, in a space of becoming where the old and new are available if one approaches them in a mode of vigorous contemplation of the about to be actual.

Defending Thinking

Michel Foucault took up and experimented with the challenge of critical thought in many different ways over the course of his intellectual life. Almost all of Foucault's writings could be called an inopportune and vigorous contemplation, a critical contestation perpetually in search of new forms of criticism and invention. Whatever else criticism or critique was for Foucault, it was not the denunciation associated with the speaker's benefit, for example, Bourdieu's Pascalian overview (*surplomb*) of others' irremediable *illusio*.[6] Whatever else critical thought was, it always concerned one form or another of examining, in-close and in-detail, an existing (often historical) state of affairs in an affectively engaged but yet contemplative way. Like Nietzsche, Foucault, almost always in an uneasy and restless fashion—*Pour une morale de l'inconfort*—strove to invent and practice a form of asceticism, by which he meant an active attention to work on the self, on those he worked with, and on the material he was considering as well as the price to be paid for forging a different mode of relationship among and between these elements.

Foucault experimented with a number of different forms of criticism and inquiry almost always in the attempt to find ways to connect them. As is well known, he frequently recast his previous efforts as if they had ineluctably led him to the work he had just finished. As is equally well known, he changed course multiple times, wary of the complacency inherent in repetition, yet not embracing an avant-guardist stance for its own sake, although writers such as Raymond Roussel and Maurice Blanchot did hold an attraction for him during a certain period. For example, Foucault told an Italian interviewer, "Each one of my books is a way of dismantling an object, and of constructing a method of analysis toward this end. Once a work is finished, I can, of course, more or less through hindsight, deduce a methodology from the completed experience."[7] This claim alerts us to the privileged status of objects and of analysis for Foucault as well as the secondary standing of method as either a guide or a guarantee, a theme he would take up explicitly and to which he would give great significance in his lectures of 1981–82.

One mode of analysis was the "history of the present," characteristic of Foucault's work during the middle 1970s, culminating in *Discipline and Punish*. The task of the history of the present was essentially a diagnostic one: to trace out—*analysis*—the sedimented concepts, practices, and organizations of knowledge and power—*objects*—that made it seem coherent and plausible to build prisons and to claim that the prisons were reforming those imprisoned while, at the same time, contributing to defending another new object, *society*. This analytic dismantling, this production of estrangement, entailed detailed work in archives as well as a rereading of conceptual texts of people such as Jeremy Bentham not as academic philosophers but as producers of programs for social reform, at the time a distinctive *practice,* with a long future ahead of it. These programs were the proper objects for Foucault's analysis to the extent that they had established a specific type of rationality as reasonable. Whether a type of rationality had been taken to be reasonable was a question not for the historian to answer but, rather, for the historian of the present to pose. The reason for making this distinction and underlining it is that the work to be done was diagnostic, the work of freeing up the recent past to a concerned objectivity, an untimely attention to objects and practices.

Discipline and Punish occasioned intense, often negative, reactions from psychiatrists as well as from some leading historians in France and the United States. Fortunately for us, Foucault's white-hot counters to these attacks or, as he says later, these "reproaches," are of an uncommon directness and lucidity. For example, in 1980 Foucault accepted an invitation to participate in a roundtable encounter with a group of prestigious historians assembled by his friend, Michelle Perrot, a historian of women. The encounter was not peaceable. From our perspective, the assembly was an extravagant success; Foucault was angry (*thumic*) enough to generate marvelously scathingly demonstrations of his mode of analysis, his chosen objects, his diagnostic practice, and his goals.

In a written response to the historians, "*La poussière et le nuage*," Foucault forged the famous analogy according to which what he was doing was deploying "*fragments philosophiques dans des chantiers historiques*" [philosophic fragments in the workshops of history].[8] His elaboration of what precisely he intended by that entrancing analogy is lucid. Primarily and fundamentally, it was a demand that the principles on which his work and that of the historian-interlocutors proceeded required more careful attention. Technically, therefore, this intervention was a critical contestation, styled in a *thumic* affect, vigorously analytic. To me, the most striking countermovement is found in the following challenge: "Perhaps we should also investigate the principle, unexamined and taken for granted, that the only reality to which history must attend, is society itself."[9]

This challenge to focus on the tacit baseline, the unquestioned and assumed to be self-evident, ontological reality—society—opens up a vast terrain for exploration. The way Foucault laid down the challenge, it was clear that it would be met with a counterchallenge, which, of course, he had anticipated. If the order of things was not social, then what was it? Obviously, Foucault was not going to substitute "power" or "ethics" or "governmentality" as some of his followers would later assert with their habitual lack of acuity. The demand for naming the "really real" required first a refusal: a steadfast rebuff to the mode in which the question was being posed. It then required inquiry.

As Hans Blumenberg has argued in *The Legitimacy of the Modern Age*, a cornerstone of this antisubstantialist mode of thinking requires the reflective recasting of certain older questions and concepts (as well as objects and practices) that had been honed in a different problem space.[10] Philosophic fragments forged in the workshops of history and historians could not be taken over unexamined. Furthermore, at times it was vital that certain older questions should not be left unanswered. That stance, of course, is not a general negation of past concepts and practices but only a reflective and critical questioning, a marking of the problems previously posed to which concepts and practices had constituted answers or solutions.

Thus, Foucault's task consisted not only of making what was self-evident contingent but also of analyzing how it had been linked in complex ways with "multiple historical processes, many of them recent."[11] The task was to make visible the appropriate objects of analysis. Among those recent and multiple processes that needed to be taken into account were the histories of the processes in question, then and now. "To make or do a history of 'objectivation,' of those elements that historians consider as objective givens (the objectivation of objectivations, so to say); it is that circle that I wish to follow out."[12]

It follows that in many cases the parameters of the question needed to be rethought, so as to make them pertinent for addressing a different problem: one susceptible of being investigated, reflected on, experimented with, learned from, and recast. High on the list of objectified givens was society: "My problem is not to propose a global analysis of society. . . . My general theme is not society but rather is true/false discourse; the correlative formation of domains, objects, and the discourses that are verifiable and falsifiable in relation to them; and furthermore it is not only that formation that interests me but the effects on reality connected to them."[13]

An example can be found in an interview titled *"Est-il donc important de penser?"* which was conducted in May 1981 with his friend the journalist Didier Eribon at the time of the presidential election of the socialist Francois Mitterrand. In the interview, which occurred during a time when the Socialist Party was calling for intellectuals to back their programs or be considered, if not class enemies, at least betrayers of social justice, Foucault presented a theme he would return to repeatedly with increasingly urgency in his remaining three years, formulating variants over and over again. The theme was the defense of thought when the pressing demand was for political action: "To begin from the outset by accepting the question of what reforms I will introduce, is not, I believe, the objective that an intellectual should entertain. His role, since he works in the register of thought, is to see just how far thought can be freed so as to make certain transformations seem urgent enough so that others will attempt to bring them into effect, and difficult enough so that if they are brought about they will be deeply inscribed in the real."[14]

For Foucault this challenge followed from what he had gradually come to define as his vocation and his problem: to think. The work to be done entailed leaving totalities behind, specifically the taken-for-granted totalities to which certain French politicians were dispositionally attached. A critical analytic task, therefore, consisted in changing not society or culture or power but thought. This task, Foucault held, was analytic, certainly, but the goal of such critical work was pragmatic in the largest sense of the term: to make changes in the near future subject to thought. "We must free ourselves (*s'affranchir*) from the sacralization of the social as the unique instance of the real and stop diminishing that essential aspect of human life and human relations, thinking.

Thought exists well beyond the systems and edifices of discourse. It is something that is often hidden but always animates ordinary human action. There is always some pinch of thought in the stupidest of institutions. There is always some thought in the most silent of habits."[15]

Critical work is diagnostic and analytic. This work might open up with more clarity that which was a necessity and that which was an obstructive luxury.

But where and how?

In Search of a Venue

I do not believe we are locked in by history; to the contrary, all my work consists in showing that history is crossed by strategic relations which consequently are mobile and can be changed; upon the condition, of course, that the agents involved in these processes have the political courage to change things.
«MICHEL FOUCAULT[16]»

The Collège de France is not exactly a teaching institution as it grants no degrees and has no general curriculum, only the lectures of the professors, who are free to explore any topic on which they are doing research. Consequently, it is a distinctive kind of institution. Professors are paid to do research and to present their work in public to whoever decides to attend their presentations. An appointment at the Collège de France is the ultimate, and much coveted, pinnacle of academic prestige in France.

In this light, and in stark contrast to his inaugural lesson in 1970, the tone of Foucault's opening lecture of 1976 at the Collège de France took the form of an odd, pathos-toned colloquy. "I would like to be a bit clearer," he wrote, "about what is going on here, in these lectures."[17] Somewhat petulantly, yet with a tone of resigned resolve, Foucault was quite uncharacteristically blunt, informing the hundreds of auditors facing him, as well as those listening in an adjoining room: "So, I do not regard our Wednesday meetings as a teaching activity, but rather as public reports on the work I am, in other respects, left to get on with more or less as I see fit. To that extent, I actually consider myself to be under an absolute obligation to tell you roughly what I am doing."[18]

He then asserted that those who attended the public reporting were free to do whatever they would like with the material he presented. His frustration and resignation were clear: "These are suggestions for research, ideas, schemata, outlines, instruments; do what you like with them."[19] But Foucault was obviously not entirely comfortable with that arrangement. Having just told his audience to do as they liked with his public lectures, he admitted, "It does concern me to the extent that, one way or another, what you do with it is connected, related, to what I am doing."[20] But how they were connected, in what way, was not clear to him; given the structure of the situation, he had no way of knowing what was being done with his material, how the lectures were being received, used, distributed, distorted, and so forth. Given these uncertainties and contradictions, Foucault adopted a tone of resigned consternation.

He observed to his audience that they, the large throngs that attended his lectures punctually and regularly, for whatever reasons, were obliged to arrive early, and half or more of those attending had to sit in a different room and listen to the lectures over a sound system. He proposed shifting the time of his lectures from the late afternoon to 9:30 in the morning because, as he remarked, he was told that students had trouble getting up that early. Clearly, the situation was not a source of either pleasure or gratification for Foucault. Again, uncharacteristically, he spoke frankly about his unhappiness with the arrangement: "The problem for me—I will be quite blunt about it—the fact that I had to go through this sort of circus every Wednesday was really—how can I put it?—torture (*supplice*) is putting it too strongly, boredom (*ennui*) is putting it too mildly, so I suppose it was somewhere in between the two."[21]

The "circus" atmosphere stood in stark opposition to the spirit of the lectures he spent so much time and care constructing: research in progress, forays in thinking and clarification, unsettling of certitudes, unexpected ramifications. What was supposed to be a venue characterized by the utmost freedom to conduct and report on current research in progress, the chair in the History of Systems of Thought, had increasingly become the obligation to perform, at least in part, so as to please or amuse or simply distract an anonymous overflow audience over which he had no control and with whom he had no contact. Although there were no registered students at the Collège de France, there was also no procedure to exclude anyone. Whoever showed up, the public, had a right to attend. "So I said to myself: It wouldn't be such a bad idea if thirty or forty of us could get together in a room. I could tell you roughly what I've been doing, and at the same time have some contact with you, talk to you, answer your questions and so on, and try to rediscover the possibility of exchange and contact that are part of the normal practice of research and teaching."[22]

Although Foucault had sought an appointment at the Collège de France, increasingly he felt trapped by its form. In Paris, there was no other obvious outlet with which he felt comfortable. Apparently obtaining a position at the École des Hautes Études en Sciences Sociales was not something he seriously entertained even though Pierre Bourdieu and Roland Barthes (among others) accumulated positions, as the French say, at both institutions. Foucault did have a small research seminar at the Collège de France for a number of years, which yielded a certain amount of collective work such as *I, Pierre Rivière* or work on the birth of the hospital. But for reasons that are not entirely clear, petty personality disputes among them, the seminar seemed to have exhausted itself.[23] During this period Foucault attempted to start a publishing series of scholarly "works," and although after a series of rebuffs he ultimately succeeded on a smaller scale than he had hoped for, the experience of trying to establish it had been discouraging and the results limited.[24] The discouragement was a product not only of the limited results but of the lack of response, enthusiasm, and adventure among those in a position to support new things.

Of course, in order to contextualize Foucault's mood, his growing sense of feeling trapped and ground down, I should describe the broader political situation of France in the late 1970s (and the biographies provide the elements to do so) as well as some of the restlessness he was undergoing in his personal life. Foucault's political activity during the late 1970s and early 1980s basically took the form of direct protest. He spoke out, joined demonstrations, appeared on panels with other Parisian figures, and even signed petitions. Among the causes he championed: he took a stand against what he took to be the French government's arrogant refusal to back the Polish Solidarity movement; he expressed his dismay and anger at what he took to be the Socialist Party's political program and its media attacks on independent intellectuals—Jack Lang referred to Foucault as "a clown"; he displayed an unexpected affirmation of the political importance of human rights campaigns as well as the nascent humanitarian movements in France.[25] That being said, Foucault experienced political activity during this period as deeply frustrating and judged the harvests of his and others' efforts to be at best frugal.

By the late 1970s, Foucault was thoroughly fed up with France, discouraged by the French political scene as well as all by the petty obstacles to his scholarly work that he encountered regularly. He had stopped using the one great public library in France, the Bibliothèque Nationale, because of the impediments imposed on accessing materials.[26] At the Bibliothèque Nationale, one submitted request slips for the books one wanted to use and then had to wait until they were delivered. One could submit only a certain number of slips at one time; the unions were not infrequently involved in job actions that extended delivery of materials beyond the habitual delays. In frustration, Foucault shifted his routine to a Dominican library where all the primary texts in Greek and Latin that he was beginning to work on were readily available for his use.

Although these and other such blockages and impediments appear petty in and of themselves, they are not insignificant. Micropractices, as Foucault had demonstrated in *Discipline and Punish*, can be used as dividing practices, as insidious annoyances, as techniques of subordination, and so forth. Lest these details appear anecdotal and trivial, it is worth underscoring that this period was one, for example, in which Foucault was discussing suicide as an option worthy of praise as an ultimate act of freedom.[27] Thus, remembering Deleuze's admonitions about the uses and abuses of history, one can see that these conditions of existence were, of course, not determinative of Foucault's personal and political actions or of the extraordinary twists and turns of this thinking. The fact that these conditions were not causal, however, does not mean that they had no importance. Without determinations, both local and general, after all, actions would have no constraint and would be thoroughly inchoate. Without conditions, no becoming. Without context, nothing to be inopportune about. The effort to derive something singular requires countermotion, and there is no method to decide how to accomplish that.

Foucault's visits to the United States, which increased in regularity during this period, gradually, and no doubt inchoately at first, can be seen to demonstrate a growing eagerness to find a different way of practicing his thinking and a nascent program in which the care of the self, his own as well as those close to him, began to emerge. Foucault being Foucault, he explored this theme both existentially and conceptually. The question of a venue—a scene or setting in which something takes place—a place to come to work with others, to undertake research, to teach, to learn, to question, and to contest findings and methods with some earnestness and excitement, unquestionably formed a problem of concern. It was in the United States, and especially in Berkeley and San Francisco, that Foucault committed himself to the program of the care of the self and its inextricable reformulation of relations with others.

As Didier Eribon pithily puts it: "The United States for Michel Foucault was the pleasure of work."[28] To his great pleasure, the classical texts were readily available at the Berkeley library or through interlibrary loan. Furthermore, in Berkeley he could actually take them out of the library. In addition, many people were eager to help him. Berkeley provided him with enthusiastic students at all levels—the man insisted on having "office hours"—imagine! He had extended discussions with Hubert Dreyfus and me that provided him a venue in which he could examine his work from a different perspective and with a different ethos. There were as yet basically no Foucaultians or for that matter anti-Foucaultians in the United States, although that would change rather rapidly.

During this period of 1979–83, the great sexual revolution was taking place in San Francisco, just before the dawn of AIDS. As Foucault wrote in a number of essays at the time, his previous battles to argue to himself and to others that sexuality was not the deepest meaning or the key to the self was being demonstrated before his very eyes. Sex was practiced openly, defiantly at first but soon casually, as was the identity politics constructed around it, both unimaginable in Paris at the time. Foucault was fascinated by these events, yet his dry humor (in English)—"There are so many gays, and I am a homosexual!"—revealed him to be seeking the locus of significance elsewhere than in the clubs and sex discussions. "Every gay is writing a book"—again, his humor was deployed not so much as to distance himself from what he was seeing per se but rather to think about the distance he felt. Again, Eribon, only slightly ironically, concludes: "Foucault's American happiness: a reconciliation with himself finally realized. He is happy in his work. He is happy in the pleasures of his body. From the beginning of the 1980s Foucault was seriously considering leaving France and Paris, which he tolerated less and less well, to move to the U.S."[29]

Of course, the Golden Age of American Happiness in the California Paradise was not to last very long. It was fated, tragically, in San Francisco, or, more banally, in Berkeley, for more somber times.

In Search of a Mode, Practice, and Form of Spirituality

Unexpectedly, the concept that Foucault settled on to characterize the dimension missing from modern philosophy, the component whose elimination (or marginalization) had produced centuries of misplaced assurance arising from and instantiating (quite literally) a quest for method, that theme was "spirituality": "the search, practice, and experience through which the subject carries out the necessary transformations on himself in order to have access to the truth."[30]

Foucault's introduction of the term "spirituality" in the 1981–82 lectures at the Collège de France was unanticipated, even startling. Although he had used the term "political spirituality" briefly in his journalistic writings about Iran, and although it is true that he had intended to return to it as a central theme (along with governmentality) of a proposed longer-term research project on the sixteenth century and the 1920s with colleagues at Berkeley, he had not found an occasion to return to it during the late 1970s. Rather, during those few years, he had devoted himself to analyzing other topics and concepts (liberalism, governmentality, security, population, and so on).[31] By the early 1980s (and to a degree in the late 1970s), however, the growing consideration Foucault was giving to ethics, to practices of the self, to questioning the function, mode, and purpose of thinking, to the worth of his work, drew him into an exploration of different conceptual terrain (half existent and half imagined). Initially, at least, Foucault did not realize as he entered into these explorations that they would occupy and preoccupy him during his few remaining years of life.

This chapter is not the place to survey the vast and varied riches of the last three sets of lectures Foucault gave at the Collège de France. It is worth underlining, however, the importance Foucault gave to two of the major organizing themes (eventually concepts) that he identified as significant during this historical period: "frank speech" (*parrhèsia*) and "care of the self" (*epimeleia heautou*). Foucault hypothesized, argued, and, to his own at least partial satisfaction, demonstrated that both terms had been important themes around which many of the practices guiding philosophic activity in the period (roughly following Plato and up until Gregory of Nyssa and the rise of Christian asceticism) turned. Foucault's own attention to these themes, and to the long-since marginalized practices associated with them, at the very least shows his absorption with them. It also indicates, it is safe to say, that these themes constituted for him a possible way forward—an *Ausgang,* an exit toward maturity, to use Kant's term—in own life and work. To be more precise, these themes (in relation to the turmoil and transformations he was undergoing in his own life), as well as his analytic and genealogical work devoted to explicating and delineating them, allowed Foucault—in many ways for the first time—to pose to himself, and for himself, the question: what form would a philosophic practice take that would be salvational?[32]

The cornerstone of his lengthy explorations of the rise and fall of the care of the self as an integral part of Western philosophic practice proved to turn on the concept of spirituality. The identification of the significance of the term led Foucault to delineate not only how and why it had been understood conceptually but, more important, how it had been transformed into a series of practices. This exploration constituted his primary research terrain during the 1980s.

In his lectures of 1981–82, Foucault formulated a series of broad, general hypotheses (accompanied by detailed explications of philosophic texts) concerning the relations of philosophy and spirituality.[33] Pivotal among the claims Foucault posited was his contention that in the pre-Christian philosophic tradition of the West, a defining principle of philosophic activity had been that "spirituality postulates that the truth is never given to the subject by right."[34] Although the Christian tradition did something quite different theologically and practically beginning with approximately the same starting point, both the pre-Christian and Christian corpus can be seen to concur on the assertion that gaining access to the truth always requires transformative work on the self. Such work, grouped under the rubric of ascetic practices, consisted in means and modes of changing, transforming, shifting, and modifying the individual so as to make him into a subject capable of receiving the truth. Foucault chronicles and analyzes (in the literal sense of breaking something down into its elements) a large array of techniques and practices developed historically to perform this preparatory transformational work on the subject.

These ascetic techniques were not exercises in virtuosity (as Max Weber described in other traditions), nor were they ends in themselves (as they have frequently become today). Rather, these ascetic techniques functioned to make the subject susceptible to return "effects." Foucault names these effects "'rebound' (*de retour*), effects of the truth on the subject. . . . The truth enlightens the subject; the truth gives beatitude to the subject; the truth gives the subject tranquility of the soul."[35]

Foucault's introduction of this terminology is surprising, even disconcerting. Today, we contemporaries might readily imagine that we could understand what "enlightens" means; we might tender respect to others' search for "beatitude"; and we might even imagine ourselves, with appropriate updating of the concepts, desiring to attain a "tranquility of the soul." Such a range of topics, however, was hardly familiar terrain for Foucault. Even in his series of essays on Kant, Foucault never posited a state of enlightenment or maturity, only the affect driving certain citizens of the world to imagine a way forward—hope, enthusiasm—or preventing them from doing so—laziness or cowardice.

Foucault did not return to beatitude or tranquility of the soul, but he did insist on the importance of "salvation" as the goal of spirituality. Again, this claim startles at first hearing or reading. During his lecture, it is as if Foucault realized how bizarre these terms must sound to the sleepy students at 9:30 in the morning who populated the overflow auditoria in which his amplified voice reverberated. Foucault hastened to reassure them; he was not talking about Christian salvation. "Salvation," he said, was simply "no more than the realization of the relationship to the self."[36] He then concisely distinguished the Christian thematic of salvation and the one at issue among philosophers such as Seneca or Marcus Aurelius. The meaning of "saving oneself," Foucault wrote, "is not at all reducible to something like the drama of an event that allows one's existence to be commuted from life to death, mortality to immortality, evil to good, etc."[37] That semantic field and those meanings were, of course, the Christian ones.

Having cleared that ground, Foucault proceeded to present a philological exercise, a technique that was gaining increasing importance as a means of exposition and demonstration in his later lectures. It was through his calm examination of terms that Foucault apparently sought to loosen them from the accretions of meaning and affect they had accumulated over the centuries, thereby allowing a different understanding and apprehension of past historical forms. No doubt such an exercise had as its horizon the intention of making future historical forms possible as well. As opposed to the strategy of the history of the present, the goal was not to show the contingency of naturalized or taken-for-granted terms, concepts, or practices but rather to trace their previous branching or ramifications as a partial guide to their historically variable potency as well as their contemporary potential (virtuality).

Thus, the Greek term *sozein* (to save) or the substantive *soteria* (salvation) covers a range of different meanings, all of them this-worldly. Thus, for example, *sozein* had many meanings, some of them quite ordinary; for example, one could be saved from a shipwreck or an illness. The verb could also mean "to guard, protect, or keep a protective shield around something."[38] Shifting from that rather literal or material sense of protection, the verb could also mean "to preserve or protect something like decency or honor."[39] Furthermore, the verb had a juridical meaning: to acquit or exonerate. Finally, and this was the most pertinent of the verb's meanings for the problem Foucault was addressing, "*sozein* means to do good. It meant to ensure the well-being, the good condition of someone, or something, or of a collectivity."[40] In sum, the verb denoted a type or form of activity: a proactive taking care of, guarding, perhaps nourishing, and the goods of one's life, material and spiritual. Understood in that manner, there was nothing exotic about the semantics or the practices directed at facilitating these quite worldly goals.

Foucault provided a synthetic overview of the functions of the techniques more or less coherently assembled into the ascetic and spiritual practices. He devoted many of his lectures, parts of the last two volumes of *The History of Sexuality*, as well as a number of lectures and interviews on various occasions during the 1980s to the technologies and practices of spirituality, salvation, and asceticism that had been developed in the ancient world.

In the 1981–82 lectures, for example, he identified several functions of the care of the self. First was the "curative and therapeutic function." Perhaps one could say that Foucault's experience in California had set him on a curative trajectory or, at the very least, had helped him to recognize that such a trajectory was conceivable. Second, Foucault identified a "critical function." By critical here he did not mean anything like the Kantian sense of inherent limitations or the more current sense of denunciation of evils or abuses. Rather, the critical function at issue turned on the demand to "unlearn," *de-discere*, what one had been taught or the way one had been trained. Likely, one had had bad teachers, perhaps bad parents, and many other practices and understandings no doubt needed to be examined with an eye to "unlearning" them if one was to proceed toward an adequate transformation of the self.

In addition to the curative and critical functions, Foucault identified the prominence within this tradition of "a function of struggle." This function did not consist in either the Christian preparation for the one last struggle to save one's soul or the struggle to free oneself from illusion or pollution. Rather, this Hellenistic struggle had entailed a mode of lifelong practice and exercise, a form of perpetual vigilance and training. The object of the struggle consisted in part in focusing attention on and unlearning the myriad bad habits and dispositions that one had accumulated and continued to accumulate. It consisted in part in the therapeutic or curative dimension mentioned above.

More appositely, such struggle aimed at providing the subject with a mode of vigilant preparedness for encountering any and all events throughout his life. Its goal was to bring those events into the present and to live with them as actualities, not eventualities. To the degree that the philosopher accomplished or approached this goal, he would be able to know; as Foucault quotes Seneca, "I await the day when I will pass judgment on myself and know whether virtue was only in my words or really in my heart."[41] It is significant that this sentence closes his course summary of 1981–82, a summary, we know, to which Foucault had devoted careful attention.[42]

Seneca's world obviously was not Foucault's. We are given a strong sense of the distance between them in Foucault's presentation of the goals of these Hellenistic philosophers. The purpose or telos of these practices, these exercises, these principles, these modes, these techniques, turned on "the two great themes of *ataraxy* (the absence of inner turmoil, the self-control that assures that nothing disturbs you), and *autarchy* (the self-sufficiency which ensures that one needs nothing but the self) . . . the two forms in which salvation, the acts of salvation, the activity of salvation carried on throughout one's life, find their reward."[43]

Although scholastically the identification of *ataraxy* and *autarchy* as central goals of Hellenistic thought is uncontroversial, their status in Foucault's own life and works is far from obvious and deserves more attention. It seems patent to me that these goals, at least in their Hellenistic form, were not shared by Foucault. After all, if the challenge had been to achieve *ataraxy* and *autarchy,* there would have been no need to leave France. Quite the opposite, France would seem to have offered Foucault an exemplary field of aggravation and disturbance in which to put himself to the test. One thinks of Seneca faced with the plotted Roman alternatives of retreating to his villa (remember Foucault had sought to purchase an abandoned abbey in Poitou) or returning to face the fate Nero's crazed sovereignty held in store for him. For Seneca there were no other choices (although he fantasized about returning to the Athens of his youth where he had been schooled in rhetoric, he knew full well that returning to the Athens of old was an unrealizable fantasy in the present). Nero ordered Seneca's suicide (Foucault returned insistently to suicide as a topic and ultimate act of freedom during this period) as well as that of his wife; Seneca complied, his wife, having failed in her initial attempts, was spared.

The Hellenistic options in a literal sense made no sense because their meaning would have been totally different then and now. The challenge of "struggle," however, perhaps could be given a contemporary form. For Foucault, salvation could be thought of not only as a deliverance from sin but also and rather as an activity of self-transformation. It consisted in "the subject's constant action on himself, . . . the vigilant, continuous, and completed form of the relationship to self. . . . The self is the agent, object, instrument, and end of salvation. . . . Salvation ensures an access to the self that is inseparable from the work one carries out on oneself within the time of one's life and in life itself."[44]

Although to contemporary ears such claims can sound individualistic, nothing could be further from the original subject matter itself or from Foucault's reasons for bringing it back to light. Perhaps the simplest proof of this claim can be found in the fact that Foucault's 1982–83 lectures were devoted to explorations of "the government of self and others." His final lectures, the following year, dealt with a genealogy of the critical intellectual, specifically a series of lectures on the cynics, who spoke truth to power in public, at the risk of their own well-being and even their lives. All of the genealogical and archaeological work on Hellenistic philosophy provided a means of reintroducing a set of concepts and terms (salvation, care of the self, equipment, and so forth) that held the promise of being useful today. It provided a vast thematic panorama with parenthetical digressions that could clearly have become courses or books in and of themselves (on Hegel, on Faust, on the nineteenth century, on the sixteenth and seventeenth centuries, on science and theology, and so on)

We should be clear, however, that what Foucault did not provide was a solution. During the time when Foucault was working in the mode of the history of the present, the refusal to outline solutions or propose directions for others was an ethical and political principle. By the 1980s, Foucault was uneasy with that mode of subjectivation. He was in quest of a different way forward when time ran out. What we do know is that, at least in his lectures and discussions during the 1980s, Foucault was once again problematizing philosophy as a practice and a way of life. The questions that Foucault posed and reposed during the 1980s remain challenging: What difference does today make with respect to yesterday? How do we find an exit toward maturity? How do we give form to our impatience for liberty? It is certain that had Foucault lived longer, these and other unexpected questions would indeed have drawn his attention and concern. What that work would have looked like, though, we will never know.

4

Michel Foucault: A Philosopher's Morality? Toward a *Bios Technika*

A little bit more than a professor and less than a militant, a little bit more than a scholar and less than an ideologue.

«FRÉDÉRIC GROS[1]»

Michel Foucault's last courses at the Collège de France, especially the last two years (1982–83, 1984), are far more ambiguous and far more uncertain—albeit fascinating, penetrating, and exhilarating—than even the most astute and eminently qualified observers interpret them as being.[2] For example, in the epigraph given above, Frédéric Gros, author of the admirable summaries at the end of the published versions of these courses, attempts to capture Foucault's pervasive, dissident discomfort in settling on a subject position for himself and others. In an essay, Gros concludes by saying: "It is a question of . . . the rigor of an ethic that pursues truth and denounces lies. It is not a philosopher's morality; it is an ethic of an engaged intellectual."[3]

Regrettably, I think this claim is wrong, or at the very least misleading. It provides a narrative of familiarity that is far too comfortable. There are several reasons for my dissatisfaction with Gros's seemingly uncontroversial and gratifying assertion. First, if one can find any denunciation of lies—or any denunciation at all—in the hundreds of pages of these luminous lectures, then one is an extraordinary literary detective. And if by any chance from time to time any such tropes appear in these lectures, then I would argue that it is simply a slippage, sloppiness, on Foucault's part. The tone and mode are resolutely nondenunciatory. Second, in these lectures, as elsewhere, the stipulation of the intellectual is far from clear; at times Foucault explicitly refused the label of "intellectual," although he did employ it as shorthand with some regularity in his interviews.[4] And, regardless of his own self-description (after all, what term would have been better?), the historical rise and fall of the figure of the intellectual had been well charted by one of Pierre Bourdieu's students; the figure arose in France in the later nineteenth century and was probably coming to a close by the end of the twentieth century. In any case the status of the intellectual in France during the 1980s was certainly being contested, especially after the election of the Socialist president Francois Mitterrand. Third, Foucault did not claim to be an engaged intellectual in the standard French sense of the term. "Engaged" is an existentialist trope associated for decades with Jean-Paul Sartre and later for politically situated rhetoric as in the later writings and speeches of Bourdieu. For most of his career, Foucault sought to distance himself politically and scientifically from Sartre (although there was some convergence politically in the early 1980s around defending Vietnamese boat people), and Foucault's writings during Bourdieu's transformation into a universal intellectual could not be more different in tone and content.

Whatever "engaged" might have meant for Foucault, it was never a direct translation of his intellectual (*sic*) work and form of writing and speech into direct political engagement. One such quote is the following (but there are many others): "I don't think that the intellectual can, starting only from his erudite and scholarly research, pose true questions concerning the society in which he lives."[5]

In sum, it seems to me to be more accurate to say that in these lectures Foucault was indeed guided by "a morality of a philoso-

pher" that he knew to be a preliminary ethos that permitted him
to assemble the concepts that might (or might not) contribute
to an ethic of philosophy, an ethic that might ultimately form
an integral part of a philosophic life, a *bios philosophicus*. In fact,
it is plausible to argue that Foucault's core diagnosis in these
lectures is the search for the location and timing of how and
when the long-standing rupture of truth and ethics as syner-
gistically interconnected took place. Foucault was attempting to
contribute to a reproblematization of the practices of reflection
and knowledge. But that labor was guided by discomfort, un-
easiness, and certainly self-doubt about the objective conditions
for such a transformation as well as his own ability to shape it.
The activity in which Foucault was engaging was most certainly
a singular form of genealogical questioning. That questioning,
as well as the form and parameters of that genealogy, however,
were being given a quite different and distinctive form from his
previous genealogical work.[6]

Thus, Michel Foucault was not an engaged intellectual in the
Sartre or Chomsky or Bourdieu mode. Furthermore, I do not
think that in his lectures at the Collège de France Foucault was
speaking as a *parrhesiaste*, a truth speaker, even though the guiding thematic of the lectures was, in fact, truth speaking. After
all, in the simplest terms, Foucault tells us that the *parrhesiaste* is
someone who (1) believes firmly that he is speaking the truth and
(2) places himself in a situation where speaking the truth entails
a risk. The range of that risk bifurcates between twin poles: on
the one hand, of being attacked (or put to death) for what one
says as well as the manner in which one declares it, or, on the
other pole, of indifference.

Although Foucault does provide a magnificent set of discussions of the past problematizations of frank speech, genealogically analyzing their elements—and not providing a comprehensive history of ideas—it must be said that it would be hard to
claim that there was any risk of being put to death for fulfilling
his statutory obligations at the state-funded Collège de France
by lecturing before several hundred auditors on largely textual

expositions of Greek and Roman philosophy. Rather, long experience had taught Foucault that the risk he ran would not be that he would encounter danger or indifference but rather incomprehension and distortion. He had come to expect and regret such predictable misunderstanding as the price to be paid for the luxury of his position at the Collège de France.[7]

Foucault was keenly aware that the venue he was operating within provided few, if any, overt dangers. In his lectures he explored previous venues in which frank speech did entail risk: the assembly of the polis, the sovereign's chambers where his counselors advised him, as well as an initial indication of the Christian transformations of these venues and practices. In sum, if there was any risk involved for Michel Foucault in lectures at the Collège de France it could only be that the thinker would lose his own way.

History of the Present: Cautionaries

The work of an intellectual . . . by the analyses that he produces in his own domain can re-interrogate the postulates and taken for granted assumptions . . . and starting from that re-problematization (where he plays his role in his craft of a specific intellectual) can participate in the formation of a political will (where he has the citizen's role to play).
«MICHEL FOUCAULT[8]»

Foucault is well known for his periodic recasting of the trajectory of his own work, providing framings that often appear to be in manifest contradiction to prior framings. As one might expect, the practice gains in prominence in each of his last three years of lectures and in his intense intellectual activity. These refigurations mark time. They also aid and abet the thinker in gathering his strength, in surveying in an almost literal sense the conceptual terrain so as to find a possible way onward. Many of the most interesting statements in these overviews (*surplomb*) are clearly meant as markings by Foucault for himself as much as for any audience, even if several hundred auditors sat before him at the Collège de France. Foucault in these years might well have been wandering, but his goal was not to follow forest paths that lead nowhere, nor was his wandering leisurely. Time seemed short, and finding the right direction for himself felt pressing. He was clearly in search of an exit. And, as was usual with Foucault, he began searching for the exit by looking backward.

Intensified versions of this survey-and-synthesis genre are present throughout Foucault's later years. Their significance should not be underestimated. Thus, for example, in the beginning of the 1983–84 series, in a footnote that Foucault did not read aloud, he asks: "What sense should be given to this enterprise?"[9] Although the forceful answer he provides is of great interest in and of itself, its mode of presentation is equally worthy of attention. Foucault's compressed statements should be read as guidelines, a kind of methodological and ethical signposting. Such guidelines themselves belong to a tradition. One of Foucault's quests was to identify a means to connect to and renew that tradition. These embodied signposts, these markers, had been identified by Foucault as *equipment* or *paraskeuē*. In the ancient world, these ready-at-hand maxims (*logoi*) were an essential component of the philosopher's *habitus*, his daily and bodily practice.[10] They held an essential place in the practice of the care of the self, which itself constituted an integral element and goal of philosophy as a practice. They should not be confused with a method in the modern sense in which the means of making connections and verifying them is presented and defended in terms of epistemology. Rather, these *logoi* were guiding maxims for the practice of thinking and living a life of philosophic activity.

As will be obvious shortly, the maxims Foucault presents are thoroughly modern, as no Stoic or Epicurean philosopher would have imagined them or could probably have even understood them. Although Foucault characterizes these maxims as "negative," perhaps the better word is "cautionary." The first is a *historicizing* caution: "Instead of recourse to a *theory* of knowledge, power or the subject, substitute the analysis of specific historical practices."[11] Of course, theory and method go together. Hence, if other thinkers had followed this maxim, a substantial part of the secondary literature on Foucault would be relegated to an analytic (dust) bin. His cautionary about the dangers of theory was relegated to an unspoken footnote better left unsaid unless his auditors take it for a more subtle theory. So, instead of theory, this cautionary leads one to ask a different question of historicism: "what have been the effects or could be the effects of such a historical [mode of] analysis in the field of historical thought?"[12]

The second cautionary is nominalist: just as specific historical determinations should be substituted for theory, so too the "analysis of experiences which constitute singular historical forms should be substituted for universals (such as sexuality, madness, crime)." Likewise, in a nominalist mode the following question should be posed: "what have been the effects of nominalist critiques in the analysis of cultures, forms of knowledge, institutions and political structures?"[13]

The third cautionary is nihilist: once again, "it is advisory not to line up (*indexer*) practices to systems of values but rather to inscribe value systems in the play of arbitrary practices while taking into account that such practice are intelligible." And again, for a ground (system of values, theory, method, and so forth) one should substitute a question as to the effects of nominalist critiques in practice.[14]

Foucault identifies the enduring object of his work as *foyers d'expérience*. The French word *foyer* literally means "home or hearth," but it can also mean the "seat" or "site" of something, and it is in the latter sense that Foucault is using it. The experiences Foucault names are the ones one would expect: sexuality, madness, punishment. These "seats of experience" can be broken down into three axes or elements.[15] They are the intersection of:

- Forms of possible knowledge
- Normative matrices of conduct (*comportement*)
- Virtual modes of existence of possible subjects.[16]

This set of distinctions maps fairly easily onto other such triads (e.g., knowledge/power/ethics) Foucault had experimented with earlier. What is distinctive and novel in the lectures of the 1980s is a modal change: the introduction of the terms such as "possible" and "virtual." These qualifications might be understood as additional aspects of the types of genealogical loosening up of taken-for-granted beliefs, concepts, and practices that Foucault regularly practiced. However, given that the last three years of lectures can be said to be engaged in a modified form of genealogy, one must note (because Foucault does not explicitly elaborate on this shift) that the "possible" and the "virtual" apply to the near future as well as to the historical present or past.

In addition to these intellectual or scientific cautionaries, Foucault adds two related care-of-the-self *logoi*. The first clarification is noticeably the distillation of many years enduring the experience of his critics and their criticism. It underlines the important function of these maxims as enabling one to proceed amid incomprehension and malice. Foucault counsels a resolutely firm attitude of refusal when confronted with certain types of reproaches. The standard Web definition of "reproach" covers two terrains: "To criticize somebody for doing something wrong. Discredit: shame or disgrace that somebody or something incurs." A reproach therefore implies not only a mistake that could be corrected but equally, or above all else, a moral failing. Such moral failings presumably were committed intentionally or due to systematic blindness; they implicate the subject in their commission.

Such reproaches (masquerading as criticism) often take the form of what Foucault had called elsewhere "blackmail" (*chantage*)—are you for or against the Enlightenment?—in which the terms of the debate are set in advance, and one's only choice is a binary one. Thus, when one hears, "You are a nihilist, nominalist or historicist," Foucault counsels, one should turn away because to respond on the terms of the one who is posing this reproach can only be a losing strategy; by so doing, "one is fatally trapped into accepting their distinctions." Rather than accept that bind, Foucault advises (himself) to respond by attempting to deploy a "historicist/nominalist/nihilist analysis" of the reproach.[17] Yet once again, the practitioner of cautionaries has learned to respond to situations of stress or confusion by turning a presumed given into questions: How did this form of criticism develop? What are its historical determinations? What value system sustains it, and how did it happen that such a moralizing mode came to stand in for inquiry? In sum, what effects does this mode of reproach produce in the games of truth and ethics?

GENEALOGIES: *EPISTEME*, APPARATUS, PROBLEMATIZATION

Foucault experimented throughout his life with developing modes of analysis sufficient for diagnosing and conceptualizing historical breakpoints and the various machineries of stasis that preceded them. Although he never settled on a fixed approach—in part because the problems he treated were diverse and as he gradually came to thematize they needed to be approached in different manners—his consistent, if not unique, goal was to contribute to a "history of the present." In that project, a certain understanding or mode of presentation of the past might provide a means of showing the contingency of the present and thereby contribute to opening the possibility of a different future. How the past apparatus came to be assembled, which problems it was designed to address, and how it became taken for granted figure prominently in all of Foucault's genealogical analyses. By so doing he opens up a space for change and rethinking that is not an abstract gesture of rejection but a historically informed and nuanced diagnosis. Because the apparatus had been assembled from heterogeneous elements over a period of time, showing its contingency required a detailed diagnosis of how it came into being. It was implied that such knowledge would provide assistance in assembling something better: not just a refusal but a critique.

For Foucault, the metric of thought did not consist uniquely in an act of diagnosis (or representation) for its own sake but rather included the effort to achieve a modal change from seeing a situation not only as "a given" but equally as "a question." Thinking is an act of modal transformation from the constative to the subjunctive: from the singular to the multiple, from the necessary to the contingent. Such a modal shift seeks to accomplish a number of things. It asserts not only that there are always multiple constraints (as well as possibilities and virtualities) at work in a situation, but equally that multiple responses exist as well. Foucault underscores the task of identifying conditions of heterogeneous, if constrained, contingency—"this transformation of an ensemble of difficulties into problems to which diverse solutions are proposed"—in order to initiate a particular style of inquiry that makes these conditions available for rethinking and, eventually, intervention.

Although Foucault practiced a form of genealogy throughout his writings, the object to which it was applied changed. Thus, in *The Order of Things*, the object was the *episteme*, whereas in *Discipline and Punish* it was the apparatus (*dispositive*). In both of those instances, Foucault remained broadly steady about the historical parameters and the periodization with which he was dealing. Although both were explicitly histories of the present of different types of objects, the analysis began basically in the seventeenth century and moved to the early/mid-nineteenth century.[18] During what turned out to be Foucault's last set of works, the object was *problematization*, and the time frame extended from approximately the fourth century BC to the second century AD, with forays into the seventeenth century.

What is a problematization, a term Foucault introduced only late in his work?[19] A problematization, Foucault writes, "does not mean the representation of a pre-existent object nor the creation through discourse of an object that did not exist. It is the ensemble of discursive and non-discursive practices that make something enter into the play of true and false and constitute it as an object of thought (whether in the form of moral reflection, scientific knowledge, political analysis, etc)."[20] The reason that problematizations are problematic, not surprisingly, is that something prior "must have happened to introduce uncertainty, a loss of familiarity; that loss, that uncertainty is the result of difficulties in our previous way of understanding, acting, relating."[21] Foucault's own analysis, it is clear, was meant both as a diagnostic and as a means of making such problematizations more visible, available, and open to remediation.

A problematization, then, refers both to a kind of general historical formation as well as a nexus of responses to that formation. It also refers to a mode of approaching historical formations by the genealogist or historian of the present. The diverse but not entirely disparate responses, it follows, eventually form (an increasingly significant) aspect of the problematization to the degree that stable formations emerge and are sustained. The responses are a dynamic component of stabilization as well as the formation of leverage or contradiction points for its destabilization (remembering such destabilization is never uniquely discursive). Thus, Foucault is seeking a means of characterizing a historical space of conditioned contingency that emerges in relation to (and then forms a feedback situation with) a more general state of affairs, one that is real enough, but neither fixed nor static (although it may be stabilized over long periods of time). Thus, the domain of problematization is constituted by and through economic conditions, scientific knowledge, political actors, and other related vectors. In sum, what is distinctive is Foucault's identification of the problematic state of affairs (the dynamic of the process of a specific type of problem description, characterization, and reworking) as simultaneously the object, the site, and ultimately the substance of critical thinking.

VOCATIONAL VIGILANCE

What was the test (*épreuve*) or standard by which Foucault measured the worth of his works? One source of confusion is easy to identify but not so easy to specify. Foucault always talked about the past in his books, yet he was consistently criticized, reproached, and even vilified by historians. The genealogist, however, was not a historian even if his material and even if in a specific manner his mode of working were historical. In his practice Foucault seemed relatively clear about this distinction, although he did not make it sufficiently explicit to either satisfy his critics or instruct his readers. Thus, to take a straightforward example, Pierre Hadot, a French classicist, while acknowledging the interest of Foucault's work on the care of the self, especially in the Roman period, was nonetheless scandalized by Foucault's omissions and distortions of past historical reality. Thus, although Foucault devoted long lectures to Stoic philosophers where he analyzed their relationship to power, to themselves, and to others, he says little or nothing about the fact that the Stoics all assumed there was a rational cosmos and that there was a fatality about the course of affairs. Obviously Foucault knew this, and obviously he left it out because he was doing genealogy, whose metric was not loyalty to the things as they really were, to use Ranke's famous mandate, but to the tenuous genealogy of philosophy as the care of the self and of *parrhesia* that he was attempting to construct.

If the standard against which Foucault measured the success or failure of his work was neither a traditional positivist nor an (existing) academic disciplinary one, while nonetheless remaining resolutely empirical and historicist, what was it? Foucault had been asked variants of that question many times, although almost exclusively in terms of the status of the relationship between his work and political action. Perhaps the most extensive set of answers he provided can be found in the long set of interviews he conducted with an Italian journalist, published in English under the partially misleading title (because many other topics are covered) *Remarks on Marx*.[22] Foucault succinctly sums up one of these interview sessions on how he envisioned the political engagement of his books by providing one standard (he will provide another in one of the book's later interviews). The first standard is largely subject oriented and experiential: "The book is merely inscribed in something that was already in progress. . . . The book also worked for this transformation; it has been, even in a small way, an agent. That's it. This, for me, is an 'experience-book' as opposed to a 'truth-book' or a 'demonstration-book.'"[23]

As was his wont, Foucault used these interviews to get clearer about what he was doing or had done; the "that's it" is a telling example of such a moment of clarity, of self-clarification, taking place. "I consider myself more an experimenter than a theorist; I don't develop deductive systems to apply uniformly in different fields of research. When I write, I do it above all to change myself and not to think the same thing as before."[24]

But whose experience was he talking about? Whose experience was he experimenting with? On the one hand, to experiment, correct, and adjust in rhythm with the ramifications of one's inquiry would count as normative in the natural sciences, in the university humanities, and in social science disciplines; however, it is rare to encounter such a risky approach, although there is a small current of avant-gardism in which newness and shock are an author's trademark. But, of course, avant-gardism was not what Foucault is up to in these later years, despite an American reception that frequently understood him in those terms.

In his genealogical approach to the history of the present, Foucault maintained a position that he had held (with modifications) for an extended period of time. This subject position was simultaneously scientific, scholarly, political, and ethical. In Foucault's formulation, the historian of the present stood close to but separate from the material he was examining, interacting with, challenging, reflecting on, and perplexed by. As his genealogical analysis took form, the substantive distance from the present increased, albeit with the goal of superior clarity. A central benchmark, or stabilization of a long-term problematization, is one in which each of the terms changes its meaning and its associated practice. The ratio of this practice is the relation—always a fraught one but always a relationship—between philosophy and politics, between the citizen (as "*l'homme moyen sensual*," to use Albert Camus' phrase) and the critic.

For Foucault the primary task of the analyst was not to proceed directly toward intervention so as to repair the situation's discordancy, as one could imagine those in the pragmatist traditions advocating, but rather to pause, reflect, and put forth a diagnosis of "what makes these responses simultaneously possible."[25] Therefore, one reason that Foucault's work was consistently cast as historical and historicist was that such a positioning provided him with an ethical parameter to mark the legitimate limits of his work. This combination of a concern with the history of the present and a resolute distancing from immediate questions and challenges while keeping them in his sights introduced a "ballast" (*lester*) to the demand (and desire) to respond in a direct and immediate fashion. In that way, the vocational intellectual could conscientiously refuse the temptation to tell other citizens what to do or how to do it, only to contribute conceptual and analytic clarity that might lead to better questioning and even action. For example, Foucault says: "The book on the prisons stops in 1840. People often tell me: this book is such a scathing attack (*un réquisitoire*) on the penitentiary system that one does not know what to do after one has read it. To tell you the truth, the book is not a scathing attack. My question consists simply in saying to the psychiatrists and the penitentiary personnel: 'Can you stand your own history?'"[26]

This stance was not entirely without slippage. Obviously, Foucault thought that the conditions in French prisons were terrible. Such a self-imposed boundary maintenance yielded its own chagrin because the incessant demand from many quarters on the left to propose solutions was tempting; clearly, Foucault thought that many of the positions held by self-styled French intellectuals were underwhelming or worse. But the asceticism seemed to stand the test of integrity and of scientific insight.

Philosophy: un foyer d'expérience [*A Crucible of Experience*]

L'histoire des hommes est la longue succession des synonyme d'un même vocable. Y contredire est un devoir. [The history of man is a long succession of synonyms of the same term. To contradict this claim is one's duty.]
«RENÉ CHAR[27]»

Could the figure of the philosopher as *parrhesiaste* and as citizen be recast? It would not stretch the imagination very far to read the titles Foucault gave to his last two courses—*Le Gouverne-ment de soi et des autres* and *Le Courage de la vérité*—in this light. To do so would seem to imply the necessity to move beyond the traditional forms of genealogy with their disruptive metric and their backward-facing positionality. But if the standard of proof in the older genealogical method was the effects it produced in both a general and a specific subset of the citizenry, it might well be hard to apply the same standard when it came to a remediated and reconstructed philosophy. In any case, the first task was to reimagine the figure of the genealogist thinker and to explore its parameters. Foucault's insistent leitmotif was general enough to be worth trying to give it new forms: "Let us try together now to elaborate new modes of criticism, new modes of putting into question, to try something different."[28]

Taken at face value, the close to one thousand published pages of the last three years of Foucault's courses were devoted to identifying concepts, terms, and themes as well as their processes and series of assemblage, stabilization, loosening, and transformation. The goal of these exercises and experiments, it seems to me, was to open up the prospect of treating *philosophy* as *a site of experience*. Genealogically establishing the venues, forms, and modes of previous philosophical practices was at the heart of Foucault's labor in these lectures. At the very least, his historicist/nominalist/nihilist genealogy of philosophy as a practice established that philosophy had previously been given different forms: ones in which truth speaking, care of the self, and a political role had been connected or at least related. In sum, Foucault was uncovering and reconstituting the fact that there were historical precedents for problematizing philosophy as an ethical practice and not just a morality. His goal was to turn philosophy once again into a critical and spiritual practice of transformation of the self and of others.

Late in the 1982–83 lectures, Foucault declaimed that he had rejected two of the currently prevalent approaches in France to the history of philosophy. The first is clearly that of Heidegger or of French Heideggarians in which one seeks to find the "radical origin" of something forgotten. The other is the more academic approach, which takes the history of philosophy as a story of progress or as the development of a specific rationality. A third approach is possible, however, and it would consist of taking up the history of philosophy as a series of episodes and forms without either a defining origin or telos. Such a nonprogressive, nonoriginary series consists of "recurrent forms, of forms that transform themselves, of veridiction. The history of philosophy, in sum, as a movement of *parrhesia,* as a redistribution of *parrhesia,* as diverse games of *dire-vrai* [truth-speaking], philosophy envisaged thus in what one might call its illocutionary force."[29]

As he had begun to analyze in his lectures of 1981–82 on *The Hermeneutics of the Subject,* and as he had discussed in interviews, Foucault underscored philosophy as a practice. It followed that the philosopher as subject had to constitute a part of the mode of veridiction. Furthermore, it was the elimination of the separation (and even elimination) of care, action, and thought as mutually implicated in the philosophic life that Foucault identified diagnostically as the central site of reproblematization, which he hoped to contribute to remedying.

To take one example, Foucault argues that for Plato (and other Greeks) the object of philosophy was embedded in the term *pragma.* This term covered at least two distinct concepts: *pragma* as a referent and *pragma* as a practice. The mode that privileged the task of philosophy (or later science) as analyzing and demonstrating the nature of the referent was a long-standing one throughout the Western tradition, albeit undertaken in different forms and covering a diverse range of objects. It is the second concept of *pragma* that interested Foucault. He was seeking to reintroduce it as a means of reproblematizing philosophy as a central component of the questions and eventual solutions that would and should arise in such a problematization. So, what are the *pragmata?* They are "the affairs, activities, difficulties, practices, exercises, all the forms of practice on which one must exercise and apply oneself and for which one must extend oneself because they are hard. . . . The *pragma* are the activities to which one must apply oneself. And, in this sense, the *pragmata* are opposed to the *skhole*, which is leisure. To tell the truth, philosophic *skhole*, philosophic leisure, consists precisely in occupying oneself to a certain number of things which are the *pragmata* of philosophy."[30]

Hence, to be philosophically pragmatic, as it were, is to have the leisure to practice a second-order activity, one in which the challenge consists of taking up questions of reflection on activities in the world and of turning that reflection into a practice. Or perhaps a better formulation would be to introduce into the world a distinctive form of pragmatic practice depending on a certain freedom from direct needs of an ordinary sort and to transform those practices in such a way that they become everyday practices of a philosophic life.

Although thinking certainly entailed a type of truth claim, if truth claims per se were separated from a principle of freedom or from a practice of the care of the self, they would not contribute to Foucault's attempt to reproblematize philosophy. Foucault described it thus: "The history of philosophy, at least what I would like to do, must be conceived as a history of ontologies tied to a principle of freedom, where freedom is defined not as a right to be but as a capacity to do."[31]

Without some dimension of freedom, there is, strictly speaking, no action, and without freely chosen action there is no consciously accepted risk for the truth speaker (although there may be many dangers). Of course, self-evidently, there can be the most pronounced and odious risks and dangers to citizens and to noncitizens, but those would fall, it seems, into the realm of direct politics and not into Foucault's much more restrictive sphere of philosophy. Without risks to the truth speaker, there can be no rebound effect of his practice.

On what site did and should these philosophical practices operate? The answer is strikingly simple: on one's life (*bios*). The form that one strives to give to that life constitutes the practice and the testing ground for philosophy as a site of experience.[32] We are not dealing with a disconnected autonomy here. Rather, the test of what Foucault calls philosophy's reality lies in its relationship with politics, with the sciences, and with its own self-formation.

It follows that a contemporary philosopher would be losing his way by acquiescing to demands for a first-order practice in any of these domains. To use the language of Alasdair Macintyre, the goods of a first-order practice, its virtue, differ from that of a second-order practice, its virtue. The price to be paid for the form and mode of the practice of philosophy that Foucault was in search of creating was to remind oneself constantly that one had to refuse the incessant request to tell politicians how to govern, tell scientists what is true or false in their disciplines, or tell another individual how to liberate oneself from one's alienation. Once again Foucault declaims a set of cautionaries: "Philosophy . . . has to be in a mode of a permanent and refractory [*rétif*] relationship with politics and it is only by maintaining this position [of adjacency] that philosophy remains real. . . . Philosophy's problem is not to divide the true from the false in the sciences. . . . Philosophy's problem is not to liberate the subject."[33]

The preconditions for this practice, to use a different repertoire of concepts, depend on gaining access to such venues and establishing a position of adjacency. One must prepare oneself beforehand for the fact that such a principled and pragmatic refusal of the demand for first-order responses will bring reproachful, often dismissive responses: threats of withdrawal of access or support; charges of irresponsibility, indolence, and irrelevance; and, most commonly, irritated dismissal and self-confident indifference. Of course, only those in a dominant position, or what they take to be a dominant position, can afford themselves such negligence.

It would be hard not to hear echoes of Nietzsche in the distance. As he writes at the end of *On the Genealogy of Morals*:

"And here I touch on my problem, on our problem, my *unknown* friends (for as yet I *know* of no friend); what meaning would *our* whole being possess if it were not this, that in us the will to truth becomes conscious of itself as a problem? . . . As the will to truth thus gains self-consciousness—there can be no doubt of that—morality will gradually *perish*."[34]

PART TWO

In Search of a Contemporary Anthropology

Suddenly, I became indifferent to whether or not I was modern.
«ROLAND BARTHES[1]»

The contemporary is the untimely.
«ROLAND BARTHES[2]»

The literary critic Geoffrey Harpham, in a book titled *Shadows of Ethics*, provides a cutting but tempered set of observations on the topography of literary criticism at the end of the twentieth century. The book is persuasively worthwhile in and of itself, offering a deflationary yet attentive examination of the leading figures in cultural criticism at the moment the wave of theory had crested in the United States. It is also interesting and relevant here because Harpham argued that the self-styled elegiac of their own marginalization while reaping the rewards of academic superstardom was both disingenuous and irresponsible. There was an ethical imperative, he argued, to stop pretending one was marginal (or at least define more precisely how and where that marginalization operated and where it did not) and to accept the less glamorous task of intervening in the institutions of one's field. Harpham took his own advice to heart as he subsequently accepted the position as head of the Humanities Center in North Carolina.

Harpham provides elements of an approach to ethics that is resonant with and apposite to my own. "The real paradox of ethics," he writes, "is that a discourse that seems to promise answers is so obsessed with questions." He also writes, "Ethics does not solve problems, it structures them."[3] We find here an echo of the various forms of problems and problematization addressed in this book. This formulation, however, could well lead to an anthropology of ethics that stands, or hopes to stand, permanently outside of that which it is inquiring into.[4] Although such an approach has much to teach us, it is not the one I am pursuing as I have resolutely attempted, in the experiments described in this book, to imagine, invent, and occupy different subject positions, ones in which intervention and observation are joined or at least brought into proximity in an assemblage.

For Harpham, ethics not only structures problems from afar but can only do its work when it understands that it is in a dependent relationship to the world of practices and institutions. Using a different analytic vocabulary than my own, he formulates this claim as follows: "Ethics is where thought itself experiences an obligation to form a relation with its other—not only thoughts, but other-than-thought. Ethics is the ought in thought."[5]

Thus, the practice of ethics is not an autonomous one. It is, to switch vocabularies, an essential element for a form-giving orientation of inquiry. Thus, ethics is neither a doctrine nor a metric fully independent of the situations in which it is brought to bear; nor, however, is it fully dependent on those situations. Ethics is neither an answer to a general question with a universal form nor an ethical practice designed to function as a stopping point to observation and inquiry.

One consequence of this situatedness, this dependency, this adjacency, this second-order mode of operation, is the relative place and weight it assigns to reason. Harpham observes, acutely I believe, that "what makes the fact of over-determination truly interesting is that ethical reasoning powerfully appears to be, in Stuart Hampshire's phrase, 'under-determined by the arguments,' predicated on norms and ideals that stand beyond reasons and must simply be accepted or rejected."[6]

In that light, it seems to me, there is a strong connection to be made to a form of anthropological practice. The traditional objects of anthropological research qua objects are, of course, beyond reasons in any formal sense. They may be coherent semantically. They may well be a product in part of a process of reflection, debate, and recursive formulations and testing. Ultimately, it is hard to disagree, however, with Pierre Bourdieu's analysis of the scholastic mistake—the approach that takes social life to be essentially and at base a matter of theorizing.[7]

Bourdieu, however, does not carry his insights far enough. His claim that, through an epistemological break and a set of severe ascetic practices, the sociologist can free himself from the *illusio* and social constraints of all other actors is guided by his passion to make sociology into a modern science and the sociologist into a modern scientist. I cannot accompany Bourdieu along that well-trodden path. The practices of an ethical science lead elsewhere.

Experiment and Experience

To place knowledge where it arises and operates in experience is to know that, as it arose because of the troubles of man, it is confirmed in reconstructing the conditions which occasioned the troubles. Genuine intellectual integrity is found in experimental knowing. Until this lesson is fully learned, it is not safe to dissociate knowledge from experiment or experiment from experience.
«JOHN DEWEY[8]»

On the basis of a long experience of varied fieldwork situations, I agreed with Dewey that, at least for the kind of work in which I wished to be engaged, "genuine intellectual integrity is found in experimental knowing." What exactly this formula meant today for the kind of work I was drawn to, however, remained unclear. There were no obvious candidates in fields close to mine of others leading the way whom I could readily and willingly accompany. Nonetheless, the conjuncture seemed right to take up Dewey's abstract assertions and to see whether they could be made into an orientation to a practice of inquiry into contemporary problems in a contemporary mode.

For me, this challenge had both a scientific and an ethical aspect to it. My diagnosis of the contemporary blockages and discordances was that if Dewey's assertions were to provide good guides (*logoi*) for inquiry, they would need to orient us in exploring a direction in which anthropology had to acknowledge that it was doing more than observing; it had to recognize that it was already participating in the production of knowledge. Furthermore, anthropology had to recognize that some modes of observing and participating were better than others. Of course, the metric for deciding which practices were better than others itself posed significant scientific and ethical challenges. Following Dewey—and (as we have seen in chapters 3 and 4) Foucault—it seemed compelling to associate knowledge with experimentation and experimentation with an ethical and epistemological experience.

The goal of that experience and those experiments was to bring scientific and ethical—in the sense of practices taken up in a mode formative of the self and of others—practices of knowing and governing into a relationship with each other that maintained their difference while bringing them into a dynamic proximity. In a word, these efforts were an attempt to give form to a practice that at one time—and in multiple forms for millennia—had been called, as Foucault had shown us, a *bios philosophicus*. My aim was to identify, take up, and reshape elements of this now marginalized tradition into a contemporary anthropology. Achieving anything like such a goal would clearly require inventiveness, resources, imagination, a modicum of goodwill and good fortune, and, above all, sufficient companions to make the work and labor worthwhile. It was in light of that conclusion (buttressed by a negative evaluation of the dominant practices and evaluative modes of the profession and more forlornly of the university) that during the middle of the first decade of the twenty-first century I decided to experiment intensively with collaborative work.

The first task was to invent new venues in which such work might develop with a certain structure and a certain freedom. I felt strongly that current venues had been designed to accommodate and facilitate a different type of inquiry and a different existential relationship to the materials and people with whom one is engaged. The goal was to see whether it was possible to demonstrate a different kind of relationship between knowing and caring. At the very least, the situation needed remediation. The term "remediation" has two facets: improvement of a deficient situation and change of media. I thought that the situation had a certain urgency, given the state of inquiry and of its leading practitioners. There was a felt need to create venues to facilitate the sharing of approaches, insights, and results in a collaborative and constructive manner that would allow for recursive evaluation of interim results.

The overall experiment has now lasted for more than four years. It has had three distinct, if interrelated, venues: (1) an experiment in reconstruction that centered on new venues for collaboration and remediation of the forms of graduate pedagogy; (2) an experiment in putting into practice and evaluating the collaborative use of the Internet for conceptual work; and (3) an experiment with a different form of participant observation as a principal investigator in the Synthetic Biology Engineering Research Center (SynBERC). These interconnected and overlapping but yet distinct experiments continue in a scaled-back form. The present conjuncture, however, seems to be the right one to document elements of the experience as well as to offer some lessons learned. Like any true experiment, some things worked as planned and others did not, or they worked less well or not in the fashion that one had anticipated. These experiments, after all, were designed to yield experiences in modes of knowing and being. Although one expected them to ramify in unexpected directions, when they did, reaction, reflection, and redesign became the order of the day.

Remediation: Experiments in Venue and Practice Construction

An important catalyst to undertaking these experiments was my encounter with Roger Brent, a molecular biologist. Brent was the head of the Molecular Sciences Institute (MSI), a U.S. government–funded Center of Excellence in Computational Biology, devoted to developing technologies for the quantitative and predictive analysis of the genomic physiology of yeast. Brent, a man of many parts, and I developed and taught a course titled "Genomics and Citizenship" together during a three-year period (2003–5). Among other things, Brent was passionately concerned with the state of security—or, more accurately, insecurity—especially as concerns bioweapons. Through the passionate discussions with Brent, the experiments that led to the two technologies to be described began to take place. His good offices, his ardent challenges to explain, and his generosity of resources, both intellectual and material, provided the initial push to attempt the experiments described here.

The most significant aspect of this experiment was an eminently successful collaborative working relationship with Gaymon Bennett. Bennett was a student in theology at the Graduate Theological Union in Berkeley when we first encountered each other in one of my graduate seminars ("Bio-power and Biopolitics"). Bennett was an active participant and a keen contributor. He engaged seriously and positively in the experiments with reconstructing the graduate seminar form mentioned above. As he finished his doctorate in theology, he entered the graduate program in anthropology at Berkeley. Given his credentials and his experience, Bennett was not a typical graduate student. As I became more actively engaged with trying to imagine and implement a participant-observation practice in SynBERC, I saw that a single-researcher model (while teaching and carrying out normal duties in the Department of Anthropology) to keep adjacent to and chronicle the development of this unique center was not feasible. Hence, we developed a form of collaboration that was closer to the type of lab organization that existed in molecular biology or bioengineering. We met almost every working day; we concentrated on experiments with diverse forms of presentation of material.

The second and simultaneous engagement was my acceptance of principal investigator status within SynBERC. This center, funded by the National Science Foundation, was the first of its kind in the United States (and in the world). It grouped researchers and facilities at the University of California at Berkeley, the University of California at San Francisco (a medical school and research facility), Harvard University, and the Massachusetts Institute of Technology. It also included Prairie View A&M in Texas, first as a research partner and later on as an educational associate. The main challenge and gamble for an anthropologist, a longtime practitioner of participant observation, was to alter the ratio of participation and observation. This reproportioning was itself an experiment; again, like all real experiments it had its ratio of successes and failures. Collaborative work with the biologists and engineers was trying on many levels, some trivial and others not. I provide an analysis of some of these openings and blockages below.

Despite three years of efforts to find some kind of middle ground between what is eerily familiar from C. P. Snow's *Two Cultures*, it basically never happened. This result is especially significant in that previously I had had excellent relations in a series of fieldwork sites with cutting-edge genomics laboratories. Colleagues in the history, anthropology, and social studies of science had remarked to me with a certain perplexity that they never seemed to find these open and philosophically oriented scientists and managers that I described in a set of books.[9] Given the skills that I had developed in more than a decade of experience, it was particularly surprising to find myself and my colleagues consistently treated with indifference or, if we insisted on over-coming that indifference, belligerence. We were reminded on myriad occasions of our unequal and inferior status, of who was paying for our work, and what the biologists and engineers took to be our arcane words and thoughts. This American Babbitry was especially irritating because basically none of the biologists with whom we worked were personally especially belligerent. Something else was taking place; I came to conclude that we were simply not contemporaries.

Schematically the venues developed consisted of the follow-ing: (1) experimenting with reconstructing the graduate semi-nar to move from individual projects and performance to shared problems and a range of capacities assembled together; (2) ex-perimenting with a different ratio of participant observation than is traditional in anthropology, with more emphasis on par-ticipation without neglecting observation; and (3) experimenting with Web sites as venues for work at a collaborative level. These topics are introduced below.

- *Labinar:* The graduate seminar format had been a frequently intense testing ground for ideas, for refining research proposals, and for providing a haven from a miasma of other priorities in the department, the university, and the discipline. That being said, there was a gnawing sense that grew over time that a great deal of what had taken place in these seminars had been lost or, despite immediate reactions, merely ephemeral. It gradually emerged that finding a means of making the graduate seminar more collabora-tive and rigorous and less personal (in terms of the performance of individual brilliance and its correlative production of individual and collective anxiety) might provide a key to remediation. Ongo-ing discussions with George Marcus and others provided at least the idea of a template for how we might proceed. Somewhere, we hoped, between the lab meeting of the biosciences and the critique or studio presentation of the art and architectural worlds there seemed to be a space of possibilities for the human sciences worth exploring. So, we did explore it, baptizing our efforts "the labinar." Variants of this effort continue as of 2011.

- *Anthropology of the Contemporary Research Collaboratory:* We made an attempt to explore the possibilities of the Internet as a venue for intellectual collaboration and a form of community of interests, of sensibility, and of concern. The long buildup to this effort involved intellectual, aesthetic, and ethical frustrations with existing venues, whether institutional, disciplinary, or national. One of the original sparks came from Tobias Rees's accounts of Hans Blumenberg and his friends meeting in Heidelberg to discuss their work and share each other's company. Another was an unexpected opening for collaborative research on security that provided a stimulus for Stephen Collier, Andrew Lakoff, and myself to write a grant proposal together and then develop a means to work together at varying distances. Those efforts grew into a Web site, www.anthropos-lab.net, built on a usable but bare-bones WordPress template. The effort to make the Anthropology of the Contemporary Research Collaboratory (ARC) into a venue for inquiry and collaboration continues as of 2011.
- *Human Practices:* From 2006 forward, we have been engaged with SynBERC. The center was funded with the proviso that it include a human sciences component; the attempt to build one has taken up most of my time during this period. It has also provided sufficient funding for the first time in my career to support graduate students. Variants of this effort continue in 2011.

Frustrated with the different degrees and types of limitations for rigorous thought and inquiry for each of these experiments—which have succeeded on other registers—Bennett, along with Adrian van Allen, a Web designer then working at the Exploratorium in San Francisco and now a graduate student in anthropology at Berkeley, and I started a new Web site, www.bios-technika.net, in which conceptual work can be visualized differently. Such remediated work will, we hope, increase our capacities for thinking and working together.

What follows is a synthesized description of the process of design and implementation of these experiments. It is not meant to be comprehensive but rather to highlight experiences and experiments that might form the basis for more design and implementation work by us and by others.

Bracketing Truth and Seriousness: An Untimely Return

The first three chapters in this part of the book (chapters 5, 6, and 7) are devoted to presenting an account of the conceptual elaboration of these experiments and their trajectories. Hence, I have adopted here an account that privileges the formal over the substantive. During this period of time (2006–2011), the core of my substantive work has centered on the emergent field of synthetic biology. That work is presented in a separate book, *Designing for Human Practices: An Experiment with Synthetic Biology*, cowritten with Gaymon Bennett.[10] Thus, taking one step back, we can see these three chapters as a description of attempts to move beyond the history of the present into a practice adequate to the anthropology of the contemporary. More background description of how we came to understand the mode in which this problem came to take shape and be taken up in anthropology can be found in *Designs for an Anthropology of the Contemporary*, a series of discussions with George Marcus, James Faubion, and Tobias Rees.[11]

In the subsequent three chapters (chapters 8 and 9 and the conclusion), I return more explicitly to the themes of truth and seriousness that I first raised twenty-five years ago (see chapter 1). At the heart of the diagnosis then was a critique of the manner in which Geertz's anthropology bracketed the truth claims of the subjects of anthropological research as well as the seriousness of their semiotic systems. By so doing, I argued, he ultimately bracketed these registers of concern as serious and consequential for the anthropologist and anthropology as well.

Returning to these themes this time, however, I approach them from a different mode of observation/intervention. My diagnosis is that we are faced once again with a double bracketing—this time performed in a distinctive fashion by the actors themselves. As concerns the biosciences, the price to be paid for attaining a modern form of truth has been the bracketing of seriousness. As concerns the art world, the price to be paid for attaining a type of (political and ethical) seriousness has been the bracketing of truth that the arts had previously been understood to attain.

Where do these bracketing operations in adjacent domains leave the anthropology of the contemporary? In order to pose that question in a mode such that it might be made operational in an inquiry, some further specification is required. One thing, however, is clear: whatever relationship one establishes to the dominant modes of truth and seriousness—especially if one hopes to bring them into a relationship—it will have to be untimely and contemporary. The untimeliness is not a blanket rejection of reigning forms and modes, only an attempt at reconfiguration and possible reassemblage. The contemporary presents a more complex challenge because the term is currently in quite common usage. Remembering that a term is a word + a concept + a referent will facilitate the task of unpacking the different concepts and referents the word currently encompasses.

Chapter 8 argues that the biosciences are resolutely modern and modernist. To the degree that such a claim is plausible, it would follow that the biosciences cannot provide either the venues or the modes of veridiction for a contemporary anthropological practice. That being said, once again one must reaffirm that elements, concepts, and practices from the biosciences might be available for other uses. Because the price to be paid for achieving their form of truth has already been paid, as anthropologists we have an obligation and an opportunity to learn something from that tacit transaction.

The subsequent chapter on the art world accepts the claim around which leading arbiters have formed a consensus: modernisms (and postmodernisms) are now dépassés. The reigning signifier is currently "contemporary art." Hence, an exploration of how the term is being used in cultural theory as well as art practice and criticism is helpful as an orientation to the present. There is a broad consensus that "the contemporary" is an ever-expanding cover term bringing into visibility and critical discourse an ever-widening universe of subjects and objects whose seriousness derives largely from claims about their political and moral significance. To the degree that such a claim is plausible, it would follow that the bracketing of truth in the name of seriousness weakens any claim to scientific status. Once again, as anthropologists we have an obligation and an opportunity to learn something from that tacit transaction as well.

Each of these experiments was approached with a clear sense that whatever form and practice we arrived at was to be neither simply traditional nor avant-garde. On the one hand, there is always a sense in the academy that existing forms, practices, disciplines, and institutions are fundamentally worthwhile and simply need to be updated or protected from one or another force currently sweeping through the environment (fashions in thought, severe budget deficits, and so forth). On the other hand, many think that the institutions and practices are essentially spent and that it is only through a radical reformulation that a relevance and vigor can be achieved. Although this distinction would need to be filled out for any particular topic or debate, broadly speaking it would be easy to find many examples of these poles and their oppositions.

The term "the contemporary," it has seemed to me, offers an alternative that is not just a tepid compromise. It provides an orientation that seeks out and takes up practices, terms, concepts, forms, and the like from traditional sources but seeks to do different things with them from the things they were forged to do originally or how they have been understood more recently. The core idea is that concepts arose from and were designed to address specific problems in distinctive historical, cultural, and political settings. When the settings change, and as the problems differ, one cannot take these things up once again or simply reuse them without changing their meaning and efficacy. To meet a present problem they need to be reconfigured, modified, rectified, and adjusted. But revisiting traditional settings can provide fertile examples of concepts, forms, and practices from which to begin a process of conceptualization and eventual redesign. In like manner, the avant-garde mandate of refusing stultified forms or the felt urgency of creation (and destruction) is frequently diagnostically pertinent. Frequently, however, it depends to varying degrees on a sense that the new is always more interesting than the old (and so on). The contemporary as an orientation or ethos is skeptical about the implicit metaphysics of the avant-garde or the tendency toward nostalgia (or worse) of an unconditional allegiance to tradition.

The painter Gerhard Richter makes more or less the same point when he responds in a provocative fashion to an art critic who asked him how it was possible that he liked the landscape painting of certain German Romantics. Richter replied: "A painting by Caspar David Friedrich is not a thing of the past. What is past is only the set of circumstances that allowed it to be painted: specific ideologies, for example. Beyond that, if it is any 'good,' it concerns us—transcending ideology—as an art that we consider worth the trouble of defending (perceiving, showing, making). It is therefore quite possible to paint like Caspar David Friedrich today."[12]

Richter's remarks should not be taken too literally; a look at any of his landscape paintings is sufficient to show that the actuality he refers to is a major transformation of Friedrich's actuality. No one would mistake one of Richter's landscape paintings for one of Friedrich's; that being said, Richter's point is suitable, untimely, and contemporary.

Collaboration, Concepts, and Assemblages

Judgments are said to be warrantably assertible or not—a third notion distinct from either affirmation or truth. As for what warrants a judgment, a theory of inquiry will have to include a number of criteria for gauging the success of inquiries. Such criteria would include various epistemological and methodological considerations such as whether or not the subject matter of the inquiry is being articulated in a coherent way, whether or not the expected results of ongoing activities are satisfied, whether or not there are better ways to proceed, whether or not the results are useful or otherwise applicable to other inquiries, and so forth.
«TOM BURKE[1]»

An essential goal of my research and teaching is to contribute to a more rigorous and powerful interpretive analytics. In order to do so, there needs to be a reworking of the conceptual and pragmatic conditions of what is called the human or social sciences. Both the terms "the human" and "social" pose definitional problems. I use the term "social" in a restricted fashion, locating it in a particular historical formation and hence making it unavailable as a generic cover term.[2] The same restrictions apply to "the human." The term "science" poses more problems—English has developed its own idiosyncratic use of the term that differs from the French "*la science*" or the German "*die Wissenschaft*," both of which are broader than the English "science," covering a broad swath of scholarship and knowledge production that includes the human sciences.

The overall goal has been and remains to rethink and remediate key aspects of the forms, venues, and practices of the interpretive sciences, that is, aspects of the pragmatic and material conditions of contemporary knowledge production, dissemination, and critique. As such, rethinking is a practice; it entails doing things differently in an embodied, materially located, and historically situated manner. Above all, it entails controlled experimentation. In its initial stages, "experimentation" simply means trying out different configurations of inquiry and critique. "Controlled" means subjected to punctual examination and reexamination. In the natural sciences, formal institutions for the form, practice, and legitimate venues for what counts as experimentation have been invented, implemented, and enforced for a long time now. This institutionalization includes genres of writing that are strictly policed (chapter 8). Although there are existing norms and practices in the interpretive sciences, they are more diverse and less controlled.

In an anthropological fashion, therefore, it seemed worthwhile to experiment with the invention and refinement of practices of venue construction and modes of presentation, as well as concept formation and clustering. To the degree that such innovation could be accomplished, a platform for further experimentation, shared at least by a small cohort in the present and a possible future "we" of unknown proportions, would make it possible to establish a practice through which rectifications and remediation could be identified, practiced, and refined. The activity of experimentation—the manner in which it was carried out—was as much the objective as specific results.

A Look Back

It is quite remarkable that the history of anthropology has produced—and thematized as exemplars for further research—so few examples of collective work. It is remarkable because the discipline has actually been the site of many such experiments. For example, Rebecca Lemov, in her book *World as Laboratory: Experiments with Mice, Mazes, and Men,* documents several of the most significant attempts at coordinated research in the social sciences.[3] Throughout the twentieth century, many experiments in collective projects have been undertaken, including a longstanding tradition of collaboration with those one is seeking to understand. Today, in any case, these efforts are either forgotten or discredited (e.g., the work during World War II of Ruth Benedict). My goals, however, are less directly instrumental (and less utopian) than those of many of these projects, although I agree with Max Weber that the social sciences have been linked—and will continue to be linked—in multiple ways with policy and politics for as long as they have been (or are) in existence.[4]

There are any number of possible reasons for the historical amnesia. One possibility is that directly collaborative work with other researchers in qualitative and interpretive inquiries is neither desirable nor plausible. Such a position has been sustained tacitly in anthropology, a discipline that has a long history of (rugged and romantic) individualism. Today, however, the social sciences and humanities need to be made more explicit and strengthened while their limitations acknowledged. Such evaluation and redirection, after all, is what critique consists in; it is a key marker of scientific, understood broadly, seriousness about truthfulness.

It is not surprising that individual research, writing, and knowledge production has received support—and instilled a habitus, an enduring dispositional change, that has been wary of challenges to its form—in a discipline that has based its authority on participant observation, existential immersion, in what were taken to be more or less isolated sites. The narratives of quest, "anthropologist as hero," and the like continue to carry symbolic weight even if essential aspects of that authority are dated.[5] Dated does not mean irrelevant, however, only in need of reexamination, further specification, and, when relevant, remediation.

Regardless of the ambiguities of fieldwork as a technique of research, it remains unexplained why researchers returning from their fieldwork are obliged to produce a quite restricted range of types of articles and monographs. Why did the discipline of anthropology (and related sister disciplines) not develop more distinctive modes of evaluation and accumulation of knowledge? It seems entirely plausible that the rugged individualism of the fieldworker with data could have been combined with different norms and forms for what counts as a fact, an argument, or a scholarly advance. Especially in the United States, the poles of ethnographic authority and a methodological formalism have rarely been brought into a successful relationship. And none has succeeded in becoming normative. Now that both poles have been placed under sustained challenge for decades, it is time once again for experimentation and invention.

The Present

The claim put forward for close to a century of anthropological inquiry that the discipline has been stuck in a takeoff stage preliminary to a mature discipline that would finally achieve a positivistic scientific rigor (presumably like economics) has proved to be little more than an elusive hope and a thwarted, if constantly renewed, object of desire. Consequently, it must be underscored that what is described here is not an attempt to prove that anthropology can or ought to be a natural science just like any other—quite the contrary. Alternatives to that pathetic mimesis, however, are most definitely worth exploring. Said another way, bringing truth and seriousness into a worthwhile relationship is a problem and challenge of a certain urgency.

Given that the current form of the social sciences and humanities disciplines in the U.S. university system is essentially the one institutionalized during the late nineteenth century or early twentieth century with the birth of the modern research university, and that there is scant motivation from within the disciplines to reform themselves as, for example, the biosciences have done, I am not optimistic that work bringing together truth and seriousness can be based exclusively in the university. The university, however, remains a source of employment, of resources such as libraries, and of pedagogical practice; it provides elements of a venue worth constructing. In that light, we imagine new hybrid assemblages, adjacent to and parasitic on, the university. Today, full-scale reform within the university seems both unlikely and probably dangerous given the dominant political trends in the United States. Rather, the efforts described here focus on giving form to a rigorous collaborative practice at a microscale; this project derives in part from lessons learned from the wave of challenges to the form of anthropological writing undertaken during the 1980s and 1990s.[6] These efforts include conceptual work and attempts to invent a venue or venues that would facilitate these efforts.

A central pedagogical parameter is to avoid the capital letter debates about theory that have garnered so much attention over the last several decades and to concentrate instead on the level of work focused on concepts and experimentation (Bachelard, Canguilhem, and Hacking); on historical conditions of knowledge production rather than universal truths (Koselleck and Shapin); and on the diversity of scientific practice and results rather than their unity (Foucault and Galison).[7]

Consequently, and as a preliminary step, it has been helpful to investigate the wave of interest over the last two decades or so in the history and current status of spaces of critical practice that exist in other disciplines (including the arts). Although there are evident (and not so evident) epistemological and pragmatic differences between disciplines (past, present, and future) that must not be overlooked, some practices that have been experimented with in various places might, with appropriate reworking, be helpful in advancing an interpretive analytics worthy of the name. To use our jargon, "equipmental platforms" and "practices" might well be transferred with appropriate modifications from one form of apparatus to a different assemblage.⁸ Once that possibility is identified, multiple possibilities become visible, and the challenge of remediation is posed explicitly and self-consciously.

A necessary if not sufficient first step in that direction is to invent practices of knowledge production, dissemination, and critique that resolutely refuse the (liberal and symbolic capital-laden) individualism of the reigning social sciences and humanities. This impulse had a history: a hallmark of early modernist experimentation in the twentieth century was the effort to go beyond the figure of the artist as genius or lone creator and to find ways of working that combined both an artisanal and industrial manner. Whether in the Bauhaus or in the Soviet workshops of the 1920s, multiple experiments were undertaken to create a new work environment that blurred the traditional oppositions of theory and practice, private and public, pure and applied, and so forth. Although these movements and experiments were defeated politically by both right and left, they have left a legacy and an archive of experimental techniques and results.⁹

Objects and Objectives: Concepts and Assemblages

The post-Kantians concentrated on a universal encyclopedia of the concept that attributed concept formation to a pure subjectivity rather than taking on the more modest task of a pedagogy of the concept, which would have to analyze the factors of the conditions of creations that remained singular.
«GILLES DELEUZE AND FELIX GUATTARI¹⁰»

The founding dream of *Wikipedia* was that a universal encyclopedia for the twenty-first century had become feasible through the medium of the World Wide Web. Such an encyclopedia would be composed largely of concepts available for perusal and modification in a flexible and expansive manner. If Deleuze had lived to see *Wikipedia* and had been in a sufficiently sardonic and ironic mood, he might have labeled it neo-Kantian. Its principles of organization, after all, are unabashedly pure subjectivity (tempered over time by legal limitations and a growing sense of the comic absurdity of equating all opinions). Deleuze's students, with his consent, might even have contributed portions of his "Abracadabra" to *Wikipedia*.[11]

In addition to the universal encyclopedia and the pedagogy of the concept—to which we return shortly—Deleuze and Guattari identify a third possibility for the form and mode of philosophy (by which Deleuze and Guattari mean thinking): the concept as a product to be communicated. For them the turn to communication of information as concept work is the most degraded and degrading form of intellectual work. They diagnose this turning as follows: "The most shameful moment came when computer science, marketing, design, and advertising, all the disciplines of communication, seized hold of the word *concept*. . . . The concept has become the set of *product displays* (historical, scientific, artistic, sexual, and pragmatic), and the *event* has become the *exhibition* that sets up various displays and the 'exchange of ideas' it is supposed to promote. The only events are exhibitions, and the only concepts are products that can be sold."[12] One can easily recognize the prevailing uses of the Internet in this characterization. Google's massively successful algorithms, bringing in billions in advertising revenue, treat Deleuze, after all, in exactly the same way as they treat Ben & Jerry's.

Surely, however, the medium (despite the hard work devoted to reducing it and everything in it to information and communication) is not exclusively received by humans as a uniquely digital output. Even if one mode of production and reception thoroughly dominates, surely there are a multitude of minor modes operating. Why shouldn't the minor practices of this medium be amplified and remediated? Why shouldn't these minor practices be modified, improved, and motivated to include the problem of thinking among the multimedia potentials? Why shouldn't they be used to increase capacities to think, collaborate, and flourish? Why, after all, shouldn't they be used to facilitate a modest pedagogy of the concept? Perhaps some of these minor modes and practices might even open up a small exit toward a contemporary maturity?

Having probed the strengths and limitations of a localized

experiment in design in the labinar, the new vector—the Internet—held out promise as a vehicle for testing to establish whether it could be made to contribute to the form of production, collaboration, and dissemination that seemed necessary, lacking, and temptingly close at hand. My hope was that we could use the new technologies to build a platform that was neither local nor directly inflected by the peculiarities of specific personalities. It seemed possible that some of a range of trained incapacities of the academy could be countered in this form. It seemed almost certain that new assemblages were increasingly going to include the Internet as one of their vectors. Living in northern California, I was aware of the hype, prophetic claims, utopian dross, and the like that saturated the discourse around the Internet. Yet, other things of value were taking shape as well, and, in any case, I was neither a technological determinist nor a venture capitalist and believed that things could ramify differently than the major players drove them to do.

One can only imagine that many others have posed similar questions. No doubt many, many diverse responses might well be remediative in diverse ways. That being said, in our experience, the scarcity of experimentation on the Internet with conceptual forms of creation is startling and unanticipated. The causes of this poverty—if such it be—can certainly be found in the role of the massive forces that Deleuze and Guattari indicate: the predominance of global capitalism, the valorization of technical virtuosity per se, the ease of access to information, the fetishization of "apps," and so on. Among these grand and much discussed aspects, however, is another that has received less attention: the habits and customs of the professorate. Isn't it the case that the majority of the professorate is using the Internet at most to produce exhibits and products, a digital version of their courses, vitae, and syllabi? And isn't it the case that it is still nearly impossible to get tenure for a dynamic, multimedia, interactive project on the Web?

My projects were driven in the hope of increasing collaborative capacities without simultaneously betraying thinking. I hoped to create a venue or venues that would facilitate the functioning of inquiry in compelling, distinctive, and significant ways. A copse of concepts guided these initial efforts, concepts drawn from the corpus of work of Dewey, Weber, and Foucault, as well as, in this instance, Deleuze. The challenge has been to make these concepts function in an assemblage different from the ones in which and for which they were created. Here as elsewhere in this book, I introduce a concept—assemblage—and then describe how it could be taken from the work it had been designed to perform originally and remediated so as to address a different set of problems in another time and place. Concepts, as opposed to theory, need to be constantly adjusted, remediated, and ramified. The modest pedagogy of the concept, in my understanding, lies in that work.

THEORY

In two books dedicated to systematizing Deleuze's work, the theorist Manuel DeLanda provides a systematic reconstruction of his core conceptual repertoire while readily admitting that Deleuze never presented his works in this fashion. This analytic work is helpful pedagogically because Deleuze's texts are notoriously esoteric. DeLanda, however, does not seem to pose the question of why Deleuze changed terms as he moved from problem to problem, one book to the next, one set not necessarily consistent with the previous one, and whether Deleuze's mode of operation is more than merely accidental or perverse. My answer would be: DeLanda is a theorist and Deleuze a thinker or, in his own terms, a philosopher. Theorists perform a valuable function in bringing (or attempting to bring) discursive order and coherence in a logically systematic manner. The relation, however, to the world of what John Dewey called "facts" is to use them as examples of the theory.[13] In contradistinction, Deleuze and Dewey would agree that thinking does not start with order and find examples to exhibit it. Rather, thinking arises when problems are encountered in the world and it seeks concepts to assist in working through those problems: this is done not necessarily in order to resolve them in a definitive fashion but rather to make them visualizable and discussable. From that point on, further inquiry becomes possible: one learns things and is changed by doing so, as are the things one is learning about and as is true during the course of inquiry.

CONCEPT: ASSEMBLAGE

The first two chapters of DeLanda's book titled *A New Philosophy of Society: Assemblage Theory and Social Complexity* lay out the argument for why *assemblages* are not the type of things traditionally identified in Western philosophy as totalities or essences. Several aspects of this presentation are directly pertinent to the problems I have been seeking to identify and address. Hence, I present the barest liniments of this concept cluster that I have found to be promising as a tool to advance inquiry rather than as ends in themselves or as steps in theory building.[14] Therefore, the first distinction is that an assemblage is not a totality, a seamless whole, a preexisting thing of the world with given and fixed properties (even if they are not all activated at any particular time or in any particular situation).

Assemblages, however, are equally themselves things in the world, things characterized by a specific form of functional coherence and efficacy. Assemblages have an ontological status, albeit a variant of what Ian Hacking has called historical ontology.[15] Once one starts looking for them, and one can begin to start that search, once the concept is articulated and made available, one discovers that assemblages abound in the world even if the conceptual vocabularies and sensibilities to notice them have been obscured by one variant or another of tradition and training.

In sum, assemblages are real; they have existence, forms, and effects, and certain assemblages include affects. They make some other things and events possible and others improbable. They differ, however, from what has been traditionally understood as "a thing" or "an object" by being composed of heterogeneous parts that retain, as they are combined and recombined into new interrelations, to a degree, their original properties.[16] They retain these qualities because they enter into an assemblage through establishing relations of exteriority—not interiority—with the other entities with whom they have been brought into proximity and with whom they interact. Assemblages are composed of preexisting things that, when brought into relations with other preexisting things, open up different capacities not inherent in the original things but only come into existence in the relations established in the assemblage. DeLanda states, "While [an entity's] properties are given and may be denumerable as a closed list, its capacities are not given—they may go unexercised if no entity suitable for interaction is around—and for a potentially open list, since there is no way to tell in advance in what way a given entity may affect or be affected by innumerable other entities. In this view, being part of a whole involves the exercise of a part's capacities but it is not a constituent property of it. And given that an unexercised capacity does not affect what a component is, a part may be detached from the whole while preserving its identity."[17]

Thus, an assemblage is not an organic unity as such entities have been understood in traditional terms. Today, of course, new assemblages of organic things are being brought into the world. New fields such as synthetic biology are dedicated to experimenting with the limits, potentials, and capacities of these entities. Nature is being engineered; once its engineers discover the manifold diverse forms existing in the world beyond the computer chip, they will become better engineers.

Thus an assemblage brings together entities in the world into a proximity in which they establish relations among and between themselves while remaining external to each other and thereby retain their original properties to a degree. This state has a number of characteristics. The first is that the order of an assemblage is "contingently obligatory instead of logically necessary."[18] It follows that "while logically necessary relations may be investigated by thought alone, contingently obligatory ones involve a consideration of empirical questions."[19] By "thought," DeLanda means "theory." Anyone familiar with Dewey or Foucault understands the distinction. Assemblages, it is true, certainly require consideration. Consideration, however, is itself not a uniquely discursive operation; it is material, affective, and embodied. Given that conclusion, it would seem obvious that the practice of thinking about and with assemblages would itself have to be more than discursive or theoretical.

Finally, Deleuze uses the term "singular"—as in "conditions of creation that remained singular"—in a distinctive and idiosyncratic manner.[20] The "singular" refers to a unit that retains its multiplicity of heterogeneous elements and brings them together into a common vector while modifying but not eliminating their diverse properties. The term has an ontological referent: it points to things and processes in the world. The term, however, is not merely descriptive of a given situation but incorporates an act of creation. For Deleuze, when there is concept work and creation, one is in the domain of thinking.

The pedagogic work of the concept therefore consists in conceptualization as an act of creation; this act of creation, however, contributes to bringing together diverse elements into a form— an assemblage—that both preserves their diversity and opens up hitherto unknown capacities.[21] The challenge and the work of recent years has been dedicated to understanding heretofore ignored entities in the world—especially emergent assemblages— and in inventing practices and venues in which and through which thinking as remediation and eventual reconstruction can be facilitated.

From Objects to Objectives: Assemblages

The name objects will be reserved for subject-matter so far as it has been produced and ordered in settled form by means of inquiry; proleptically, objects are the objectives of inquiry. The apparent ambiguity of using "objects" for this purpose (since the word is regularly applied to things which are observed or thought of) is only apparent. For things exist as objects for us only as they have been previously determined as outcomes of inquiries. When used in carrying

on new inquiries in problematic situations, they are known as objects in virtue of prior inquiries which warrant their assertibility.
«JOHN DEWEY[22]»

The following list of objects follows Dewey's logic: they are both the product of previous inquiry and the objectives of a new stage of inquiry. Each of these objects is a distillation of a wide range of other inquiries. In order to proceed toward collaboration in our variant of the human sciences, they must be set within a new problem-space. They can thereby function as topics of further inquiry where inquiry is understood as addressing *discordances* and *indeterminacies* in a delimited situation.

Object one: Object one is to invent a form of collaborative work that not only allows but requires attention to common problem formulation. Do it in such a way that the common focus, and the collaborative work, requires attention to individuation where it is appropriate and to deindividuation where it is appropriate. Individuation would concentrate on attention to individual skills, interests, projects, experience, maturity, and the like. Common problems should be a factor of both cohesion and individuation. Achieving this work entails renewed analytic and ethical attention to the nature of different tasks at different moments of life and career.

Object two: The first object is strengthened if at the outset a strong and clear distinction is made between projects and problems. The collaboratory qua collaboratory works on problems. Hence, there is an outside as it were to the space and reach of the collaboratory; it follows, however, that there is an inside and intensity to the work of the collaboratory. A reflective and recursive return to this point, these limits, and those processes must be built into the workings of the collaboratory more generally or the labinar more specifically.

Object three: The insistent recognition that one is part of a constituted tradition, one that is reconfigured with some regularity, establishes both a source and a site of authority beyond the immediate group—hence freeing the professor from having to occupy that role uniquely and freeing other participants from the Romantic imperative of genius. This relation to history (or tradition) is radically different from the biological sciences, whose time span is extremely limited, and from the more artistic undertakings in which originality is primed. Although tradition is essential to orientation, by definition it can never be adequate in and of itself. This relation to the past—recognition, renegotiation, and renewal—opens up a range of possible relations to the future.

Object four: A central dimension of the work is to construct and elaborate in an intensive and expansive fashion a conceptual toolkit. Concepts are to be used; hence, they need to be adapted to changing problems and changing uses. On the other hand, there is a long history of attempts to understand things human and vital; much of value has already been produced. Starting de novo makes no sense and in any case is not possible. Therefore, there is an archaeological dimension to the elaboration of an appropriate inventory of concepts; there is a genealogical dimension that serves the critical function of requiring work and questioning before deciding whether a particular concept is adequate and appropriate. There is furthermore an elaborative dimension of testing the limits of categories that were developed in other contexts for other purposes. And as one moves from the history of the present to the anthropology of the contemporary, the challenge of further elaborating concepts is joined by the critical work of judging their limits of applicability. Inquiry into the contemporary will almost always require both old and new conceptual work and elaboration. Hence, timeless theory or universal concepts are unlikely to be very helpful.

Object five: Object five is to proceed from the maxim, that is, increase capacities while not increasing relations of domination.

The conceptual process had now arrived at a stage in which design could be undertaken. In order to proceed with that process, experiments had to be set in motion. That is the subject of the next chapter.

Venues: The Labinar and the Anthropology of the Contemporary Research Collaboratory

A problematization occurs when forces of an infrastructural kind (including scientific ones) become realigned in a fashion such that those organizations, dispositions, and practices long taken for granted must be reexamined and, more positively, when the possibility of rethinking and reworking them becomes explicit as an opportunity and a challenge. Such moments of problematization and possible reconfiguration are underdetermined in the sense that many vectors contribute to them and that many responses to them are in principle possible. With regard to *Writing Culture,* to take an example that by now is historical, a number of varied responses did take place. Pertinent here is what was put into question by *Writing Culture* and how it has faded from actuality. What was put into question and made an object of thought was "ethnographic authority." Although that topic could have been approached in many ways, it was primarily the moral authority of the subject of ethnographic reports that was challenged by a far-reaching and insistent hermeneutics of suspicion. The time for that mode of criticism has passed.

Today, in the second decade of the twenty-first century, an increasing number of graduate students in anthropology have had experience working in nongovernmental organizations or international agencies. Many of these young adults come to their current work in graduate school with a felt need to understand conceptually what it is they had already experienced proximally (contact with war, epidemics, poverty, social suffering, and the like) while working on a team that was a part of a larger organization. Consequently, whatever *rite de passage* fieldwork may have been previously, it can no longer be based solely on the deprovincializing of the middle classes, although that goal retains its merits. However, achieving it today requires more than travel and theory.

If a graduate student group in a seminar, for example, is working with students who already have a rich set of experiences (women's health in Uganda, refugee camps in Darfur, AIDS hospitals in Thailand, children in favelas in Brazil, social exclusion and rehabilitation in Vietnam, and so forth), then a question like "what is it that one wants to know about these places?" demands attention. How can we best design or redesign the next field trip to get at that understanding? Today, for multiple reasons, both significance and design are pertinent in a different way than they had been previously. Today they are foregrounded as topics that must be reflectively addressed and with which experiments need to be conducted and the results disseminated.

The Labinar

After a series of stimulating, energized, and intellectually successful graduate seminars in the Department of Anthropology at the University of California at Berkeley (2004–5)—one on biopower, another on security, and a third on forms of contemporary anthropology, "we" (a core group of graduate students and I) began to discuss what might come next. These informal discussions began to yield an orientation about how we might attempt to create and implement a different form to the work. The motivations were multiple: too many insights (or what felt like insights) evaporated once the session was over; too many different things were going on at the same time; the traditional authority structure of elite humanities seminars (professor centered, performance dominated) had been attenuated and made visible but despite that had remained basically unaltered. The immediate satisfaction of sustained discussion (the seminars often lasted four hours, with graduate students continuing from there over food and drinks), a sense of mutual support for projects being thought through, a tentative formulation of concepts beyond the ones such as "biopower" or "liberalism" that we have been bequeathed, and possible interrelations of projects and concepts led to an impatience, even an urgency, that we devote some energy to inventing (i.e., imagining, conceiving, practicing, and revising, in recursive spirals) a form in which more of the "insights" and the "experience" could be captured and returned to in a systematic fashion by us and by others not present at the time and place when and where these insights and experiences arose.

Among other criteria, there was consensus (with almost no debate, as the participants were self-selected) that the form to be invented would be one in which the work done must be disciplined and collaborative. There were a set of reasons and prior experiences for the centrality of these criteria. The challenge of transforming the elite graduate seminar was set against the background of two other projects that were in preliminary stages of articulation.

First, George Marcus had been talking for some time about possible modes of collaborative work that would take up some of the practices and insights from other disciplines, such as the "critique" in schools of art practice or the "*charette*" in architecture. The latter term was coined at the Ecole des Beaux Arts in Paris during the late nineteenth century; it captured vividly the practice of architecture students wheeling their design projects through the streets of the Latin Quarter to the Ecole, where they would be evaluated by the professors in a series of annual competitions. The relevant analogy here is that the students were assigned an architectural problem to solve (e.g., design a bank by the seashore, design a villa in the hills of Rome), there were something like common standards (although such standards were in crisis by this time), there was a time limit for the exercise, and there were exemplary solutions to previous competitions available for scrutiny.[1]

Another example of intense and focused group work that was likely to provide an analogy to work from, if not an example to directly imitate, was the "lab meeting" as it has evolved in various natural sciences. Again, there was a common problem, a set of more or less agreed on and more or less explicit set of standards as to what counted as a solution, and—in contrast here to the architectural pole—a consequent experiment or experiments that would be designed to address the problem. And these would yield further experiments to be worked on upon the completion of a previous experiment. Although there is a large literature on the history and significance of laboratories and experimentation, apparently there is little or no literature on the lab meeting.[2]

The analogies with the lab meeting and the *charette* help to render visible (and hence available for refinement and reformulation) several practices, techniques, and goals for work in interpretive analytics under the sign of the anthropology of the contemporary as opposed to the history of the present.[3] First, both the artistic and scientific analogies provide examples in which problems and solutions can be shared. They demonstrate that no contradiction exists between the establishment of a common problem and distinctive individual solutions to that problem. Although the idea that creativity and conformity enrich each other may appear to be paradoxical in the human or social sciences, the paradox lies in the "doxa" and not in the objective world. These seemingly opposed poles can be connected into a productive form in a number of ways. For example, the apprentice architect at the Beaux Arts was not considered to be a builder following rules but an artist imagining formal solutions. Or in mathematics, the language of elegance and brilliance is widely deployed while the objectivity and formal power of a solution is held to be an essential condition for such qualities to manifest themselves. Hence, there is no a priori reason that those of us working in a mode of interpretive analytics or the anthropology of the contemporary cannot work collaboratively while also nourishing and crediting individual contributions and projects.

There might seem to be something counterintuitive about a structured and role-defined protocol in order to foster creativity and break this bind. The idea would be that only a radically antiauthoritarian and supposedly egalitarian form could produce true innovation. Counter to this is the fact that all groups have a form that will lend itself to certain kinds of production and not to others. No space is actually free of social constraints or power hierarchies. An academic seminar is not, and it never will be. In hypothetically egalitarian setups, such as a roundtable or a group with rotating leaders, a pecking order will emerge based on the external reality of professor-student relations; natural variations in articulateness, timidity, experience, and knowledge; or perhaps those classic scourges of race and gender. A conscious refusal to predefine organization would simply accept those social constraints and interactions. We chose instead to confront them and attempted to reformulate our own ingrained mode of academic sociality.

That evaluative and accreditation process is at the heart of academic advancement and can be dispensed with lightness of spirit only by those at the top of the hierarchy. Individual credit is required for audit procedures; it must be incorporated into any new practice of inquiry and analytics that hopes to become institutionalized in any sustainable manner. So, let us bid good riddance to genius and other such nineteenth-century figures and set to work, as Max Weber would say, on creating the components for rigorous creation that takes its own conditions of production into account.

We defined our project in anthropology as an attempt to understand the following: under what conditions is thinking possible now? Thought, in our debate, was recognition that something has been contingently constituted as an object and a problem. "Now" indicated that those conditions were historically dependent, partially established in institutions, laws, and scientific statements and partially in motion. Broadly, we referred to goings-on and problematizations in the world. But, specifically, we considered what kind of pedagogy fosters thinking. If our work could make the conditions of thought more explicit and hence more open to intervention, how are we to proceed when our own inquiry and diagnoses are caught up in the same contemporary framing as what we study? Could our biases be offset by the multiple perspectives available in a group, utilized in the rigorous practice of second-order observation?

LAB NOTES: WRITE-UP OF AN EXPERIMENT IN
COLLABORATIVE ANTHROPOLOGY (*by Meg Stalcup*)

In the spring of 2006, our group began an experiment in collaborative anthropology. There was a dual impetus to our efforts: a desire to deal head-on with inadequacies in our academic environment and a strong feeling that the classic norms of qualitative inquiry needed to become contemporary. Collaboration struck us as potentially key to both. The core of our group comprised members from the disciplines of sociocultural and medical anthropology, medicine, law, and sociology. Although most members were affiliated with UC Berkeley, one student commuted from Stanford. Another participated via speakerphone and Web cam from Yale Law School. A senior anthropology librarian and the director of the molecular biology research institute where our meetings were held often sat in.

What are the actual practices of intellectual colaboring? We had had some successful experiences, magic moments when thought seemed shared, an insight captured and made tangible. We were also cognizant of consistent challenges: groups were too large, students were competitive rather than genuinely cooperative, and the work accomplished seemed to evaporate at the end. We wanted to create a space where intense intellectual synergy could take place on shared problems. We hoped that sharing our fieldwork would facilitate concept work. We wanted to speed up in order to understand what was happening in the world, as it happened. Over the course of the semester, we designed a protocol for a graduate seminar around these goals. Our attempt was to turn the existing obstacles into guidelines for a better form.

We were constrained by the socialization of graduate school. The seminar provides a space to compete and posture for the professor. Students are trained to perform rhetorical thrusts and parries, and the performances show what one already knows. Such performances move a group away from thinking new thoughts or focusing together on a chosen topic. They also compound the variation in participation styles among students who think out loud or to themselves, who are assertive, or who are reserved. Collaborative thinking, we decided, would require a very different environment.

Yet despite these constraints, past seminars had allowed moments of discussion that went beyond reproduction and performance to breakthroughs. Sometimes these moments built on each other throughout the semester, and we ended up feeling that indeed we had attained something—extracted conceptual tools from Niklas Luhmann's denser texts or defined the limits of Foucault's biopower and biopolitics as explanations for today's events. More frequently, the breakthroughs were tenuous; as we grasped them, they evaporated, and the semester ended. We wanted to develop a way to work in a relatively large group, to learn the skills of cooperative thinking while retaining the ability to critique, and to capture the results of our labor.

For each challenge, we developed a corresponding response, mixing small innovations with proven approaches, such as close textual reading and reflective awareness of group processes. We were vigilant about grounding these techniques in the fieldwork seminar participants had engaged in so as to make the discussions focused and practice oriented. What we wanted to do would involve work on ourselves: training in procedures and retraining in how to approach the classroom experience.

We drew a parallel to laboratory experiments. In the textbook version, one begins with a question, formulates a hypothesis, and then tests it by adapting or inventing techniques and practicing them. With a certain irony, we nicknamed our experiment the "labinar," "lab" plus "seminar."[4] From the beginning, we understood the labinar as an experiment in venue construction. We understood it as an intervention into pedagogic practice, as well as anthropological inquiry. We reasoned that the world is different than it was when the standards of qualitative human or social science became codified in the heyday of traditional anthropological fieldwork. Even multisited ethnography, obviously necessary for many phenomena, is limited by what a single individual can manage intellectually, logistically, and interpretively. Because we advocated field sites being chosen according to a problem, there were severe limitations to the traditional practice of the individual anthropologist. Furthermore, we wanted to work on what was potentially emergent instead of the search for holistic systems either as objects in the world or in an academic construction. Yet anthropology still follows the disciplinary model of the lone researcher, toiling for years to produce a definitive statement on a specific group or phenomenon.

We were, of course, all engaged in our own specific research projects. We wanted to conduct an experiment in which we put together all of our work in order to discover whether those projects shared a common problem. The field sites and topics represented in our group were, in a sense, aleatory. We took this diversity as a necessary substrate: our hypothesis was that the problems, as defined by our subjects and in our analyses, might together indicate identifiable shape, a problematization.

In this light, we began with a text from Michel Foucault in which he sketches the term "problematization" as "the analysis of the way an unproblematic field of experience, or a set of practices, which were accepted without question, which were familiar and 'silent,' out of discussion, becomes a problem, raises discussion and debate, incites new reactions, and induces a crisis in the previously silent behavior, habits, practices, and institutions. The history of thought, understood in this way, is the history of the way people begin to take care of something, of the way they become anxious about this or that—for example, about madness, about crime, about sex, about themselves, or about truth."[5]

First, we took up Foucault's text as an exercise in *explication de texte*, close reading. We wanted, in our lab seminar, to study problematization in real time. The next step was to examine our own work by using Luhmann's distinction between first- and second-order observation. Observation, for Luhmann, meant both to notice in a disciplined sense and to register significance. First-order observations tell us *what* is happening. Second-order observations shift frames so as to tell us *how* the first-order observations are made. Second-order observations mark criteria and distinctions, assumptions, and the limits of categories. Neither type of observation is privileged: they have different objects and provide different kinds of information. The distinction proved useful for the labinar on two levels. We wanted to understand the way that our subjects understood, classified, and categorized their own problems. Our primary data were their first- and second-order observations, which we would observe, mark, and order. If there were indeed an emerging problematization, our mode of inquiry would stand a chance of identifying it.

Drawing on the Anthropology of the Contemporary Research Collaboratory and previous seminars, we began with the premise that major changes were occurring in relation to "security." Transformations in the U.S. government, such as the establishment of the Department of Homeland Security, responsible for both natural-disaster preparation and counterterrorism measures, or the description of severe acute respiratory syndrome and avian flu as issues of biosecurity, indicated that conceivably disparate elements were being understood as linked. We intended to see whether a reproblematization of security could be discerned by examining our projects for common problems.

PROTOCOL (*by Meg Stalcup*)

Paul Rabinow and a small group of students who had taken classes together for several years wanted to transform the graduate seminar into a different venue that would facilitate our goals. We planned to spend the semester intensely focused on fieldwork and developing concepts that would help us make sense of what we were finding in the field. With students in different stages of graduate work, we wanted to both analyze the work that they had done and think about how to improve the design for future projects.

In 2006, thirty students shopping multiple courses showed up to the first semester meeting. We declared that the criteria for entrance were familiarity with a repertoire of concepts and an active research project; about half the students returned. Then we requested help from an improbable source, a specialist at the research and consultation firm Global Business Network. He was a PhD graduate of Berkeley, was familiar with some of the readings, and was willing to help. We asked the following questions:

- What are the different models for how a meeting is run? Which model makes the most sense for the kind of thought we want to foster? What is the director's role? Literally, we asked, "Where should he sit?"
- What kinds of roles/ positions are there in a meeting? How should these be divided among participants—by experience, by personality, or by volunteers? Should they rotate or be set for the semester?
- What are some proven ways of structuring time in a three-hour meeting? Is there an optimum division? Are there activities that are always best done before break? After break?
- What is the best way to structure a large group? What kinds of participation are there? Are subgroups useful? How would subgroups relate to the whole, in terms of labor, reporting back?
- What are the best techniques for producing a useful record of the meeting and for preserving ideas that come up?

The answers we received, we later realized, were up-to-date training methods honed in high-tech industry.

Up to this point, conceptualizing and planning a different kind of seminar had taken place on the sidelines of other conversations and through e-mail exchanges. Realizing that we were going to constantly reevaluate and adjust the setup, we wanted to establish a time and space for informal conversations and a system for making decisions about the seminar. Yet, because this was to be an experiment in what types of interactions a specific form might engender, we needed to not just talk about the experiment but also conduct it, do work, and discover and evaluate whether the forms were productive.

We came up with several solutions and implemented all of them. One was creating a specialized committee that met weekly to calibrate the seminar in a continuous second-order fashion. After the meeting with Global Business Network specialist, who approved the idea of a committee and suggested that we orient and name it the "design group," we convened and spent several hours of frenzied protocol planning for differentiated time, designated roles, and small break-out groups. Finally, we decided to set aside time at the end of each session for the group as a whole to make second-order observations, discussing how the particular session had gone, as well as the overall progression, and designated specific weeks in the semester to the synthesis and modification of our practices.

We carried out this attention to micropractices in another way. We were accustomed to seminars in three-hour blocks and had considered them something like a blank white sheet on which we were free to draw out our ideas. We switched instead to structuring our time with neatly defined beginnings and ends. In the same way that a deadline for a project or paper obliges productivity, we tested whether structuring our time would force us to make explicit and agree on an insight, which we could then refine.

We knew we needed to counteract the tendency for classroom behavior to revolve around Rabinow's approval. Our experiences in previous semesters and our attempt during the labinar's first week to have a roundtable approach had made it clear that student-professor relations needed to be modified. Again reverting to the level of micropractices, he moved to a chair placed outside the circle in the back of the room. This effectively shifted the balance of attention; it also elicited humorous student contortions in the effort to glimpse his facial expressions during the discussion.

We further attempted to destabilize the regular balance of power by separating out the procedural tasks of running a classroom. We began the semester with a timekeeper, a facilitator, and a "concept tracker," but after a week or two we saw that the facilitator needed control over the time in order to make calculated judgments as to when to cut things off and when to let them run their course. As well, the temporality of these chores was different from that of the group's conceptual work. We were losing the contributions of too many participants to aspects of a too rigid form. The first plan was to rotate roles. With weekly reprogramming, however, it was impossible to keep track of what was supposed to happen unless one was in the design group. Hence, these duties were consolidated for the rest of semester.

We had to figure out how to order the proceedings when we met as a large group without defaulting to the traditional "seminar mode." A surprisingly powerful tool turned out to be using a distinction between clarifying and expository questions. The first was signaled with a finger in the air and was limited to "Is this what you mean?" or "Can you clarify this point?" The second served to state an opinion or address broader issues and was indicated by signaling with a hand or two fingers or catching the facilitator's eye to enter the line to make comments. The whole process might seem trivial, but openly indicating the kind of question or comment was important for a number of reasons. On the practical side, everyone could hear the points of clarification while they were formulating their thoughts. Confusion about factual matters could be taken care of before we entered into a different kind of discussion, and we were more likely to all be talking about the same thing. More fundamental, the act of evaluating one's contribution, reinforced of course by the group's response (because it became obvious when a question was not really clarifying), was an integral part of training ourselves in how to think of the discussion collaboratively. A comment might request a point of information, or it might offer insight. We learned to think before asking whether a question would take the group in a useful direction.

Dealing with the size of the group brought out several facets of the experiment and the work we were doing on ourselves. Having between four and six participants seemed to be the critical point where people could easily speak in turn and be productive. Large-group interaction was the core, but we wanted to maximize contributions by accepting everyone's participation style. We tried to provide a different kind of interaction by going into small groups for a period of each class. These were chosen by counting off. Then, in circles of four or five, we discussed, depending on the week, projects or concepts. In project sessions, the people whose work was being examined were in different groups. In concept sessions, the groups drew on the collective research of the projects. The idea was a back-and-forth movement to constantly refine our conceptual tools to our inquiry.

As the semester progressed, we settled on three concept clusters to use as a filter on our data. These were as follows: (1) the figure of the human and humanitarianism; (2) biopower and the social; and (3) preparedness and insurance. After a breakout session, one person from each group would give a summary, and then we continued with the discussion. The shyer students still held back during this time, but the idea that their thoughts could come out in the smaller groups and then be shared by the designated reporter was fairly successful.

At issue was how to preserve the labinar's results in an ongoing manner without that process interrupting the labor itself or becoming too onerous. We established a rotating note-taker position. This person had the right to interrupt and say, "Can you repeat that?" or "Is this what you meant?" Having a designated note-taker let everyone else concentrate on the discussion; it also guaranteed that a shared record of what happened could be given to someone who was absent that day. These notes were posted online. We also made digital audio recordings of the sessions with the idea that we could go back to them if it seemed that something useful had been said and that the exact phrasing was relevant, although regular transcription would have required too much time, labor, and resources. We used the university instructional technology platform to store the notes and the audio recordings with the intention of creating an archive. The platform, however, was phased out, and the documents were retained only by students.

Each student wrote a "reaction" paragraph, which could include reflections on form, on projects, and on problematization. It could also be a place for complaints or venting. The task was required, but the choice of topic was open. The previous week's notes were read as a summary at the beginning of class to put us all on the same page to begin again.

We had chosen specifically to look at the problems presented in the data from everyone's fieldwork. We designed the protocol, however, with an eye to future seminars and undergraduate lecture classes and sections. We wanted the format to be adaptable to other matters that might be addressed collectively and envisioned using it for courses on the development of dissertation projects or analysis of fieldwork or texts.

INITIAL LESSONS LEARNED

My evaluation of the results of the three-year experiment in new venues and new practices demonstrated a proof of concept: it is perfectly possible to remediate the practices of the graduate seminar. It is perfectly possible to remediate the pedagogy of the concept: how concepts are introduced, discussed, used, disseminated, and criticized in the service of learning and inquiry. The emphasis on problems rather than projects, the exercise of collaboration, and the practice of observing and rectifying those habits and dispositions that have been taken for granted are all part of a toolkit that has nothing either mysterious or arcane about it. The meetings were intense, and the seemingly constant switch between groups and activities made them seem rapid. We did not entirely eliminate the performative, but we did shift the norm so that the metric of the good was that individual brilliance contributed to the group's collaborative thinking. Our objective was to harness our collective perspectives to challenge, to critique, and to encourage each other.

As an isolated experiment, however, the form is probably unsustainable. It simply requires too much willpower, or what the French call *volontarisme*. At the beginning, and sporadically thereafter, we had a plenitude of energy, goodwill, and personal and collective investment. For these experiments to succeed, however, these effervescently collaborative charismatic moments had to be routinized in one fashion or another. Such slowing down, norming, labor was hard to sustain. An example is the design group: in its initial iteration the labinar had a separate design group of three or four people who met a day or two prior to the labinar meeting and agreed on the design of the particular sessions given the material under consideration that week. This work undoubtedly facilitated orientation, discussion, and clarification. It was, however, another obligation to fulfill and to fit into busy schedules. Although we experienced bountiful goodwill and a willingness to be charitable in interpretations in the earliest labinars, as things progressed and the familiarity and trust were not as evenly distributed, we needed to address the suspicion that one was being governed too much by an in-group.

The issue of governance and form was imminent to almost all aspects of the experiment. Here is one of the key differences with both the architectural *charette* and the bioscientific lab meeting. Many more of the rules of the game as to what counts as authority, evidence, value, and the like have been long settled in broad strokes in these other domains; this is not to say that there is not incessant contestation or disgruntlement elsewhere, only that the form it takes is commentary on specific individuals, claims, and the like. More research on the dynamics and metrics of *charettes* and lab meetings would be required to elaborate on these intuitions.

Furthermore, it was hard to sustain the practices and affects given that none of my colleagues were engaged in similar or parallel experiments in any explicit form that would allow for interchange. There was simply no carryover for the students from one seminar to another. For there to be a habitus, there needs to be reinforcement and variation in multiple situations. Decades ago, I experienced these mutually reenforcing conditions at the University of Chicago. The conditions for an invention of something resonant but different simply did not exist, either, at the University of California at Berkeley. This social fact is especially irritating given the extraordinary quality and dynamism of Berkeley's graduate students and its faculty. I regret to say that not a single colleague has approached me for more details on the experiment; they have of course approached the students. Here, as elsewhere, personality issues and characterizations were the fallback explanation of differences of pedagogical strategy and forms of inquiry.

One of the characteristics of today's practices in the qualitative human sciences has been its encounter with theory. As this enthusiasm has waned in recent years, concentration and identification with certain terms—neoliberalism, governmentality, sovereignty, secularism, citizenship, and so forth—have become more the norm. In a university such as Berkeley, although outstanding work is being undertaken by many colleagues, the terms have become identified with the professors. They have also become markers of difference, inclusion, and exclusion. Of course, this mode of silo maintenance could not be more foreign and nefarious to a community of inquiry. I can affirm, and other colleagues can do so as well with equal sincerity, that the intention of our work is not maximizing symbolic capital, inventing dividing practices, advancing reification, and the like. Yet, techniques and reflection—and, above all, venues—on how to counter these all-too-present phenomena are missing.

The labinar experiment, in a word, was untimely. It swam against the grain of a period in American political economy of the infamous dominance of neoliberalism in which individual careers were "enterprised up" to draw from the insights of Nikolas Rose and Marilyn Strathern. In my experience at Berkeley, it was less the neoliberalism that so many of my colleagues were analyzing and denouncing in multiple locations around the world that they were studying; rather, it was a more classic form of political formation that stood in the way: liberalism. For example, on the rare occasions that curricular reform and admissions policy were discussed, there was general agreement that some form of streamlining and efficient process management was probably a good idea, but the next step, which would involve implementing such steps, was met not so much with reasoned criticism (which might well have been appropriate) but with a dispositional return to what Michel Foucault has called the political rationality of liberalism: are we governing too much? A different political rationality and a different ethical ethos of science as a vocation would be required for the general project to flourish.

The labinar, then, can be said to have entered into the domain of warranted assertibility in Dewey's sense. We showed that a venue could be constructed in which inquiry of a collaborative sort would be discussed, organized, and pursued, at least in a preliminary fashion. Our object, as it were, had been constructed in such a manner that it became an objective of further design and judgment. We demonstrated to ourselves that it was possible to practice inquiry in a collaborative fashion guided by an ethic of care. That ethic, understood broadly in the sense mentioned earlier as the other and object of thought, was not external to thinking and inquiry. Rather, we provided a proof of concept, as it were, that a modified form of truth (warranted assertibility) and a form of seriousness (an inquiry that was ethically informed) not only did not need to be bracketed but, quite the contrary, constituted the very parameters for a mode of anthropology appropriate to addressing at least some of the indeterminacies and discordances of the contemporary situation.

The need for a new form of collaboration was instigated by the desire to redesign a form of anthropology to be more adequate to the contemporary. We demonstrated that it was possible, perhaps even necessary, to undertake this ambitious task of reconstruction through one form or another of collaboration. To the extent that such a judgment is warrantable, it follows that the search for companions is itself both an end and a means of an ethical science.

Anthropology of the Contemporary Research Collaboratory

The Anthropology of the Contemporary Research Collaboratory is a collaboratory for inquiry into contemporary forms of life, labor, and language. ARC engages in empirical study and conceptual work with global reach and long-term perspective. ARC creates contemporary equipment for work on collaborative projects and problems in the 21st century.

The term "collaboratory" gained currency in the early 1990s referring to a "distributed research network articulated by means of information technology." For us a collaboratory is a dynamic and emergent form for inquiry and exchange. We seek to re-imagine and remediate the norms, standards, and mechanisms of critical rectification that make it possible to conduct inquiry. The aim is to contribute to the production of knowledge and tools for thought in a mode of collaboration and care.

« *Statement on ARC Web Site*[6] »

The goal of the work on the Web sites we have built and experimented with has been to create a venue in which and through which we could bring into being an assemblage. The goal was to bring together a set of diverse people, projects, and properties into a common facility in order to remediate the practices, forms, and determinations of inquiry and pedagogy—and thereby make new capacities possible. The sought-after function was not unanimity of doctrine, opinion, or even a common research object.

That is not to say there was nothing in common; we shared an experimental ethos and a broad understanding of what constitutes a domain of significant problems today. The challenge was to see whether a Web site (or eventually an assemblage of more than one Web site) could mediate—but not eliminate—the distances between and among us and by so doing open a space of new capacities.

We have found it striking that few Web sites actually engage in the modest task of the pedagogy of the concept as opposed to training, classifying, or exhibiting, not to mention the dominant mode under which so many operate, communicating. No doubt the reasons for this state of affairs are diverse, but one can point to a currently limited sense of pedagogy (understood as primarily either instruction or demonstration) as well as an understanding of concepts as discrete entities, often presented as simply referential and consequently easily representable as exhibits or displays. Finally, although many Web sites are organized as collectives, there are apparently few outside of the natural sciences and engineering that operate as collaboratories.

Although the actual timing of the experiments with the labinar and the Web site collaboratory overlapped, here it is analytically easier to treat them as sequential. The labinar was located in one place, Berkeley, and in a specific venue, the graduate seminar. Because many of the more general goals, especially conceptual ones, were not inherently restricted by place and space or the status of participants, it was logical that we should experiment with a venue that was not as limited spatially and temporally, with participants who did not all have the same status and whose topics and themes were even more diverse than those of the labinar. It is in light of these limitations and in the spirit that serious intellectual work should be possible on the Web that we developed our own Web site.

THE PROCESS

By 2005, academic and scientific Web sites were becoming common. The price of making one was dropping, although it was still expensive. The idea of using these sites as venues for serious work began to seem less exotic and out of reach for academics with limited resources and skills. It was only slightly later that open-source programs such as WordPress began to be truly functional as well as be facilitated by a community of users. Having some funds from a National Science Foundation grant and having been generously allotted space and some technical support at the Molecular Sciences Institute, a group from the labinar and former graduate students located in several cities and I took the plunge: These are the material conditions under which we undertook the work on the first Web site, www.anthropos-lab.net.

Eventually we settled on WordPress as our technical platform. WordPress is a simple, open-source program, well designed for basic thematic design, blogging, and document presentation. In our experience we found that a team seeking to use it should employ an undergraduate to keep it running because there are always minor glitches to cope with as well as quantities of spam to ward off.

With the usual fits and starts characteristic of a new domain and fledgling practitioners, it took over a year to design the site (long delays in delivery of the promised beta version) and make it operational (long discussions about what should be in it). Although such delay seems lengthy today, things were different then in terms of a scarcity of technology as well as competent and affordable technicians and designers to carry out the work. What has not changed significantly in the ensuing years, despite the vast proliferation of Web sites, is clarity about the capacities of a Web site for concept work and collaborative inquiry.

It took time, pedagogical and chronological, to form a group of practitioners, to define objectives, and to remediate the conceptual work we were used to doing as academics—even with the experience of the labinar—into another medium. Today, the core set of blockages—both discordances and indeterminacies—continue to be unresolved even after extensive experience with three Web sites. That being said, a reason to continue our efforts is that we can think of no inherent impediment that could not in principle be overcome or remediated. The power of the Internet for connection, dissemination, and exhibition remains daunting; moving beyond the encyclopedia or communication mode, however, remains an open challenge.

We had several specific objectives over the course of the development of the site. These were as follows: (1) to create a blog space for commentary both on scholarly work as well as on current events in domains such as security, biopolitics, epidemics and public health, and the like; and (2) to create an archive of published articles, conference presentations, working papers, and so forth that would constitute a resource both for ourselves and for what we hoped would be a larger audience of associates and visitors. These objectives were established and successfully implemented. There has been interesting blogging of a serious kind at sporadic intervals, usually linked to an event such as the emergence of the H1N1 virus.

The main shortcoming, however, was that the contributions were sporadic; they did not follow the kind of regular rhythm that would draw people back to the site with a considered regularity. My expectations, I have been told by experienced bloggers and Web site aficionados, were exaggerated. In a formal sense, the second objective also has been fulfilled; many articles, presentations, and working papers are available on the site. That being said, it is not clear how and if this archive has functioned in facilitating research and inquiry both directly and indirectly in the greater blogosphere.

LEARNED CAPACITIES AND INCAPACITIES

The guiding goal of the Web site was to facilitate conceptual work, pedagogy, and inquiry. We imagined the Web site as a venue that would assemble concepts, problems, practices, and qualities and bring them into a proximity that would make new capacities and affects come into being. Exactly how this would function and where it would lead, we naively assigned to the process itself.

Advancing on that objective—abstract as it may have been—

has proved to be the most daunting obstacle of all. At its base the challenge amounts to a dare to academics to change the habits they have painstakingly acquired through training and performance in graduate school and in the venues of professional meetings and the like. Furthermore, we were asking them to take the risk of transforming these newly acquired or long-unquestioned habits into new practices whose goals were lofty but whose rewards were largely symbolic. With an abundance of goodwill, it has still proved onerous to alter the academic habitus of expecting one's work environment to accommodate extended time delays, lengthy responses, and carefully worked out, guarded, and reworked interventions. Although each of these habits and their associated norms do offer an entirely appropriate and worthwhile counterweight to the blogging rule of opinion and expression for its own sake that characterizes so much of the content of the Internet, it remains an obstacle to the type of academic collaborative work and labor that I envisioned.

I had encountered a parallel unwillingness (or inability) to alter dispositions in my encounters with the synthetic biologists. The main difference between the bioscientists and the human scientists, however, was that the bioscientists did not feel or recognize either ethical discordance or scientific indeterminacy as arising from the way they practiced their science and formed their lives. Their star was rising, and other of problems of ethics or venue was in their eyes simply not among their concerns (see chapter 7). Although all of the founding members of ARC shared, to one degree or another, some dissatisfaction with the current disciplines, professions, and institutions, their career base was still to be found within those entities. Because most of the collaboratory members were at the beginning or relatively early stages of their careers, the demands and pressures of the way of life to which the professions and institutions disposed them weighed heavily and legitimately on their allotment of time. At the end of the proverbial day, there were few external rewards for devoting extended periods of time working on ARC projects.

In retrospect, the starting attempts at ARC sought a kind of delocalization of the seminar form. Although it built on a background of familiarity and trust, it generally lacked the face-to-face interaction that provided a stimulus (and a certain force of shame or pride) for preparation and performance. Furthermore, although the work held an analogical connection to a laboratory meeting, the analogy did not extend very far. There was no authorized lab head; there were no available external sanctions (renewed grant proposals and the like); there was no defined common problem even if there was a shared interest in a broad problematization of *anthropos* and *bios* in their actuality. There was no obligatory regular temporality to discussions or contributions.

Accepting (to a degree) the reassurances of participants and observers friendly to the experiment that it had achieved a certain level of success, I was nonetheless dissatisfied. It seemed appropriate to learn from these experiences of both the labinar and ARC and to put them to use differently. In a word, it seemed worth the effort to assemble things in a different manner. This remediation included a major design and concept review of ARC in June 2010. It also included the completion of another Web site on which a great deal of labor and love had already been expended.

BIOS TECHNIKA

One lesson learned from the ARC experiences was that small groupings, two or three people, demonstrated the most cohesion and productivity. In such groupings, in our experience, there was a sharp problem focus, a collaborative division of skills and capacities, the reenforcement of trust and friendship such that blockages and interruptions could be weathered, an enhanced possibility of moving work into venues that would receive professional recognition, and the like.

In that light, it seemed promising for Gaymon Bennett and I to attempt to remediate the architectural conceptual work in our "diagnostic" that we had undertaken into another form. We had tried some of this extension on ARC, but the Web site itself had not been designed as a venue for such specific conceptual work arising out of a specific set of inquiries (synthetic biology).

Furthermore, our experiences with Web design and designers at ARC had demonstrated that bringing this quite heterogeneous set of skills, dispositions, resources, and affects into a functioning assemblage was far more difficult than we had anticipated. That being said, Bennett and I had developed a range of conceptual work, thereby providing us with a better sense of at least the general parameters of the kind of design that would make our work visible and provide a venue for its enrichment—or so we thought.

It was at this point that we began to be fully engaged with a gifted artist and Web designer, Adrian van Allen. She was working full time at the Exploratorium in San Francisco, where she had been employed for close to ten years. Among the many projects she had designed at the Exploratorium were several dealing with earth sciences, archaeology, and various aspects of biology. Her ability to render scientific work visible was impressive. Her ability to work to deadlines and operate under an authority structure that was hierarchical and often demanding was impressive. Her well-concealed frustration at not being able to broaden and deepen these experiments due to time and financial and audience constraints gradually became evident. Her skill set and impressive talent presented itself as a potentially collaborative complement to the highly satisfying and productive working relationship Bennett and I had achieved.

Working first on a common project for the Synthetic Biology Engineering Research Center, we gradually came to see that we needed to have more independence. We also gradually came to see that we had a unique and precious opportunity to make something striking and incisive come into being. It seemed possible and plausible that together we could collaborate on the creation and construction of a venue in which concept work, visual design, and a dynamic functionality could converge. Experiments and experiences had shown us that achieving such collaboration to be more challenging than we had imagined.

We had the heterogeneous entities—an experienced and road-tested set of concept and inquiry practitioners, an experienced project manager, and a brilliant designer—the challenge was how to formulate a project, bringing these diverse skills into a proximity such that distinctive capacities would flourish that would go beyond anything we could do individually or in the institutions in which we were employed.

We drastically schematized a year's worth of work, and our first attempt to bring the conceptual work, inquiry results, programming challenges, and a multitude of other demands on people's time demonstrated to us that we had built up enough familiarity with each others' temperaments, strengths, and limitations that we could both work together and eventually evaluate in a rigorous fashion what was successful and why.

This work achieved a high degree of elegance of presentation. There is much to be said in its favor. It remained, however, in an exhibit mode. The two main causes for this partial success were as follows: (1) Bennett and I greatly underestimated the difficulty and originality—and hence the time and cost—of building a sophisticated Web platform that could have the kind of functionality we imagined corresponded to the work of incessant refinement and rectification that our own thinking and inquiry entailed; and (2) an ongoing sense that we were all engaged in a contractual arrangement (which we were) with deadlines, directives, and deliverables. Van Allen was reluctant to force the issue, and hence a certain gap arose between what was being hoped for and the resources required to bring it into the world. One might say that there was cooperation at a high level but not yet collaboration. Because the Web site—www.bios-technika.net—will have evolved and mutated, to continue the organic language, by the time this book is published and read; consequently the best solution is to advise readers to explore whatever its current form will be.

RAMIFICATIONS

Ramification: (1) Complicating result: a usually unintended consequence of an action, decision, or judgment that may complicate a situation or make the desired result more difficult to achieve. (2) Branching: the process of dividing or spreading out into branches.[7]

Not surprisingly, on reflection, things developed differently from we had imagined or planned. They ramified. We should have expected this curl because ramification is one of our key concepts. We have been using it for several years now as a replacement term for "consequences" or "implications" as developed and institutionalized as a national, and eventually international, policy as part of the genome mapping and sequencing projects. The model of ELSI, the ethical, legal, and social implications (or consequences) of "name your techno-science" continues today, although it is under increasing contestation.

Inquiry and second-order knowledge-producing and knowledge-observing practices in general operate in troubled and uncertain situations. One of their characteristics is to orient, diagnose, and establish objectives, which leads to the identification and specification of objects, which opens the possibility of an altered set of objectives. Inquiry ramifies; it does not apply a theory to an example. Recall DeLanda's formulation: "While logically necessary relations may be investigated by thought alone, contingently obligatory ones involve a consideration of empirical questions."[8]

One blind spot we had as we entered into our Web site work, to use Luhmann's vocabulary, was to mistake our intentions for what we actually did. We intended to build an assemblage—a set of entities that remain exterior to each other while being brought into proximity and achieving a distinctive functional dynamic. In fact, we did achieve something like that.

Seen from the outside, however, and at times confusedly from the inside, the assemblage apparently appeared as if it was designed to be an organic whole or totality whose entities bore internal and mutually dependent formative relations one to the other. Said another way, we were seen as an ingroup, using an esoteric discourse and simply displaying insincerity in our proclamations to the contrary. Part of the reason for this misapprehension was insufficient attention on our part to how we were appearing while we were attempting to construct our operation. In fact, one of the innovations in the labinar when it was operating at full throttle was to assign a participant at each session to be a second-order observer. That person's observations would be posted on a class Web site and would be taken into account by the design group.

Another contradictory aspect of this apprehension from the outside was that we propagated our materials in an exhibit mode on both Web sites. To compound matters, when we became aware of these discordances and distensions and the way they were being received (mainly through hallway gossip and random cutting comments), we attempted to remedy the situation by introducing improved communication. Not surprisingly, in retrospect at least, these interventions succeeded in only further obscuring the blockages to us and reinforced them to others. In this instance, as elsewhere, professions of goodwill and sincerity can constitute a part of a blockage as well as or perhaps even more than their opposites.

In that light, we also mistook the desire for collaboration for the fact of cooperation. We had assembled a set of entities (actors, skill sets, concepts, problems, media, and so forth). We wanted them to provide a venue for the emergence and flourishing of capacities, but we remained at the level of properties most of the time. Properties differ from capacities in that they attached to the entity and not relationality; they are preexistent, not emergent; and they can be enhanced or diminished but do not reveal new things.

One way to remediate this situation is to pay heightened attention, in the next iteration, to a different mode of relating properties and capacities, relations of interiority and exteriority, and relations of exhibit and inquiry. Clearly, in order to allow our assembled things to ramify, we need to include these parameters in the design and practice of our next iteration. It seems like enough work has been done, albeit with partial success, on bringing diverse entities into a relationship on the interior of the assemblage. The challenge, however, is, having established these relations on the interior, to remedy their functionality as internal to each other when that had been neither the goal nor the means we had set out to put in motion.

Another way to remediate the situation and to foster ramifications is to turn outward—something that many of us had been doing all along in our specific inquiries into diverse domains such as synthetic biology—and thereby to move the assemblage closer to those domains to which our research was adjacent. This altered relation might allow for an animation of centrifugal ramifications. Once that motion was established, the relations formed and de-formed could then serve as objects to be inquired into, and perhaps, here and there, to be remediated and even reconstructed.

7

An Experiment in Discordancy: Reflections on Familiarity, Trust, and Confidence in Synthetic Biology

Reflection appears as the dominant trait of a situation when there is something seriously the matter, some trouble, due to active discordance, dissentience, conflict among factors of a prior non-intellectual experience. . . . Given such a situation, it is obvious that the meaning of the situation as a whole is uncertain.
«JOHN DEWEY[1]»

All knowledge, as issuing from reflection, is experimental.
«JOHN DEWEY[2]»

After more than a decade and a half of anthropological observation and writing about genomics, postgenomics, and biotechnology, I found myself, first by accident and then by design, as an official participant, a principal investigator, in a new venture in the biosciences, the Synthetic Biology Engineering Research Center, which comprised, as noted earlier, a five-university consortium (Berkeley, the University of California at San Francisco, Harvard, MIT, and Prairie View A&M) funded by the National

Science Foundation as a flagship center of innovation in synthetic biology.[3]

The accidental part was that I was initially only tangentially interested in synthetic biology. I had just finished a project on postgenomic molecular diagnostics and was not intending to pursue any other such work. With some reluctance, I had accepted a molecular diagnostics project because of a unique invitation to observe the early days of a new company, Celera Diagnostics, and a new field, postgenome-sequencing molecular diagnostics. The chief scientific officer of the company, Tom White, with whom I had worked on a previous book and with whom I had become friends, proposed that I follow the emergence of what they were quite confident was going to be a set of major discoveries. For both personal and scientific reasons, it was an offer I could not refuse. I decided, however, to see whether I could turn it into an experiment in the anthropology of the contemporary, a term and a program I had recently committed myself to developing. As described elsewhere, I set the challenge of attempting to do the research and to write a book within a year, before any definitive results in the company would have been achieved. I designed the challenge first as a methodological one and second as a narrative one. In order to have a hope of attaining these goals, I knew I needed to collaborate, so I decided to undertake this experiment with a gifted undergraduate, Talia Dan-Cohen.[4]

As I noted earlier, during the course of this project, I was also spending quality time with a maverick molecular biologist and autodidact, Roger Brent, who directed an independent Center of Excellence in Computational Biology in downtown Berkeley. Brent and I turned our passionate exchanges on science, security, and significance into a new course, "Genomics and Citizenship," where we attempted to design a form for teaching Berkeley undergraduates the foundations of molecular biology as well as those of the anthropology of the contemporary. Aside from the course, which we taught three times, two other significant ramifications of my encounter with Brent are relevant here. First,

Brent was convincing on the relevance and urgency of biosecurity; he had convinced me that there were genuine, significant, and long-lasting issues of concern especially for the future of the sciences in a democracy and that I had an obligation to think about how things were developing. This accidental turn of events opened the horizon of a design phase. His persuasive arguments led to a major project, titled "Global Bio-politics of Security," carried out with Stephen Collier and Andrew Lakoff, who eventually took the lead on the research and publication. Second, and this finally leads up to the accidental part of my relation to synthetic biology, Brent introduced me to Drew Endy, a young engineer, who was a friend and former colleague of Brent and then teaching at MIT. Drew was the visionary of synthetic biology, dreaming and proselytizing about turning biology into an engineering discipline.

Endy invited me to be one of the speakers at the First International Conference on Synthetic Biology at MIT; I delivered a talk titled the "Ecology of Ignorance," a term I took from Niklas Luhmann. The term referred to our contemporary conditions in which a postplanning world of contingency, emergence, and emergency required an observational mode close to the practices and focused on short- and middle-term ramifications. Such a mode and its associated ethos could not have been further removed from the rhetoric of a coming radical transformation that Endy and others had polished into a very successful set of presentations and grant proposals. I also used the term "ecology of ignorance" to refer to the fact that there was a large and, to my mind, ever-growing deficit in the overall global landscape of knowledge, particularly among the biosciences and cutting-edge humanities. Bioscientists, among others, are ever more technically competent, and ever more pressured into mastering more and more technical tools and subdisciplines, but with less and less time for anything else. In my view, the production of ignorance in the elite American academy was systematic and successful; countering that trend had been one of the main goals of the course Brent and I had developed. The reception of the talk was puzzlement, as per my intention. The reception, however, was also cordial; a few people expressed interest in what I had said, and the others simply seemed to take it as another subspecialty in which they had no competence. They knew they were living in an ecology of knowledge in which there were going to be large areas about which they were simply going to remain ignorant; that compartmentalization is a fundamental part of their education and practice. Because there were few other social scientists or humanists present, I was spared either their approval or opprobrium. Some journalists expressed mild interest but did not follow up; the venture capitalists present were too busy chasing the bioscientists to pay me heed either way.

In the following months, I began to pay attention to synthetic biology, especially its interfaces and ramifications with biosecurity issues as my contribution to the Global Bio-politics of Security project. So, when the Second International Conference on Synthetic Biology, held in Berkeley in June 2006, rolled around, I accepted Endy's invitation to give another presentation. This presentation was on the concept of "preparedness" in a situation of relative ignorance as to risks and dangers. By this point, the National Science Foundation had funded SynBERC, handsomely at least from an anthropologist's perspective. The funders had insisted that the financing was dependent on including an "ethics and societal" component. Endy and Jay Keasling, SynBERC director, agreed; they asked (or were approached by) the dean of the School of Public Policy at Berkeley (a former Clinton administration arms control specialist), who proposed appointing an adjunct professor, a lawyer with an interest in both legal and economic affairs. Stephen Mauer was named to head this "thrust." There were three other thrusts: parts, devices, and chassis. During the conference, however, Mauer and Endy clashed in a dramatic fashion, resulting in a very tense confrontation at dinner, over a governance proposal for SynBERC as well as the wider emergent synthetic biology "community." To make a short but dramatic story even shorter, Mauer was removed, and it was proposed that I become coleader of the ethics and society thrust along with a political science professor at MIT, Ken Oye.

During my second year as a principal investigator it was unclear exactly where I stood—ethically, conceptually, and affectively—in relation to SynBERC's mode of operation as well as its entrepreneurial ethos. The initial period had been filled with a mix of persistent frustration as well as ample stimulation. The sporadic but insistent pressure to clarify the state of affairs weighed heavily on myself and my lab mates at the Berkeley Human Practices Lab.[5] The following is an attempt to analyze the elements of that discordancy, to use Dewey's term, in the hope that such clarification might open up a pragmatic way forward or at least to clarify the blockages that characterized this experiment.

Human Practices: Participation

Rather unexpectedly, I found myself moving from my more habitual position as an anthropological observer to one in which I accepted the challenge of becoming an engaged participant. My acquaintance with the issues categorized as ethics (or bioethics) associated with the genome sequencing and mapping projects had been forged during my research on the French genome project—where I played the role of "philosophic observer" at the major French mapping center. These issues had taken a quite different form in France from the one that had been instituted in the United States. Given that set of experiences, I knew that I had definite intellectual hesitations about the worth of transferring the ethics approaches that had been developed around the sequencing projects to postgenomic developments. Although this is not the place to spell out those reasons (as I have done so elsewhere), what is relevant here is only that I was familiar and dissatisfied with the form and practice of ethical and social issues as they had been positioned and defined within the contemporary biosciences.[6]

Before accepting the position of a principal investigator and coleader of a component of the center, I insisted that lessons learned from prior models of "ethics and society" be taken into account. With that precondition in mind, I traveled to Washington, where I explained my understanding of the situation to the NSF officials responsible for funding and overseeing the engineering research center. They concurred that something new and innovative was desirable. They expressed support concerning my thoughts about possible ways to design a different approach, although they offered no specific suggestions as to what such a different approach might or might not look like. They made it clear that although this arena was not something they knew much about, they were open to new directions.

After some thought, I decided to rename the thrust "Human Practices" as a replacement term for one or another variant of the label "social consequences." The basic reasoning for this change in terminology was straightforward. The term "consequences" implied that only downstream results from biology and engineering were the proper domain of the human sciences. The term "social" was misleading because either the term was entirely vague, referring to all human groupings, or it had a specific meaning that tied it to the welfare state as it did in European social thought and policy; the United States, however, did not have a welfare state.[7] As neither the NSF officials nor the leaders of SynBERC expressed either interest or resistance to this name change, it was adopted without much discussion. This indifference to conceptual change and innovation from the human sciences proved to be an omen of much discordancy that was to follow. At the time, however, their casual acquiescence to the change was acceptable.

From the outset I found the other principal investigators (and their postdocs and doctoral students) in SynBERC to be devotedly engaged in their experimental work as well as in their theorizing or fantasies about what an age of biological engineering would look like. They were agreeable superficially, if extremely busy and steadfastly insular, like most American professionals at the top of their game. There were sporadic expressions of wariness, a reaction that I had encountered frequently over the years in other research projects. Such wariness was usually merely a transitory stage of caution about not having their time intruded on. I was familiar as well as comfortable with doing the work required for establishing some degree of mutual familiarity, comfort, and reassurance. In the past, the work of overcoming wariness had largely consisted in waiting out the seemingly pre-programmed clichéd jokes about my using them as guinea pigs or observing them under the microscope and then attending to the few individuals whose curiosity—and at times doubts about what they were doing—made them candidates to become informants, even collaborators.

Things at SynBERC unfolded in a similar fashion. However, I was not engaged in this project uniquely as an anthropological observer whose goal was to gain knowledge and convey that knowledge to my colleagues in the human sciences. In this instance, I was equally a principal investigator whose role was to participate formally as an equal. My role (as I interpreted it) was to deliver reconstructive proposals (to use another term of John Dewey's) about synthetic biology both within the center and beyond. What form those deliverables might take was unknown; that novelty constituted a prime reason to accept the challenge of taking up this unaccustomed role. Thus, within a traditional anthropological endeavor, the general acceptance and indifference by the majority of the bioscientists would have been normal; however, under these new job conditions they proved to be discordant.

The reasons to pursue this enterprise arose from my judgment that:

1   Moving beyond the hyperbolic and vague overstatements characteristic of an initial "manifesto stage," synthetic biology was beginning to demonstrate its capacity for intervention in biological processes, including some that are clearly beneficial. One such example is Jay Keasling's artemisinin project, where a costly antima-

laria molecule originally found in a Chinese yew tree was produced in a yeast system, dramatically lowering its cost and availability.

2 The majority of the bioscientists involved were earnest while being inextricably mired in the turbulence of careers and commerce, as is practically everyone in the elite scientific departments of the American academy. It followed that the framing and pursuit of this endeavor should not be left to them alone. The challenge was to find a form of collaboration in which interdisciplinary expertise and inquiry, accepted as essential in the biosciences, could be expanded to include the human sciences—and begin to be practiced.

3 It seemed worth enduring the expected accusations of complicity in order to achieve an in-depth evaluation of how capacities and critical limitations in this experimental venue were in fact developing or being blocked. Today, undertaking this participant-observer endeavor meant accepting a risk in the sense that its ramifications were not predictable and its chances of success uncertain and far from guaranteed.

My engagement, therefore, was scientific, ethical, and, in a more distant fashion, political.

>>><<<

For the first time in my career, this position as principal investigator provided me with funds to support graduate students. Working in a public institution, however prestigious, one finds that support for graduate students, especially non-American ones, is scarce and perpetually endangered. To have such funds available for a number of years tied me to SynBERC and gave me pause not so much about expressing criticism but about exiting from an often frustrating situation.

In sum, I was faced with a classic set of options (as outlined by Albert Hirschman) available to those who find themselves in an uncomfortably blocked situation: exit, voice, or loyalty.[8] I was clear that if my research was foreclosed, I would have to exit and pay the price of losing support for my graduate students. Access to traditional research possibilities was never a problem;

the bioscientists were willing, even generous, in answering questions concerning what their projects were and where and how they hoped the field would develop. In fact, if what I had wanted to do was to carry out a traditional anthropological project, the conditions would have been close to optimal. Because I was committed to something different than that, problems and quandaries abounded.

Leaving exit in suspension, I focused on the remaining options, voice and loyalty. Although I have been vocal about what I take to be SynBERC's shortcomings but in a situation of benign indifference, voice, initially at least, has had little impact, either positively or negatively. Consequently, provisional loyalty (tied to self-interest as well as an informed sense of beneficial scientific and technical advance at the heart of SynBERC) constituted the lead option.

Thus, the dual challenge was how to practice anthropology and ethics as a member of a collaborative research center. The anthropological challenge turned on how to transform traditional observational practices, albeit situated and existential ones, into participatory ones. The ethical challenge turned on the question of whether synthetic biology would prove itself to be worthwhile interpersonally, scientifically, and ethically. The latter challenge, of course, was more than an observational one, and it carried with it unknown dangers.

Handling Indeterminacy

A year earlier, in an attempt to orient ourselves conceptually and ethically, Gaymon Bennett and I had decided that in order to produce an orientation and an objective means of evaluation of what was going on in synthetic biology, we needed to produce a schematic analytic that would give us the *capacity* to diagnose the significant issues within SynBERC and the larger milieu in which it was operating. We felt it to be our obligation to separate out the numerous petty personality issues that always arise in any organization (but nonetheless can be all too real and obstructive) from the presumably more enduring institutional ones. We decided that once we made headway in that analytic project we would be better able to take up the original task we had accepted when we agreed to participate in SynBERC: to invent, design, and implement an appropriately innovative and responsible form of ethical and human scientific practice.

The diagnostic provides a multilevel table of topics and schemas. It is available at www.bios-technika.net. The diagnostic has proved to be surprisingly and rewardingly accurate when put to the empirical test in a variety of experimental settings and observational situations that we designed to verify its internal coherence and its external pertinence. We have discussed these issues as well as the more technical aspects of synthetic biology and SynBERC in the forthcoming book *Human Practices: An Experiment with Synthetic Biology*. Throughout the experience, there remained a fundamental disconnect between the form and goal of the Human Practices work and that of our bioscientific colleagues. Significant aspects of those conceptual interferences and indeterminations are presented, analyzed, and diagnosed in the next chapter.

>>><<<

Conceptually, we have been gratified by the results of our labor. Pragmatically, we decided that our central task during 2008 was to invent a mode of practice in which we could put these results to work. The challenge was how to transform our practice from that of a traditional anthropological observer to that of a (second-order) participant. The initial results of this experiment have been revealing and instructive. Explaining what we were doing or how we were approaching our challenge, either to the biologists and engineers involved in the center or to the bureaucrats from the NSF who provide the funding and periodically review the center, has proved to be challenging.

Although during the first three years we received positive reports from the site visit teams, the reports contained little substantive feedback. For example, the site visit report of 2008 said the following: "The Berkeley team of Thrust IV is doing some exciting, innovative work to characterize the field of synthetic biology, developing an ethical 'diagnostic' and critically analyzing the modes of human practices engagement. In many ways, the Berkeley Thrust IV team is attempting to redefine the task and deliverables of ethics research."

Walking home from my office one day, the question occurred to me: should one trust these guys? Without much forethought, and in a commonsense, citizenlike mode, I knew that my answer would be "certainly not." After all, I knew all too well that transparency in decision making was not the hallmark of SynBERC, nor was equality of influence, input into strategy, and access to information (or, for that matter, to gossip). Not surprisingly, at SynBERC there was an inner circle, an old boys club. The information shared with all of the principal investigators was a belated and at best partial accounting and consultation about many issues, such as planning events, meeting times, intellectual property, decision making, transparency on procedures, and the like. In and of itself, there is nothing scandalous about this state of affairs; elites function by controlling information flow, limiting access to decision-making processes, and emphasizing speed and efficiency rather than the more ponderous deliberation and formal procedures that an open and democratic form requires. Many of the decisions made were relatively petty, and if one insisted, one could usually find out what happened. In a word, the situation was more banal than evil.

Power, I have often taught in my seminars, is above all a question of access to and control of information, the ability to take part in informal decision making as well as the capacity of mobilizing a constituency (often of higher-level power brokers). Having learned from Pierre Bourdieu about strategic dimensions of academic power relations and from Luc Boltanski about recent changes in the managerial strategies of capitalism and their modes of adjustment and justification of differing value spheres, I understood that this lack of transparency was not simply a calculated strategy directed at excluding those of us not in the biosciences but rather a habitual way of dealing with subordinates, information, and potential competitors.[9] That being said, analytic clarity goes only so far, and this exclusion was irksome, given that I was a principal investigator in the project.

So, the question was, do I trust the enterprise of synthetic biology? Hence, in the summer of 2008, where did I stand conceptually? On the one hand, our lack of an already formed position as to the truth or falsity, worth or value, good or evil, and utility or futility of what was emerging in synthetic biology was disconcerting and not well received by either critics or supporters. On the other hand, clearly it made sense in an emergent field set within an uncertain but extraordinarily dynamic situation of a global scale that the best way forward—scientifically and ethically—was to focus on the very conditions producing this diffuse discordancy and indeterminacy. Although we had made considerable progress on the conceptual front, the participatory challenges were proving to be more intractable. How, then, to proceed?

On the one hand, formally, our mandate from the National Science Foundation, vague as it was, consisted of an unspecified responsibility to ascertain whether things in SynBERC, and synthetic biology more generally, were being done right, especially as concerned matters of ethics and security. On the other hand, I found, and continue to find, that several of the synthetic biology projects excite my curiosity and provide a deep and steady stream of edification about the malleability and limitations of living beings and their milieus. In sum, there was clearly a danger of cooptation and complicity. There was clearly a danger that the anthropological possibility of being an in-close observer of a significant emergent formation would be missed and never be documented. There was clearly a danger that a refusal to participate would prove to be not the price to be paid for truth but the elimination of the possibility of understanding.

I remain uncomfortable with the categorical opposition to biotechnology found in some quarters. Sydney Brenner's proclamation that the twenty-first century would be the "century of biology" was compelling to me both because so many discoveries and inventions were taking place and because so little was actually understood about the nature of living systems.[10] That being said, many of the criticisms leveled by critics—including lack of transparency, far-reaching patents, hyped claims for beneficial consequences, seeming conflicts of interest, and the like—clearly had some merit. Nevertheless, many opponents, it has seemed to me, left no room for a detailed understanding of what synthetic biology is accomplishing and failing to accomplish, topics about which they had preformed opinions. Although I remain irritated with the overblown, venture capital–style hype about the revolutionary wonders synthetic biology is about to bring forth in health, security, and the environment, I remained simultaneously skeptical by the imprecise and prepackaged responses of many critics.

In sum, on the one hand, continuing to work in SynBERC without publicly criticizing the project (or at least expressing concern and urging caution) posed the danger of cooptation and complicity with as of yet unknown wrongs that might be committed by a powerful organization and a burgeoning field. I knew from experience that such disinclination to prejudge a situation that was in formation assured me that accusations of sins by an array of critics both within the academy and beyond would be forthcoming. Such unpleasantness, however, went with the terrain. On the other hand, premature withdrawal might wipe out a unique opportunity to be an in-close observer of a significant emergent formation and hence the possibility of producing a sharper diagnosis of the situation. I was unwilling to foreclose that possibility. Finally, and here is where this situation and the challenge diverged from anthropological practice as previously constituted, there was a risk that the opportunity to participate actively in how SynBERC and synthetic biology ramified would be forfeited.

I was in a quandary: what was the responsible path to follow? The often petty blockages and frustrations of SynBERC were alternatively troubling or boring, simply another set of minor annoyances in daily life. Each complaint—Why were we not consulted on the meeting date? Who decided on that agenda? Why weren't we told about that change?—was met with silence, denial, or a brush-off. It was clear as well that we were gaining a reputation as troublemakers. Troublemakers, of course, are exactly the kind of people you don't want to include in your informal, minor, and often hasty decision making. What to make of these micropractices, trivial as they seemed to be (or were categorized as being), however, kept resurfacing as a kind of affective and conceptual predicament. Each instance seemed minor, the aggregate of these incidents significantly less so.

Familiarity, Confidence, and Trust

Walking home from my office another day, it occurred to me that perhaps shifting a blocked situation into a conceptual dilemma at least might make it possible to think about the overall situation in a fresh light. Conceptually, the way to resolve a dilemma is to change one or the other of the premises that structured the dilemma leading to the mutually undesirable alternatives. Our undesirable alternatives consisted in letting each one of the petty snubs or exclusions go or in drawing attention to them with the result that we increasingly were being categorized as "difficult" or, even to quote the most amusing epithet, "bleak." Although cast as a form of upbeat American Babbitry or the power of positive thinking, it was really more a dismissive gesture with overtones of threats that if we were not loyal to the corporation, there would be consequences. Because we did not have the political power to force a change in the situation, all we could do was to endure these mild rebukes and to attempt to think our way around them.

It was here that the work of the German systems theorist Niklas Luhmann provided conceptual aid, a set of terms—familiarity, confidence, and trust—as well as an idiosyncratic interpretation of them as a recursive series, that proved to be helpful in transforming the predicament into a dilemma that at least could be turned into a thought experiment. The conclusion, and I will try to explain how I got to it in a moment, is that to the question, "But do you trust them?" needed to be refined and rephrased. A better approach, one that unsettled the seemingly self-evident alternatives and conceptually freed up the dilemma, consisted in framing the situation not as a set of dichotomous alternatives but rather as a recursive series.

- Are you familiar with the situation in an intimate manner?
- Are you confident that things are proceeding in a plausible manner?
- Do you trust yourself and others to act well in this situation?

Such a series made it possible to imagine more than two responses. With the approach posed in this fashion, it became clear that there were at least three distinct positions, which we knew already, but the reason these positions were distinct yet connected lay in the series and the possible order of the valences at each step. Logically there were three variables and two valences, or 3^2 slots.

I was familiar with much (but not all) of the basic structure and practice of what was taking shape. Therefore, the challenge was to explain how it was that having become familiar with synthetic biology and biologists by dint of intellectual curiosity, professional commitment, and position with the center, that familiarity had not produced confidence, and how was it that I had come to risk trust that was not predicated on prior confidence?

The situation did not produce confidence in part because domains of practice in which decisions were being made were blocked from becoming familiar; of course, other principal investigators, bioscientists, were not in the decision-making circle either, without being bothered by the situation because what they wanted from SynBERC was little more than to be provided with some financial support and to be left to do their work. That being said, the lack of confidence in the way the organization was being run did not preclude a priori having trust in the larger enterprise. That syllogism, while paradoxical, makes sense once one gives a particular meaning to the series of familiarity, confidence, and trust.

The latter claim opens up several connections to anthropology. For instance, one of the imperatives of the anthropological method is to establish familiarity with the people about whom the inquiry is centered. The pursuit of such familiarity, seemingly always receding and requiring more than cognitive skills, is one of the hallmarks of what makes an inquiry anthropological as distinct from the other human sciences. The price to be paid for attaining whatever degree of familiarity one can achieve is the long months or years of fieldwork: the anthropological badge of character, the askesis required to attain access to the knowledge the discipline values. If anthropologists are the miniature painters of the social sciences, then the ordinary, the routine, the micro, and the nuance must be on their palette.[11]

Another credo of anthropology is that it is only by establishing such familiarity, however imperfect, that the anthropologist earns a degree of confidence in what he is doing, as well as the capacity to do it. Without some familiarity, there can be no confidence that one is heading in the right direction; without some reciprocal confidence of those with whom one is working, anthropological work is, at best, thorny.

PROBLEM SPACE

Luhmann, in a short article titled "Familiarity, Confidence, Trust: Problems and Alternatives," provides a set of distinctions that are helpful in clarifying the problem under consideration.[12] For Luhmann, familiarity is a logical baseline; without it, there can be no series. That claim does not mean that familiarity is always stable empirically. Even in a historical time when familiarity supposedly was widespread, it was not immutable or invulnerable. In Luhmann's technical use of the term, familiarity is the form that makes it possible for the unfamiliar to be incorporated into the familiar. Hence, familiarity is a condition of inquiry and evaluation rather than a simple state of acquaintance.

Having analytically established familiarity, Luhmann shifts his attention to two dependent terms: confidence and trust. Confidence and trust are action terms within a system. They are distinguished by a marked difference between tacit (taken for granted, habitual) action versus explicit decision making. Thus, in a mode of the self-reference of confidence if events prove disappointing, then there is an *attribution* to *external* factors. In the mode of trust, the cause of consequences refers to an *internal* attribution.

In society (Luhmann's ahistorical contrast term to environment), the normal condition is confidence, an expectation that things will work the way they are expected to. If I ride a tramway, to use Max Weber's example, I am confident that it will run and run safely.[13] That expectation includes the possibility of nefarious events happening as long as the cause of those events can be attributed to external factors. If the bus breaks down, I am confident it will be fixed by someone who knows how to fix it. Things may well be dangerous, but it is not my responsibility to take care of them because I did not cause them to happen; I have confidence that experts are available with the requisite knowledge, skill, and authority. Or, alternatively, no experts are available to repair things, but the dangers are still external and not within my control; if lightning strikes a bus, it is not for that reason that I stop riding buses. Hence, the form of self-reference for confidence is bringing routine/disappointment into a frame of the routine.

Trust, contrastively, operates via internal attribution. Trust "is only required if a bad outcome would make you regret your action."[14] Trust depends not on danger but on risk. Trust requires an internal calculation of external risk; there is a circular relation between action and risk. "Risk is at once in and out of action: it is the way action refers to itself. Risk represents a re-entry of the difference between controllable and uncontrollable into the controllable."[15] Hence, the form of self-reference for trust is bringing the controllable/uncontrollable into the *controllable*.

Trust is distinguished from rational calculation in which one figures out the favorable odds beforehand with a specified degree of assurance. Thus, the distinction between trust and confidence "does not refer to questions of probability or improbability."[16] The reason for this form is that trust is a question of attribution, of an action as to whether the right action was taken. It is not a question of the objectivity of the external situation; trust must include the risk of a bad outcome resulting from my actions.

Given Luhmann's systems theoretical approach, it follows that changes in familiarity will logically impact confidence and trust. Familiarity does not always simply disappear but can lose its previous social scope, scale, and standing. A decline in the scope and scale of familiarity can lead to a crisis of confidence although not its disappearance, because no social system can function at degree zero of confidence. But as trust, to a degree, depends on confidence, delimited spheres of confidence will impact trust.

Day-to-day work in the lab establishes a kind of *familiarity*, albeit, again, a privatized one. This familiarity is built on the routine activity of extensive hours at the bench (especially for younger researchers), which include a great deal of time to chat and observe as the experimental work unfolds. To the degree that the familiarity is established and sustained, it facilitates a form of *confidence* that things today and tomorrow will remain reliable or can be repaired. And it is on the basis of the twinned form of familiarity/confidence that a specific kind of *trust*, an ability to take specific risks and act on them, becomes possible. For example, who to trust among one's competitors is a prime topic in scientific banter and strategy; it is significantly more important, in my experience, among bioscientists than among human scientists. Finally, the lab meeting and scientific conferences are important institutions in initiating, testing, and sustaining the triad of terms and their milieu.

One of the achievements of the sciences in general, the biosciences more particularly, and the emergent interdomains such as synthetic biology specifically has been their ability to construct and privatize zones of familiarity; to develop and enforce practices that build specific forms of confidence in the everyday order of scientific life; and to inculcate and reward a range of specialists who are expert at risk taking in their own highly specific domains. The preeminent achievement of this apparatus and its equipmental platform has been to facilitate movement from the multitude of microsituations in which many of the elements have been standardized (lab machines, lab procedures, lab notebooks, lab meetings, lab scheduling, and so forth) to a range of normalized macrosituations of varying scales by inventing and stabilizing pathways and forms. That is to say, the biosciences, in a series of historical waves ranging from the discovery of the structure of the DNA molecule on through the Human Genome Project and now, it seems, synthetic biology, have been successful in developing forms that compartmentalize and maintain strongly demarcated boundaries between the domains marked as the external world (on which it is dependent for money, political support, training facilities, and many other things) and its own well-policed and well-demarcated internal domains. It is a major historical achievement to have developed the forms that have refigured and reenergized the series of familiarity-confidence-trust into mighty machines to make futures.

In recent decades, the forms, venues, and practices of the biosciences have not been stagnant. In fact, major modifications in the players and organization have been introduced and implemented, becoming simply part of the environment in which the biosciences operate. The first wave of changes came with the mandate and gradual acceptance of commercialization of research both within the university system and without. Following the Bayh-Dole Act passed by the U.S. Congress in 1980, once largely unknown actors such as patent lawyers, technology transfer officers, efficiency experts, and the like have been integrated into the familiarity-confidence-trust form of the biosciences. More recently, with growing strength after the attacks of 9/11, security considerations and their associated experts are becoming part of the milieu in which the biosciences operate. Consequently, there is no a priori reason that human scientists should not become familiar and trusted figures as well.

Conclusion 2011: Risking Knowing

Within SynBERC the dispositions of the bench scientists and their scientific managers, the project directors and senior principal investigators, lead them to conclude that the human sciences should serve them as corporate public relations specialists, disseminating their achievements and potential contributions while refraining from overt criticism. This view of things is simply insulting.

This corporate model is less acceptable than the ELSI model developed during the Human Genome Project. In that form, the human scientists or ethical or legal specialists were contractually obliged to remain external and downstream of the scientific and technical developments, but at least they had the duty of drawing attention to what they considered to be ethical or legal or social limits to acceptable research and development. For the ELSI practitioner, spending time discussing those limits and their foundations, however imaginary much of the content might be, and however lacking in the capacity to verify and test such limits remained, is certainly better than issuing the equivalent of tarted-up press releases.

After reading an earlier draft of this chapter, a friend wrote:

> Are you sure you really trust these guys? Perhaps it's my misimpression, but I don't take away from your discussion of how people in power and specifically synthetic biologists (and those of their high circles) in power typically operate any grounds for trusting them, but rather the opposite. Then there's the matter of being able to count on them to (intend to) "do the right thing." You're suggesting—in your extending of trust to them—that you do count on them to do so—or at the very least to regret making a mistake or committing a moral wrong should that come to pass. OK: but what you say in leading up to that apparent point doesn't really offer your reader much of a basis to participate in your gesture. These guys sound like a rather instrumentalistic lot who might not give a whit if their intentions went awry or they caused harm counter to their intentions. What am I missing?

He is not missing anything. These observations are all valid. SynBERC has not succeeded in instilling confidence as to the transparency of their organizational practice. Although such a state of affairs is troubling, it is not the end of the story. This state of affairs constitutes the reasons for withholding confidence as well as what is ordinarily understood as trust. However, in my interpretation of Luhmann's terms, trust means risk taking: neither the cool calculation of the most plausible alternatives nor an affective bond determined by familiarity.

Trust, understood as a practice of risk that is not operating according to a metric of calculative probability, nor necessarily in accord with affirmative affective bonds, is at the heart of the anthropological enterprise. Who, after all, on the basis of the rational actor theory, would spend such long periods of time hanging out, observing other people's labor and boredom, and hoping that one had chosen the right site of inquiry in order to have the opportunity to write a book that several hundred people (or eventually several thousand) would read? Thus, it seems to me that one has to trust that the practice is itself inherently worthwhile: that conceptual invention and clarification, ascetic exercise of the will in the pursuit of knowledge and insight, and forced training in listening, looking, and passivity will yield dividends for one's soul, one's friends, and that small virtual cohort of future students and readers. Having engaged in that practice for several decades, it seemed worth suffering the proverbial slings and arrows of academic insult, the pervasive indifference of policy makers, the mildly condescending tolerance of the bioscientists, and the trained incapacities of fellow social scientists to risk something different. The dangers of traditional anthropology after a certain point are all too familiar and neither very grave nor very interesting. The risks, I am relatively confident, are obscure, and therein lay the challenge.

Hence, confidence in the actors or the organization per se is not a necessary predicate of trust, although familiarity with their practices would seem to be. Rather, an essential predicate of trust as risk is a conviction in the worth of inquiry per se. Regardless of the technical successes, failures, achievements, or mistakes of synthetic biology, inquiry about it is worthwhile. In order to conduct such inquiry as a mode of ethical engagement, one must adopt a mode of uncertainty about the sufficiency of expertise, and experimentation, with regard to questions of value and worth. It is in the space of uncertainty and experimentation oriented by a metric of flourishing that it becomes possible for an ethics to become a practice of inquiry rather than a discourse of values and expertise. And once ethics becomes a practice of inquiry, the practitioner enters a problem space in which collaboration, as well as discrimination and discernment, comes to the fore. How such foregrounding might lead to an increase of capacity for reconstruction and remediation is the challenge and the problem.

Even once a situation becomes determinate, its significance cannot be reduced to or evaluated uniquely by formal conditions of internal coherence. It is at this point that a stepping back, a reflective evaluation, becomes pertinent. Its evaluative pertinence, however, can only be ultimately judged by how things work once the inquirer returns to the inquiry. Since at least 1920, broadly speaking, John Dewey had called this whole process *reconstruction*: "Reconstruction can be nothing less than the work of developing, of forming, of producing (in the literal sense of the word) the intellectual instrumentalities which will progressively direct inquiry into the deeply and inclusively human—that is to say, moral—facts of the present scene and situation."[17]

The challenge reconstruction had, for Dewey, was a pointed urgency under conditions in which the technical accomplishments of the sciences were expanding while separating themselves ever more from the older moral base in which it was held they used to be embedded. In this regard, there are some striking passages in Dewey's 1948 introduction to the reedition of his *Reconstruction in Philosophy* that bear an eerie resonance to contemporary problems. Dewey was annoyed at those who advocate that technoscience simply needs a counterweight and that all that is necessary is to institute ethics alongside science. Such a position, he argued, constituted a serious scientific and ethical evasion because it assumed that the necessary ethical responses were already available and only needed to be applied to the new and ever more powerful means that were being invented. The pragmatic difficulties of accomplishing this feat were simply being ignored. With respect to philosophy (or, we might add, anthropology) there was a more serious problem. Such a position, Dewey wrote, "retains intact the divorce between some things as means and mere means and other things as ends and only ends because of their own essence or inherent nature. Thus, in effect, though not in intent, an issue which is serious enough to be *moral* is disastrously evaded."[18]

That evasion continues today. This claim implies that the problem retains its actuality. It indicates that the problem of reflection on means and ends and the different range of capacities required to address them will not disappear through the exercise of power in specific situations, however effective these may prove to be in deferring addressing this problem. Given that this deferral has lasted for a very long time indeed, there is absolutely no guarantee that successful solutions will ever be implemented. As Dewey argued, unless there can be a return to inquiry, there cannot be reconstruction.

It follows that what seems to be required is a differently designed and situated set of experiments. What these might look like remains to be seen; however, we can conclude that the experiments discussed here have been successful to the extent that they have shown the need for a different assemblage of anthropology, ethics, and the life sciences.

8

Why There Is No Contemporary Bioscience, Only a Modern One

After Nietzsche's devastating criticism of those "last men" who "invented happiness," I may leave aside altogether the naive optimism in which science—that is the technique of mastering life which rests upon science—has been celebrated as the path to happiness. Who believes in this?—aside from a few big children in university chairs or editorial offices. Let us resume our argument.
«MAX WEBER[1]»

Almost a century after Max Weber's scornful aside to the assembled university audience in Munich in 1917, it is disheartening to realize that today so many believe more than ever in the figure of the last men who invented happiness and the credibility of the technoscientific pastors and guides who accompany them.[2] Weber was correct both in his assessment of the trajectory of technoscience and in his contempt for those who think such a trajectory will lead them to happiness, and so I return to the problem of what the modern life sciences have to contribute—an untimely concern because most people believe that the issue is settled already. The problem is contemporary in the sense that, if taken up in the way Weber proposes, it requires the invention of a different configuration of the past, present, and future.

As Weber observed as an aside in "Science as a Vocation," the limited contribution of the natural sciences to the larger cultural sphere leaves open the question of what happens once it is understood that natural science can provide no answers to the larger questions of human existence. As he says, "What shall we do and how shall we live? That science does not give an answer to this is indisputable. The only question that remains is the sense in which science gives 'no' answer and whether or not science might yet be of some use to the one who puts the question correctly."[3]

Unfortunately, Weber did not pursue this line of inquiry. Furthermore, as far as I know, there are few resonances of his challenge in the voluminous scholarly literature on Weber produced over the course of the twentieth century. In the United States and in Germany, Weber's observation was taken up (albeit tacitly) as an epistemological issue in the debates over methodology in the cultural and natural sciences.[4] Although these debates over the status of hermeneutics and natural science are valuable, they are not quite the same ones as Weber's more existential and cultural questioning.

Seeking resources to better diagnose this situation—and attempting to do this work in a contemporary mode—I turn once again to conceptual repertoire work. The first thinker whom I choose to accompany here is not generally well known—Gyorgy Markus, an émigré Hungarian philosopher. In the first issue of *Science in Context*, Markus wrote an article that has haunted me since I first read it years ago. The article is titled "Why Is There No Hermeneutics of the Natural Sciences?"[5] I know of no follow-up discussion of any substance to the provocative claims Markus puts forward as hypotheses to be pursued and enriched with further inquiry.[6] I have continued to find the article's argument haunting because it seems to be both generally perspicacious as to the overall status of the natural sciences today as well as illuminating about my own recent experiences in different positions close to and engaged with particular biosciences.

Above all, Markus provides the conceptual tools for diagnosing why the bioscientists with whom I have been working are not my contemporaries in the specific sense of the term as I have been employing it in this book. Equally significant, Markus's analysis helps me to see why, although the practitioners of the biosciences and the human sciences involved in this project continue to work in proximity, we are not actually accompanying each other.

Why There Is No Hermeneutics of the Natural Sciences

Markus provides a preliminary analytic of the elements that have been assembled over the course of the last century into a stable, largely unchallenged, and taken-for-granted genre of writing in the natural sciences. He emphasizes that his argument does not take a position on whether the claims of the natural sciences are true or false. In that, he is observing the critical limitations of his discipline and providing an excellent case study of the conditions in which statements are taken to be true or false. Furthermore, he explicitly acknowledges that he is overlooking the socioeconomic conditions that underpinned the growth of the natural sciences. He acknowledges that in a comprehensive analysis, both of these registers—the epistemological and the sociological—would require more attention.

Markus's analysis does not include insights from anthropological fieldwork. One of the defining qualities of fieldwork is its existential and experiential character. One encounters directly, and frequently not at the time and place of one's choosing, a range of problems that a text-based discipline might miss or at least would have the luxury of choosing how and when such issues should be addressed. Of course, there are always background absences in texts, and although some absences from a text can be discovered through critical and philological methods, they cannot become the site of direct intervention aimed at changing or altering them. In a fieldwork situation—or more generally in what Dewey understood as inquiry—such absences are at times encountered as discordances and breakdowns. Thinking about them, observing them, reflecting on them, and proposing alternatives in fieldwork situations in which participation is given equal weight to observation provides a critical multidimensionality to our understanding. If the fieldwork or inquiry is carried out in a mode of reconstruction, then a further level of ethical as well as epistemological engagement is brought into play.

THE GENRE

Markus argues that the current form of the scientific article emerged in the nineteenth century and has been successfully stabilized and institutionalized ever since. This remarkable achievement in genre construction—perhaps unparalleled in any other domain of cultural practice—has been so successful that it has become a taken-for-granted part of the self-understanding of the natural sciences. This mode of jurisdiction—the peer-reviewed article produced in compliance with a highly disciplined form of presentation—has facilitated a specific mode of veridiction, one in which an author function, a reader function, and a specific narrative form have been made normative.

That normativity, in turn, has been facilitated and reinforced in an essential manner by the construction and stabilization of a small number of legitimate venues for its production in the university and publishing worlds. Only by adopting these forms and these norms is one authorized to make legitimate truth claims in the life sciences. As has become evident through the course of my participant observation, bioscientists today have been successfully trained to exhibit professional indifference to, ignore, or, if necessary when the existence of alternatives is forced on them, reject as carrying no veridictional significance any truth claims that take a different form or are produced in a different venue.

The rise, stabilization, and policing of this genre of writing the truth has had many ramifications. It has functioned as the discursive and institutional vehicle for the consolidation of the greater and greater specialization and subspecialization characteristic of modern science, another Weberian theme whose validity by now is conspicuous. It is worth underlining one more time that this genre of writing, this mode of veridiction, and this mode of jurisdiction—this form—are all relatively recent cultural and institutional achievements. They are achievements that mandatorily displaced, reconfigured, and produced a historical amnesia. As Markus observes: "The *République des savants* of the eighteenth century, still loosely uniting scientists, philosophers, publicists, and cultivated amateurs, has been transformed into a multitude of separated *research communities* comprising the professional specialists in the given area and now posited as the sole public for the relevant scientific objectivations."[7]

The constraints (and concurrent strengths) of this genre are themselves normative. If a piece of scientific writing does not conform to them, it will not get published in an authorized journal; it will not count as true. It will not be, to use the striking phrase of Georges Canguilhem, *dans le vrai* (within the [domain of the] true). At best, it will be cast into the other available rubric in the prestigious journals that is adjacent to the research article—the opinion piece. Of course, access to express an opinion is itself also highly restricted to those otherwise authorized to speak the truth.

Although one could (and should) write a social history of these genres, and Steven Shapin has taken the lead in this direction, Markus emphasizes that the discursive-textual approach is not intended to expose or capture the motives, conscious or unconscious, of the actors.[8] They have been trained to write (and to read) in a certain mode—the history of the grant proposal would equally make a signal contribution to our understanding of the *Bildung* of modern scientists—and then how not to think about that mode once they have achieved a sufficient mastery of its technicalities. Historically speaking, both the practices of this mode of thinking and of not thinking required a long time to invent, to inculcate in a disposition, and to normalize. Once established and regularized, these dispositions and norms have been enforced by mechanisms that are hardly only cognitive.

Markus develops his argument directly in the line of thought articulated by Weber in "Science as a Vocation." Weber argued that the natural sciences, with their steady progress and technological prowess, have achieved unparalleled success at what they do: the development of rationalized concepts, experimental practice, and specialization. The price for that success, for that progress, however, has been a steady loss of meaning in the larger cultural arena. As the natural sciences continue to burgeon and subspecialties proliferate, the one question that cannot be posed as a modern *scientific* question is whether the ever-advancing specialization and technical mastery is a good or bad thing.

Weber's claim does not mean that many natural scientists do not have beliefs and opinions concerning the impact of their work; frequently they do.[9] They often characterize such topics under the rubric of "consequences" or "implications." Natural scientists, however, have neither the legitimate authority nor the scholarly capacity to defend their beliefs and opinions as truth claims with the same kind of discipline and rigor that their own disciplinary claims demand. The point is a quite simple one: a prestigious biologist is often capable of having his opinions on topics such as religion or poverty published. Of course, were he not a prestigious biologist, it is extremely unlikely that such opinions would be publishable in a scientific journal; in either case, they would not be publishable in scholarly journals of the humanities and social sciences as they almost certainly would have ignored the relevant scholarly literature as well as the genre constraints applying in these other disciplines. This state of affairs is perfectly normal in the Weberian sense that specialization is the price to be paid for scientific work in modernity.

A slippage occurs, however, when the scientific authority earned in one specialized research arena is transposed into the power to impose opinions as if they were authorized truth claims. When bioscientists simply ignore (or silence) those who pose questions they have neither the time nor the inclination to consider seriously, it is a demonstration (tacit or otherwise) of their superior power. In these cases we are not dealing with different claims from diverse but equally legitimate modes of veridiction but rather with unequal power relations or simply the application of force in which no rational justifications are required. Naturally, as citizens in a democracy or republic, we believe that the opinion of one citizen is in principle the equal of the opinion of another citizen. Thus, in the public sphere, the human sciences have no a priori privileged claim to adjudicate cultural affairs.

The other side of Weber's claim—updated by Markus—is that today at least the natural sciences are untroubled about their loss of meaning because they are largely unaware of this state of affairs. In fact, they are prospering financially and institutionally as never before. If there are deep conflicts of meaning adjacent to the life sciences—and there are, for example, creationism versus evolution, playing God, and so forth—their existence has not altered or significantly influenced the forms and practices of modern biology one iota. Such discussions have been successfully cordoned off into a realm of "religion," "ethics," and "culture." While bioethics commissions and their specialists and subspecialists proliferate and debate issues of seeming import, in the life sciences research continues untroubled and unhindered, at least by these cultural concerns; and, as Weber would have said, this state of affairs is as it should be. But Weber also said that for those unable or unwilling to accept these conditions, the doors of the old churches are open "widely and compassionately" to them.[10]

THE FORM: THE AUTHOR FUNCTION

The inscribed author of the natural scientific text is a depersonalized one. The use of the first person singular is *verboten;* should it be used in a submission it will be eliminated before publication by the journal's editors. This genre requirement is in tension, however, with the sociological fact that career advancements, grants, and symbolic or monetary rewards are awarded to individuals. Thus, although the normative mode of the article is deindividualized (it can be at most collective), often written in a passive voice, today this mode of presentation of truth claims is always accompanied by credit lines naming individuals. The latter now includes an obligatory specification of the contributions of each author, noting any potential conflict of interest and demarcating a clear line of responsibility should trouble arise.

The manner in which authorship and credit have been handled has successfully navigated a number of juncture points or crossroads in the twentieth century. In the biosciences, for example, the vast expansion of technological capacities and the backgrounding of many of the older craft practices and virtues of the biological sciences during the implementation of the human genome sequencing project have become normative. Among other considerations, the community has resolved the issue of how to manage the distribution of credit once tens, if not hundreds, of persons have contributed to an experiment, have interpreted the data generated, and so forth. This statement is a normative one; of course, it does not claim that empirically all tension of competing claims has been resolved successfully or eliminated but only that the manner in which such competition or conflict should be adjudicated has been given a normative and stable form. It is within that form that conflicts arise and are dealt with, to the personal satisfaction or aggravation of the parties involved.

In addition to the undifferentiated "we" that is commonly deployed and the frequent use of the passive voice (as if Nature were still speaking in the results), the genre requires a neutral narrative of how experimental results arose. Results are narrated not as a set of choices among alternatives consciously chosen by a particular research team leader in a particular lab operating under real-world constraints of timing, personnel, and the like but as a sequence of events flowing out of the experiment and its design. The actual actors involved are discursively placed in the background and replaced in the narrative account by an anonymous performer (helped by an organized lab, financed usually by the state).

Once the objectivity and depersonalization of the author is established narratively, the experimenter can then discursively occupy the role of detached observer of the results: the requisite and normative author-function. Among a list of concomitant ramifications of this narrative achievement, one is pertinent here: "Through this depersonalization of the author the experimental paper acquires its fundamental cultural trait of *report*."[11]

In point of fact, this instantiation of objectivity opens up further far-reaching genre results. As should now be clear, the genre of the report and its effects, affects, and ramifications stand in stark contrast with the genres in the qualitative human sciences.

THE FORM: THE READER FUNCTION

The intended readers of natural scientific articles in peer-reviewed journals are other expert professionals working in the same research area. Although there may be a few generalists (for example, for several years in new fields such as developments in RNA research), in order for articles to make a valid scientific contribution, they have to report new research results resulting from new research. If they do not report specific results, there would be no point in publishing them in these journals.

That much is straightforward; what is less obvious is Markus's insight that these qualities make possible, even mandatory, a further coupling: "The most important hermeneutical consequence of this professionalization of the audience consists, however, in the fact that—in conjunction with the earlier characterized depersonalization of the authorial role—it normatively posits the *complete interchangeability* of the author and the recipient."[12]

Although articles often contain a short background paragraph on the state of the broader field, they are meant to be read and evaluated only by other specialists. There are, of course, journals devoted to differing levels of vulgarization and diverse audiences; by definition, however, readers of *Scientific American* or *Popular Mechanics* are amateurs. Ultimately, however, the audience for research papers is only researchers in the same subspecialty. In the end, given this restrictive discipline, this normativity, and the capacities maximized, by definition a larger audience is of no interest or consequence: "Proper scientific publication is in this way construed as the opposite of seeking publicity."[13]

In addition to these genre constraints, there is a further reason why research reports are meant only for other researchers and not a public. Research is a practice. As opposed to the humanities and most social sciences, the natural sciences are rooted in, and assume a familiarity with, experimental-manipulative practices. This technological and tacit dimension essential to and constitutive of experimental natural sciences has been discussed in the relevant history of science and social studies of science literature, but signaling its importance in restricting the readership is, I think, a contribution of Markus's.

This insight helps to explain one of the frequent ripostes we have encountered in our fieldwork as well as in formal presentations to bioscientific groups. "We don't understand what you are saying." "Engineers are not very sophisticated." "Why don't you write in plain English?" The most generous interpretation one can give to these remarks is that there is an expectation of author-reader transposability. Of course, when a specialist in RNA folding structure describes her work, for example, a polymer chemist is not expected to understand it in detail, only to appreciate that it is advancing understanding. Consequently, this lack of reciprocity when it concerns the human sciences is comprehensible if not admirable.

Again, in line with Weber, the very strength of the mode of veridiction of the modern biosciences is also its limitation. The more the genre of research article achieved dominance, the more it narrowed its competent readership and the more it sacrificed claims to broader significance despite assertions about how the specific results contribute to broader understanding and, even more commonly, how they constitute a step toward conquering disease and pathology.

Modernism

In their relation to tradition, the natural sciences at least since the nineteenth century have been resolutely modernist. What counts is the "new." In the natural sciences, that the "new" emerges from and backgrounds what had been the previous "new" is called *progress.* It follows that the natural sciences' shallow time perspective is perfectly legitimate. Their practice depends, at least in part, on the ability to work in a genre in which a historical amnesia is itself unmarked but present—presentism facilitates progress.

In addition, and perfectly in line with this presentism, the natural sciences do not possess canonical or classical texts in the way the humanities and some branches of the social sciences do. Thus, for example, in the qualitative social sciences, it is perfectively normative to cite the work of Max Weber, whereas it would be unimaginable to cite the work of Galton or Buffon in a research article in molecular biology.

Markus underscores that there are parallels in the depersonalized and passive voice of the research article and paradigmatic forms of modernism in the arts. In both, the new is what counts; their subject matter was given a form in which the materials are made to seem to speak for themselves through a transparent medium. He notes, "The programmatic elimination of the subjective authorial voice ... aims at making these texts completely self-referential. That is, such a text normatively insists on being received 'for its own sake.' It foregrounds the language actualized in it as its *material* instead of this language's being used as a mere *means* of communication (about something real or fictitious). This is achieved ... through a conscious and systematic destruction of the identity and unity of those directly referential relations which are spontaneously evoked by any use of the language."[14]

Of course, in the arts this modernist program was explicit, lasted for a number of decades in different iterations, and was always, at the end of the day, resolutely fictional, in the sense of made, artifice, created, and so forth.[15] The materials speaking for themselves in modernist literature or painting or music were always speaking in a loud voice, calling attention to themselves, their use of materials and forms, their practice, and their own distinctive style of criticism. If there ever was an explicit genre, modernism was it!

As these conditions, this program, and this historical trajectory do not apply in anything like such an explicitly programmatic way in the natural sciences, the parallel with modernism in the arts, while evocative, is limited in its scope and applicability. In the sciences, after all, it is the research results, as well as the methods that produce them, that are intended to achieve a formal transparency. The form and language in which they are presented, while actually crucially important in achieving this goal, are not the subject of endless debate, colloquia, lectures, critical institutions, museum panels, and the like. They simply are the way things are presented if they are to take their place *dans le vrai.*

Modernism, however, has been over in the arts for many decades now. Regardless of how the issue of what contemporary art is might be resolved, if it ever is (or, as is more likely, is simply replaced by yet another series of productions and critiques, i.e., fashions), the result will no longer have any isomorphism with the natural sciences. That being said, the question remains for those of us not working in the natural sciences or the arts: what is anthropology practiced in a contemporary mode?[16]

9

The Accompaniment: On the Contemporary and the Untimely

It is not the actual interconnection of things but the conceptual interconnection of problems which define the scope of the various sciences. A new science emerges where new problems are pursued by new methods and truths are thereby discovered which open up significant new points of view.

«MAX WEBER[1]»

Giorgio Agamben titled the inaugural lecture in his 2005 Theoretical Philosophy course at the University of Venice "What Is the Contemporary?" He explained to his audience that during the course of lectures he would attempt to answer the question, "Who and how are we contemporaries?" As a disciplined Heideggerean, Agamben cautioned that the essential task required to arrive at an adequate understanding of the contemporary consisted in "the challenge of taking texts from long ago, relatively recently, and quite close to the present, and to read them as if we were their contemporary."[2] The subject matter of his lectures and ultimately of temporality itself, then, would be textual. We can find here echoes of Roland Barthes' analogy (in a paragraph that Agamben does not cite but that immediately precedes a quotation from Barthes that he does): "Like a blind person whose finger lingers on life's text and recognizes here and there what has already been said."[3]

The equation of life and texts is one Agamben and many of his historical contemporaries share. The last several decades of the twentieth century in Europe's elite academies were nothing if not discursive and textual. However, while Barthes privileges touch, memory, and speech as the mode in which one approaches a text, Agamben chooses sight.

For Agamben, there are two essential qualities of the contemporary: *déphasage* (temporal disconnection) and *l'anachronisme* (anachronism). He introduces the first term through a reading of a poem by Osip Mandelstam written in 1923 titled "My Epoch." (*vek*, in Russian). Mandelstam meditates on the disconnection between an individual life with its own singular temporality and the form and motion of the epoch in which he lives. The poet gives form to a fundamental disconnection between the two poles through a figure of striking bodily imagery; the relationship that might have existed in a healthy fashion between the individual and the epoch is disjointed literally, like a broken spine. The poet is out of phase with what has been, what is, and what is coming.

Mandelstam's subject faces backward toward the last century so as to pick out traces of the arrival of the new century and the disjoined connectivity it will bring with it. This posture and its associated figuration are by now familiar to critics through Walter Benjamin's reading of Paul Klee's *Angelus Novas*. By the second decade of the twenty-first century, such an interpretation is canonical.

For Agamben, Mandelstam is searching for zones of obscurity, not light. For Agamben such a mode of looking, or searching, is not a privative one. Those who scan the present for its obscurities rather than its lights "have taken up a contemporary position toward their time."[4] What does the poet see in the form of obscurity of his time? He sees something different from the Romantic disjunction of the singular and the historical; he sees something different from the modern scanning the future. Rather, the poet sees an untimely space: an anachronism, something foundational.

For Agamben, as for Heidegger, the *arché* constitutes an essential quality of the truth; perhaps it is even the truth itself. The philology of the term "archaic" provides the key to its true meaning: "Archaic means close to the *arke,* that is to say the origin. But the origin is not situated uniquely in a chronological past. It is contemporary to historical becoming and never ceases to act through it."[5]

Agamben switches registers and employs a virtue term—"courage"—as the quality that the poet must possess in the attempt to grasp the fundamental. Agamben's figuration is topologically complicated here; he argues that if we find the courage to look at the obscurity that surrounds us in the right way, then we will be able to see the true light. "The contemporary inscribes itself in the present signaling the archaic, and only he who perceives in the most modern of things, the most recent indices the signature of the archaic can be a contemporary."[6]

That "becoming" is messianic, an overcoming of all temporality in which past, present, and future fuse, or are defused, in a flash: time and being are one. One sees that the right "time is the eternal now."[7]

Those peering into the dark, facing backward, seeking the archaic, are not, in any case, those whom I wish to accompany, nor are they my contemporaries.

What Is the Contemporary in the Art World?

The venerable avant-garde journal *October* devoted a large portion of its fall 2009 issue to "A Questionnaire on the Contemporary." Hal Foster, writing on behalf of the journal's editors, sent out the following questionnaire to seventy critics and curators. He notes that very few curators responded. The questionnaire reads as follows:

> The category of "contemporary art" is not a new one. What is new is the sense that, in its very heterogeneity, much present practice seems to float free of historical determination, conceptual definition,

and critical judgment. Such paradigms as "the neo-avant-garde" and "postmodernism," which once oriented some art and theory, have run into the sand, and arguably, no models of much explanatory reach or intellectual force have risen in their stead. At the same time, perhaps paradoxically, "contemporary art" has become an institutional object in its own right: in the academic world there are professorships and programs, and in the museum world departments and institutions, all devoted to the subject, and most tend to treat it as apart not only from prewar practice but from most postwar practice as well.

Is this floating-free real or imagined? A merely local perception? A simple effect of the end-of-grand narratives? If it is real, how can we specify some of its principal causes, that is, beyond general reference to "the market" and "globalization?" Or is it indeed a direct outcome of a neoliberal economy, one that, moreover, is now in crisis? What are some of its salient consequences for artists, critics, curators, and historians—for their formation and their practice alike? Are there collateral effects in other fields of art history? Are there instructive analogies to be drawn from the situation in other arts and disciplines? Finally, are there benefits to this apparent lightness of being?[8]

CONSENSUS

All thirty-two responses are conspicuously staid. Although the majority of the respondents are cutting-edge academic critics (most of them employed in the elite institutions of the American university system), in their responses none takes any stylistic liberties of any significance, and none experiments with form. It is as if they had been sent a questionnaire. The tone and the undertones of disquiet in the replies reveal that there are vital stakes involved in the issues. The reason for the gravity of the responses may ride on the fact that these questions, both within the critical university establishment and in the art world of museums, galleries, auction houses, and festivals, remain unsettled and dangerous.

Although there are nuances of tone, of insight, and of fervor in the range of responses, a consistent broad thematic does run across the replies. Few, if any, contest *October*'s tentative diagnosis of the state of things in the world of art and art criticism. But at the same time, none of the respondents actually directly takes up Hal Foster's challenge to move beyond "general reference to the 'market' and 'globalization.'" This lack of engagement does not mean that "globalization" or the "market" is not being constantly evoked, only that no sustained, serious sociological or economic analysis is provided (or even referenced). This absence of scholarly curiosity, or felt necessity, to engage a vast literature on these topics is striking and revelatory: this is a self-referential peer group who has internalized the existing genre constraints at work in their disciplines. Or perhaps these critics are so dependent and connected to the turbulent effects of these myriad market forces and the venues and trends they create that to take the time to address them in an adequate manner would be to exclude oneself from the hyperaccelerated current game of contemporary art. Timeliness is mandatory; being untimely is too risky professionally.

There is broad agreement that even though there is no stable scholarly or commercial consensus on what contemporary art is or is not, the growth during the last two decades of the twentieth century of institutions to display it, explore it, and sell it has been rapid and compelling. Not only has there been an expansion of the scale of the well-known biennales but also there has been a globalization of their sites and contributors as more and more venues are created, financed, and visited by artists, dealers, curators, and critics as well as tourists and amateurs of all kinds. Even more surprising, given the dispositional and institutional lethargy of the academic world, there has been a mushroomlike establishment of university investment in contemporary or contemporary/modern art with the associated courses at both the graduate and undergraduate levels. And, of course, there has been a "transience" in the branding of the object being named, driven by a torrent of money, of artistic producers and directors, and of critics in and out of the academy, museums, and auction houses. It would almost certainly be misleading, however, to characterize the state of affairs in this part of the art world as a crisis. To call it a crisis would imply that the existence of the older art institutions are in danger, that suddenly there was a steep falling off of money and audience (as in the classical music world), or that the mood of those involved was either somber or torpid.

Thus, for an anthropologist of the contemporary, the art world's contemporary qualifies as a plausible object of reflection. Because undertaking such a study is neither my current goal nor my expertise, here I offer a few observations in order to get clearer about the current range of the term "the contemporary" and to clear some more ground for subsequent explorations.

ACCELERATIONS: THE VIEW FROM MOMA'S ESCALATOR
One of the few curators to respond to *October*'s questionnaire was Helen Molesworth—head of the Department of Modern and Contemporary Art (created in 1997) and the Houghton Curator of Contemporary Art at the Harvard Art Museum. Her reflections are among the most thoughtful and balanced of those appearing in the issue. Her core diagnosis of the current state of play turns in part on her observation that "for many, the unanswerability of questions about quality, the lack of consensus about importance, the newfound vitality of the viewer, and the perpetual influx of new art are all causes to rejoice."[9]

As a curator, Molesworth cannot comfortably embrace this state of affairs, which she nicely labels "festivalism." The reason for her discursive pitch of caution is that, as a curator, she is obliged to make choices precisely about quality, importance, and vitality about the cacophonous influx of artistic production. She laments the fact that her most distinguished fellow curators, even while they are organizing shows at the most prestigious and well-funded institutions on contemporary art, are uncharacteristically unsure and noncommittal, who, after some hesitation, have decided to make a virtue of what they take to be a necessity. She writes tellingly that even "MOMA [the Museum of Modern Art in New York] seems unwilling to narrativize what is at stake."[10] And that refusal authorizes others in less prestigious institutions not to commit to a standard beyond the numbers of people drawn to visit the museum or gallery, the experience of the art and artists, and a sense that another show will soon be on exhibit.

Johanna Burton—associate director and senior faculty member of the Whitney Museum Independent Study Program in New York City—describes her disquiet and irritation while riding the escalators at MOMA at the cascade of things on display apparently without order or hierarchy except, of course, that they are at MOMA and hence are valuable and worthy of regard. One might say that she regrets being mandated to occupy a stance of a flâneur when she was trained to be an arbiter of taste. The contemporary operates as a category, Burton writes, in two different ways: "as a category so pluralist and wide-reaching in its vicissitudes and effects that it would seem all-encompassing, *and* as a newly secured 'institutional object' recognized as particular (or at least pervasive) enough to be jockeying for legitimacy within the field of art history."[11]

The theme of the dispersion of authority is introduced by a number of respondents with notable ambivalence. Alexander Alberro, the Virginia Bloedel Wright Associate Professor of Art History at Barnard College and Columbia University, observes: "Gone is the chic collector who seeks cultural capital, let alone the connoisseur of early modernism; art collecting today is largely dominated by purchase of sheer speculation."[12] This diagnosis is linked to a broader claim that there is a near total void of a sophisticated and conceptually rich analysis of reception. What is mentioned, perhaps a little timidly and sotto voce, by a number of these art historians is the felt need to reestablish, in some fashion, the learned critic's legitimate authority to lay claim to judgments of "objectivity" and "disinterestedness." Of course, theory-driven critical discourse within the elite academy over the last several decades has itself spearheaded the deconstruction of such notions as merely historical, arbitrary remnants of modernism. In addition, the blurring or elimination of the line between high and low, or popular and elite, or individual and community, art production and art criticism has been established with a near hegemonic authority.

Some of those who championed these developments, and who still, to an extent at least, appreciate their value, are now wondering about some of the unexpected ramifications of their theorizing practice. "Current artistic practice is extremely heterogeneous, yet in theoretical and critical writing on contemporary art one often finds a quite consistent set of terms employed to analyze artistic practices. I am thinking in particular of Agamben's 'homo sacer,' bare life and state of exception; Jean-Luc Nancy's inoperative community; Jacques Rancière's partition of the sensible; Negri and Hardt's multitude; Laclau and Mouffe's radical democracy, and Balibar's transnational citizenship."[13] It seems at times as if awareness was suddenly stirring among these holders of endowed chairs that they are reaping what they, or their advisors, have sown. Among those ramifications appears a current that negates or eludes the very practice of history as the study of a past per se. "Perhaps paradoxically, then, the horizon of contemporary art history is in fact the past, not the present. The field against or on which it operates is what we think we already know. The present is not arrived at through the past but the reverse. I think contemporary art history is best when it is de/constructivist of 'contemporary,' 'art' and 'history' alike."[14]

The only paradox is that one stream of *doxa* has become dominant. And that dominance increasingly precludes, at least in certain venues, a sustained attention to and presentation of the past. The line between "presentism" and the "history of the present" is, when it comes down to it, underconceptualized and no longer controlled by those who are, or were, authorized to think about such arcane topics.

THE BEAUTIFUL CLOUD

Although MOMA's curators are apparently reluctant to name the order obtaining in the contemporary art scene, others are not so hesitant: one interpretation of the current state of affairs is Yves Michaud's short book (or long essay), *L'Art à l'état gazeux:*

Essai sur le triomphe de l'esthétique (*Effervescent Art: An Essay on the Triumph of the Aesthetic*), published in the summer of 2003.[15] Michaud, a prolific philosopher and Parisian critic, argues that the special domain of art as the privileged site of the aesthetic, which had prevailed for centuries, has come to an end. What has replaced it, gradually at first and then in an accelerated and triumphant fashion more recently, is the ever-increasing spread—like a cloud of invisible and euphoria-inducing gas—of the aesthetic into more and more realms of life.

Michaud identifies three main causes for the state of the contemporary situation. The first is the progressive undermining and eventual disappearance of the art object as the unchallenged pivot of the aesthetic experience. Michaud provides a long discussion of the gradual dissolution of the autonomous art object during the course of the triumph of modern art during the twentieth century. He traces genealogically the process's origin to the decade of the 1910s with the appearance and eventual acceptance of the *Papiers Collés*. He cites that as early as 1972, the critic and advocate of modernism Harold Rosenberg had identified the deaestheticization of the art object. These and a plethora of other examples bolster Michaud's thesis that the end of the autonomous art object does not by any means entail the end of art: quite the opposite, in Michaud's view.

As the art object became displaced and was eventually replaced by a broader understanding and practice of the aesthetic experience, it became clear quite early on in the process that there could be multiple paths leading to such an experience, not just painting and the other nineteenth-century fine arts. If it is the "effect" side that begins to colonize aesthetic experience, then the trend to more and more technical means of generating such experiences is not surprising. It follows that its production requires engineers and managers as much as artists. The twentieth century has seen a vast expansion of the industrial production of cultural and symbolic goods. Perhaps most famously in the Bauhaus, the older demarcation zones were brought into more proximity. This process certainly had its democratizing dimension; it also required more standardization and the industries that could make such products available for mass distribution.[16] The Bauhaus is emblematic of the adjacency and collaborative efforts to bring art, craft, standardization, pedagogy, and industry into apparatuses designed to reshape daily life in an industrial economy and society. Less obviously instrumental was Marcel Duchamp's readymades; they became emblematic, Michaud argues convincingly, of how an artist's gesture transferred the vast world and an ever-expanding world of ordinary objects into the field of artistic or aesthetic gravity. Once Duchamp made a urinal a museum piece, the arrow between design, art, and daily life began to run back and forth in tandem, transforming the precious status of both as well as the boundaries that had obtained between them. Michaud captures one aspect of this motion nicely when he says: "Art has spread; the children and grand-children of Duchamp have filled the world with ready-mades."[17] The generalization of this process of delocalization, production, and relocalization—former art objects sent on their way into the world of daily use by the Bauhaus and industrial objects fabricated in principle for their utility or prestige sent into museums and galleries as aesthetic objects—has proved to be expansive.

Michaud argues that this process and its associated experiences continue to be more and more pervasive. With the kind of dissolution and disassociation occasioning such anxiety among our contemporary art critics and curators, all is not lost. Today there are no fixed and a priori boundaries. Michaud's writes, "What does remain is the fact that all sorts of practices, absolutely all, can under certain conditions and timing, become part of contemporary art."[18]

Once the object domain became a museum without walls, and the walls of the museum became a space for objects without limits, the next step in Michaud's narrative is that the experience of these objects and the experience of that experience was opened up for aestheticization in a definitive fashion. John Dewey's pragmatist advocacy of "Art as Experience" has come to fruition, albeit hardly in the form that Dewey imagined.

DECELERATIONS: A DIFFERENT CONTEMPORARY

Enter, once again, contemporary art. Johanna Burton of the Whitney provides a claim I can almost agree with. She writes:

> When Roland Barthes asked in 1971, "Is not to be modern to know clearly what cannot be started over again?" he was suggesting that sometimes so-called critical distance draws a very firm line between past and present—too firm as Barthes saw it. . . . What the contemporary offers—when it is allowed to operate as a way of thinking broadly about the conditions for artistic production and reception we are ourselves experiencing—is the opportunity for praxis. Writing, thinking, and teaching about art whose consequences we cannot fully know provides us a kind of meta-exercise, one not dissociated from historical accounts but, rather, alive and awake to connections to be made between now and then while nonetheless aware of their utter incompatibilities.[19]

Why "utter incompatibilities"? Had she said, "incompatibilities," then the link to practice and reflection would seem plausible, contemporary in a different and, to my mind, better sense. If the line between past and present is so firm as to be utterly impassable, then we are, it seems to me, once again into a form of modernism or, perhaps without a faith and seriousness of a movement, simply postmodernism.

Charles Baudelaire, Foucault's emblematic modern critic, was confident that he knew what the best modern painting was; he devoted much of his time to the métier of art critic. Nietzsche also devoted himself to aesthetic criticism, especially of music, as his recurrent and frequent attention to Wagner demonstrates. His notebooks are filled with attempts to figure out what the music of his time should be and whether Wagner was the person who was leading the way forward. Nietzsche, of course, for a time accompanied Wagner, literally at Bayreuth and then, feeling betrayed, left him behind with a storm of vituperation.

Lest this reference to Wagner seem merely anecdotal, Foucault's trips to Bayreuth with Pierre Boulez (and other friends) and his reflections on the director Patrick Chéreau's staging of

The Ring cycle would indicate otherwise.[20] In a long article he wrote for the Italian newspaper *Corriere della sera,* Foucault reviews the performance of the cycle in Bayreuth in 1980 and provides a beautiful, acid-seared aesthetic of the contemporary.[21]

Boulez, Chéreau, and the set designer Peduzzi were confronted with the question: what to do with Wagner today? The question was inevitable, and no doubt its daunting magnitude is what drew these stellar and highly different artists to accept that challenge. Foucault briefly rehearses the core answers that had been given to that inevitable question. At the other pole was an attempt to avoid the history of the last century and its nefarious associations so as to get back to something in the music, staging, and power of the *Ring* that continued to make it worthy and compelling for so many. Pure mythology was one solution, but that meant focusing on Wagner's mythology, which was, for Foucault, both "explosive and derisory." After the Second World War the solutions varied between attempted historical solutions (setting the scene in one past or another, one pre-Nazi in East Germany, another with a full awareness of the awful political legacy in the West). Chéreau and Peduzzi also avoided staging the musical drama as a kind of assemblage in the manner of Bertolt Brecht, which would have entailed making the differences between chronological references apparent and inassimilable: the epoch to which the *Ring* explicitly refers; the time in which it was written; and the present moment during which it was being performed.[22]

It was in the crossroads that Boulez and company took up the challenge in 1976. Boulez was at first sight an unlikely choice. He was, after all, one of the great formalist innovators in twentieth-century music, known for his difficult avant-garde pieces and vast erudition. To choose Boulez to take Wagner's cycle, so filled with noise, fury, and images, and to "accompany" it was, to say the least, hazardous both for the festival and for the conductor. The first performance was very poorly received by the Wagner faithful at Bayreuth; it was greeted with hisses and boos. Five years of annual performances, however, gradually familiarized these faithful to what Boulez was attempting to do. In 1980, when

Foucault witnessed the performance, there was one and one-half hours of applause at the end of the performance and more than one hundred curtain calls.

What had Boulez done? His solution was a *contemporary* solution. It was, Foucault argues, Boulez's depth of knowledge and loyalty to the musical changes of the twentieth century that allowed him to find and give form to a living "meaning to musical drama," not opera, music, or drama alone. What was that meaning? Among the early criticism of Boulez and company's staging and arrangement was the charge that he had merely *accompanied* the drama with Wagner's music. Foucault agreed that that is what Boulez had done. But, he asked, "But one must understand what kind of accompaniment it is a question of."[23] And Foucault provides the elements of how Boulez chose to accompany the work of Chéreau, Peduzzi, and Wagner: "Boulez took seriously the Wagnerian idea of a drama in which music and text do not repeat each other, are not saying each in its own way the same thing; but rather one in which the orchestra, the song, the play of the actors, the tempos of the music, the movements of the scene, the decors must be composed as partial elements so as to constitute, during the time of the performance, a unique form, a singular event."[24] Through rigorous listening and mindfulness of the series of developments of contemporary music from Wagner to us, Wagner becomes "one of our own" (*une part de la notre*).[25]

Conclusion: The Demands of the Day: An Untimely Accompaniment

In anthropology, it ought to be time—although unfortunately it seems not yet to be time—to sacrifice the *individualism* as the subject position that has been at the core of anthropology's approach to research, publication, pedagogy, and, above all, thinking. According to the Microsoft online dictionary, the primary meaning of *sacrifice* is to give up "something valuable or important for somebody for something else considered to be of more value or importance."[1]

The various experiments described in this book have all been, albeit in different ways, attempts to reconfigure, remediate, and reconstruct the forms of the subject position of individualism in anthropology so as to create—or at least show the possibility of—a genre of work that would be collaborative. Whether that change is realizable under present conditions remains uncertain. Regardless, the first step has been to make the effort to identify the problem. The second step has been to experiment with the creation of a venue (or venues) in which that mode of work could be developed and improved. The effort to invent and valorize a form of collaborative sociability that would make the lonely work of inquiry more pleasurable as an experience and richer in its scientific and ethical results is—I am convinced—worthwhile.

Parameters

A parameter is a type of variable, a limiting factor. Although the Microsoft online dictionary emphasizes the restrictive functions of a parameter—"a fact or circumstance that restricts how something is done or what can be done"—one could equally emphasize the productive, form-giving contribution of parameters as an essential part of a design process.[2] Without parameters one does not know whether one is moving in the chosen direction and which signposts to follow in order to get there.

Parameters come in series. The series deployed in the set of experiments described here contains three major parameters (there are other minor ones): *reconfiguration*, *remediation*, and *reconstruction*. I have attempted to work on these as *elements*, both old and new, in such a manner that they could become *objects* of inquiry and practice. Once constituted in that manner, they can serve as the basis for the equipment required to make them available for conceptual work and design. The challenge has been how to make such interdisciplinary conceptual and design work collaborative and not merely cooperative.

To *reconfigure* something does not mean to eliminate or destroy it but rather to shift its elements, those elements' place and function within a figure, and by so doing to alter its meaning. The reasons—scientific, philosophical, associational, ethical, and political—motivating this search have been described on different registers throughout this book.

Reconfiguration in and of itself, however challenging it may be, is by itself insufficient because it might well result in an inferior or deficient state of affairs. Thus, these experiments have been designed and evaluated additionally by the parameter of *remediation*. They have been experimental in a fairly straightforward and not overly literal sense; I have been attempting in a disciplined fashion to make the process of inquiry and reflection work differently and to do so while keeping analytic and existential watch on how the process has variously unfolded: how it has worked and whether it has succeeded or not, being attentive to the why and how. This effort has been recursive to a degree insofar as the attempt has been to integrate lessons learned into the next iteration of the experiment. The work and the goal have sought to be remediative in the double sense of the term: they have been attempts to make something better, to improve it; and they have attempted to do so by introducing a different mix of media than has traditionally been obtained in anthropology.

All of this work of reconfiguration and remediation has been designed as well so as to invent and implement a form of what John Dewey has called *reconstruction*. In that light, reconstruction is another of the *parameters* deployed to organize these disparate efforts into a contemporary genre worth the sacrifice of the comforts of existing practices or the glories of avant-gardism. Dewey's definition of reconstruction is inspiring, if vague: "Reconstruction can be nothing less than the work of developing, of forming, of producing (in the literal sense of the word) the intellectual instrumentalities which will progressively direct inquiry into the deeply and inclusively human—that is to say, moral—facts of the present scene and situation."[3] The *instrumentalities*—or in our technical vocabulary *equipmental components*—of most direct relevance to remediating and reconstructing anthropological inquiry have been *concepts*, *pathways*, *cases*, and *determinations* informed by a *diagnostic analytic*.[4]

Intellectual Sacrifice

To the person who cannot bear the fate of the times like a man, one must say: may he rather return silently, without the usual publicity build-up of renegades, but simply and plainly. The arms of the old churches are open widely and compassionately for him. After all they do not make it hard for him. One way or another he has to bring his "intellectual sacrifice"—that is inevitable.

«MAX WEBER[5]»

The sacrifice that Weber was calling for was less dire than the one Seneca had to face. Weber portrays it, however, with a certain pathos. Almost a century later, one can imagine a synthetic chemist entering St. Thomas Church in Leipzig and being greeted by the sounds of a Bach oratorio; memories of Bach and Buxtehude flood into his mind, as do memories of the carpet bombings in northern Germany during the Second World War, which providentially left most of this church standing although others in the city had been leveled.[6] Later on in the afternoon, back in his office, finishing a grant proposal, our chemist knows how to forget all of that. He is a twenty-first-century man of knowledge; historical amnesia is a skill in which he was well trained and continues to practice daily in his lab as a matter of unexamined and unreflective habit. He is working on Sunday; if his team can finish the grant proposal this week, he says to himself, perhaps he and his partner can go hiking next weekend, or, if not, perhaps they can attend a concert; in either case these leisure-time activities will generate no truth-effects in synthetic chemistry. Weber's acrid affect of loss has long since dissipated into the ether of history.

In that light, by now—in the early years of the twenty-first century and as we near the end of this text—it should be obvious that the contemporary sacrifices talked about here are not to be borne in the name of the religious solace, whose dignity Weber acknowledged to his audience a century ago. Hence, it is worth attempting to clarify in which domain our sacrifices might be found and what they might look like. One can also wonder—for the sake of what should they be undertaken and endured?

Today, the division of value spheres that every major theorist of modernity from Weber to Luhmann has written about for a century now as inevitable and insurmountable is once again becoming an area of renewed problematization. That problematization (if problematization there be) is not taking place within the biosciences—they remain busily and contentedly modern and modernist. As far as they know, the division of value spheres does not present an explicit challenge either for or to their modes of practice and authority—quite the contrary. In the twenty-first century, their modernism is a social, political, and cultural fact, a thing of the world. Its apparatus of genres, forms, practices, and venues is prospering. The situation in the arts is less clear. It is arguable that a problematization of the division of value spheres is not going on (in a pronounced fashion) in many of the humanities, which remain either modernist or postmodernist in their abandonment of grand narratives or in their critical genres. That being said, we saw that when it came to the anxious turbulence over the status and boundaries of contemporary art, it is true that the relationships to other spheres, mainly political until recently, have been a topic of discussion and experiment. Of course, being untimely was the last thing anyone was attempting to achieve.

Even more recently, with the appearance of bio-art, modes of bringing the practices and productions of the biosciences into a different formal setting have become the topic of some experimentation. If one follows the line of argumentation proposed by Yves Michaud, then the art world has dissolved its object into a generalized aesthetization of all things, practices, and styles. This "art in its gaseous state" is a situation with which contemporary artists, critics, and curators must grapple conceptually and even vocationally. Even molecular biology, it seems, can become aestheticized.

In sum, the biosciences have long since sacrificed cultural *meaning* in order to achieve their form of power and knowledge. The plastic arts have sacrificed their *object* in order to enhance and protect the aesthetic over which they have lost control. Whatever the sacrifices demanded of the anthropologist, they are not the same as either that of the synthetic chemist or of the contemporary artist.

In Search of a Metric: Science as a Vocation

If the parameters of the experiments have been reconfiguration, remediation, and reconstruction, the metric guiding them has been flourishing or *eudaimonia*. The term forms part of a long tradition but seeks to transform it, taking ethics to be principally concerned with both inquiry and the care of others, the world, things, and ourselves. Such care is pursued through practices, relationships, and experiences that contribute to and constitute a *flourishing* existence. Understood most broadly, flourishing includes physical and spiritual well-being, courage, dignity, friendship, and justice, although the meaning of each of these terms must be reworked and rethought according to contemporary conditions. The question of what constitutes a flourishing existence, and the place of knowledge-seeking in that form of life, how it contributes to or disrupts it, must be constantly posed and re-posed in such a form that its realization becomes more rather than less likely.

Although the quest has been accepted as both noble and valuable, the effort required to think and inquire is extravagant. Why undertake, after all, all of this grinding labor and this exigent work? It turns out that this question is surprisingly hard to answer. Given that state of affairs, it is perhaps less surprising that few have actually attempted to answer it or to clarify the problem. Among those who have tried are some of those whom I have accompanied in this work.

Although they had no trouble publishing their own books, Michel Foucault, Paul Veyne, and François Weil fought to establish a publishing series of serious work of less celebrated authors that they felt were being squeezed out by commercial pressures and a reigning intellectual orthodoxy in France. The title they gave to the series, when it eventually appeared in 1983, was "Works." What, then, is a work? According to Foucault, "Work [is] that which is susceptible of introducing a significant difference in the field of knowledge, with the price of a certain difficulty for the author and the reader, and with the eventual recompense of a certain pleasure; that is to say access to another figure of truth."[7] To say that work, when it succeeds, gives one access to another figure of truth, and that there is a pleasure in that achievement, is as cogent and pertinent a formulation I know of for the rewards of the required sacrifices. It is also self-evidently the case that few if any of our fellow researchers and creators would frame their work using these terms. It follows that one will have to seek out contemporaries elsewhere, although by now that parameter is not a surprise.

For that pleasure and that figure of truth to be truly worthwhile, however, one certainly would want to add a further dimension, a further questioning of the elements in the series—work, signification, difference, difficulty, pleasure, figure, and truth. Exactly what that further dimension consists in remains surprisingly hard to pin down for thinkers, including those who have been my accompaniment throughout these experiments and experiences. For example, John Dewey's metric is the "deeply and inclusively human," but what that means and how to know the "deeply and inclusively human" when one arrives at it remains elusive. Dewey certainly did not hold that there was an essence or nature of the human ready to be uncovered or actualized, but what such an arrival would look like, assuming that is even possible to envision, remains opaque.

Max Weber ends his "Science as a Vocation" by evoking as his metric the Socratic god, whose divine whispering led Socrates to his search for virtue through questioning of those who claimed to know or to be qualified to lead others and equally led him to his death at the hands of his fellow citizens. Weber's closing peroration is as follows: "We shall set to work and meet 'the demands of the day' in human relations as well as in our vocation. This, however, is plain and simple, if each finds and obeys the daimon who holds the fiber of his very life."[8]

Although this defiance is impressive, it was Weber himself, after all, who demonstrated the profound irrationality of the calling to work and the utter bleakness of the methodical way of life, especially once its original theological underpinnings had long since faded away. Not surprisingly, Weber mentions neither a recompense of pleasure nor access to a new figure of truth, although he clearly valorizes the difficulties and strains required to find and obey one's own way.

Thus, these companions offer three candidates for the metric of knowledge seekers: a new figure of truth; the deeply and inclusively human; and finding and obeying the daimon who holds the fiber of one's very life. Doubts remain, however: What if this daimon is at war with the goddess Eudaimonia? What if methodical labor is simply grinding oneself and others down into a state of brutalization recompensed only by leisure and consumerist activity? What if there is no deeply and inclusively human that is linked to inquiry and logic in any essential way?

In this light, and with humility before my teachers, the only proposal I can make is to work through these doubts and uncertainties—*durcharbeiten*—as best as one can, with care and rigor, along with those others one can find to accompany one in this work, whether they be living, dead, or not yet born.

Notes

INTRODUCTION

1. Bertolt Brecht, *Stories of Mr. Keuner* (San Francisco: City Lights Books, 2001), 25.

2. Ibid., 5.

3. Martin Chalmers, "Mr. Keuner—and Mr. Brecht; or Etiquette in Dark Times," in *Stories of Mr. Keuner*, 101.

4. Hannah Arendt, "Bertolt Brecht," in *Men in Dark Times* (New York: Harcourt, Brace and World, 1968), 246. The Brecht essay appeared in the *New Yorker* in the November 5, 1966, issue.

5. Frederick Nietzsche, *On the Genealogy of Morals*, in *Basic Writings of Nietzsche*, ed. Walter Kaufmann (New York: Random House, 1968), 451.

PART ONE: MEN OF KNOWLEDGE IN SEARCH OF REDEMPTION OR SALVATION

1. Clifford Geertz, *The Interpretation of Cultures* (New York: Basic Books, 1973), ix.

2. Michel Foucault, *The Hermeneutics of the Subject: Lectures at the Collège de France, 1981–1982*, trans. Graham Burchell (New York: Palgrave Macmillan, 2005), 185.

3. *Wikipedia*, s.v. "Redemption," http://en.wikipedia.org/wiki/Redemption.

4. Michel Foucault, "Politics and Ethics: An Interview," in *The Foucault Reader*, ed. Paul Rabinow (New York: Pantheon Books, 1984), 375.

5. Michel Foucault, "Friendship as a Way of Life," in *The Essential Works of Foucault, 1954–1984*, vol. 1, *Ethics: Subjectivity and Truth*. ed. Paul Rabinow (New York: New Press, 1997), 137–38.

6. Hervé Guibert, *À l'ami qui ne m'a pas sauvé la vie* (Paris: Éditions Gallimard, 1990).

7. René de Ceccatty, *L'accompagnement* (Paris: Éditions Gallimard, 1994), 11.

CHAPTER ONE

1. Walter Benjamin, *Theses on the Philosophy of History*, http://www.efn.org/~dredmond/Theses_on_History.html, 7.

2. Martin Heidegger, "The Word of Nietzsche: God Is Dead," in *The Question concerning Technology and Other Essays*, trans. William Lovitt (New York: Harper and Row, 1977), 63.

3. George Stocking, *Race, Culture and Evolution* (New York: Free Press, 1968), 229.

4. George Stocking, *The Shaping of American Anthropology 1883–1911: A Franz Boas Reader* (New York: Basic Books, 1974), 4.

5. Ibid., 5.

6. Ibid., 6.

7. Melville Herskovits, *Man and His Works* (New York: Alfred Knopf, 1947).

8. Ibid., 61.

9. Ibid., 63.

10. Ibid., 66.

11. Ibid., 68.

12. Ibid., 76.

13. Ibid.

14. Ibid., 73.

15. Alfred Kroeber and Clyde Kluckhohn, "Culture: A Critical Review of Concepts and Definitions," *Papers of the Peabody Museum of American Anthropology and Ethnology* 47, no. 1 (1953).

16. Geertz, *Interpretation of Cultures*, 82–83.

17. Ibid., 68.

18. Ibid., 38.

19. Ibid., 39–40.

20. Ibid., 91.

21. Ibid., 92.

22. Ibid., 93–94.

23. Michel Foucault, *The Order of Things: An Archaeology of the Human Sciences* (New York: Vintage Books, 1994), 321.

24. Geertz, *Interpretation of Cultures*, 44.

25. Foucault, *Order of Things*, 321.

26. Geertz, *Interpretation of Cultures*, 15.

27. Ibid., 16.

28. Ibid., 24.

29. Ibid., 30.

30. Clifford Geertz, preface to *Language and Art in the Navajo Universe*, by Gary Witherspoon (Ann Arbor: University of Michigan Press, 1977), vii.

31. Ibid., x.

32. Ibid.

33. Geertz, *Interpretation of Cultures*, 364.

34. George Stocking, "Anthropology as *Kulturkampf*: Science and Politics in the Career of Franz Boas," in *The Uses of Anthropology*, ed. Walter Goldschmidt (Arlington, VA: American Anthropology Association, 1979), 37.

35. Geertz, *Interpretation of Cultures*, ix.

36. Ibid., 30.

37. Michel Foucault, "Truth and Power," in *Power/Knowledge: Selected Interviews and Other Writings, 1972–1977* (New York: Pantheon Books, 1981), 128.

38. Michel Foucault, *The History of Sexuality* (New York: Pantheon Books, 1978), 6.

39. Ibid., 7.

40. Foucault, "Truth and Power," 127.

41. Ibid.

42. Ibid., 129.

CHAPTER TWO

1. René Char, *Selected Poems*, edited by Mary Ann Caws and Tina Jolas (New York: New Directions Books, 1992), xvii.

2. Susan Slyomovics, *The Performance of Human Rights in Morocco* (Bloomington: Indiana University Press, 2005).

3. Jean Duvignaud, *Change at Shebika: Report from a North African Village* (New York: Pantheon Books, 1970).

4. Geertz made the Moroccan word *nisba* the centerpiece of his long article on the market and the key to Moroccan identity. Clifford Geertz, "Suq: The Bazaar Economy in Sefrou," in *Meaning and Order in Morocco: Three Essays in Cultural Analysis*, by Clifford Geertz, Hildred Geertz, and Lawrence Rosen (Cambridge: Cambridge University Press, 1979), 142–50. The publisher has not supplied the cover image on the Amazon Web page.

5. The expression is a mix of Moroccan and French argot: "Big men are never at ease." On exchange: Pierre Bourdieu, *Esquisse d'une théorie de la pratique précédés de trois études d'ethnologie Kabyle* (Geneva: Librairie Droz, 1975), translated as *Outline of a Theory of Practice* (Cambridge: Cambridge University Press, 1977).

6. Roland Barthes, *Camera Lucida: Reflections on Photography*, trans. Richard Howard (New York: Hill and Wang, 1981), 74; Roland Barthes, *La Chambre Claire, notes sur la photographie* (Paris: Cahiers du Cinéma, Éditions Gallimard et Seuil, 1980), 115.

7. Roland Barthes, *Mythologies* (Paris: Éditions du Seuil, 1957), translated as *Mythologies* (New York: Hill and Wang, 1972).

8. Barthes, *Camera*, 78; Barthes, *La Chambre*, 122.

9. Barthes, *Camera*, 12; Barthes, *La Chambre*, 176.

10. Barthes, *Camera*, 11; Barthes, *La Chambre*, 50.

11. Barthes, *La Chambre*, 48.

12. Pierre Bourdieu, *Un Art moyen* (Paris: Les Éditions du Minuit, 1965), translated as *Photography: A Middle Brow Art* (Cambridge: Polity Press, 1990).

13. Barthes, *Camera*, 27.

CHAPTER THREE

1. Foucault, *Hermeneutics of the Subject*, 15.

2. Thanks to James Redfield for his precision on the German meanings of this term as well as for his overall reading of the text. The term "remediation" follows the general sense of the term, for example, as discussed in Jean Starobinski's *Le remède est dans le mal* (Paris: Gallimard, 1989).

3. Friedrich Nietzsche, "On the Uses and Disadvantages of History for Life," in *Untimely Meditations*, trans. R. J. Hollingdale (Cambridge: Cambridge University Press, 1983), 59.

4. Gilles Deleuze, "Contrôle et devenir," *Pourparlers* (Paris: Les Éditions de Minuit, 1997), 231.

5. Ibid.

6. Foucault provides a partial genealogy of this "*surplomb*" as the act of looking down on one's own life in order to judge it rather than in order to demonstrate the inadequacy of others' self-understanding. See Foucault, *Hermeneutics of the Subject*, 281–83.

7. Michel Foucault, *Remarks on Marx: Conversations with Duccio Trombadori*, trans. James Goldstein and James Cascaito (New York: Semiotexte, 1991), 29.

8. Michel Foucault, "La poussière et le nuage" (1980) in *Dits et écrits* (hereafter referred to as *DE*) (Paris: Gallimard, 1994), 4:10–19.

9. Ibid., 15.

10. Hans Blumenberg, *The Legitimacy of the Modern Age* (Cambridge, MA: MIT Press. 1983).

11. Foucault, "Table Ronde du 20 Mai 1978" (pub. 1980), *DE* 4:22.

12. Ibid.

13. Ibid., 33.

14. Michel Foucault, "Est-il donc important de penser?" (interview with D. Eribon, *Liberation* 15 [May 1981]: 21), *DE* 4:181.

15. Ibid., 180.

16. Foucault, *DE* 4:691.

17. Michel Foucault, *Society Must Be Defended: Lectures at the College de France 1975–76*, trans. David Macey (New York: Picador), 1.

18. Ibid.

19. Ibid., 2.

20. Ibid.

21. Ibid.

22. Ibid., 3.

23. Marielle Macé, *Le Temps de l'Essai: Histoire d'un genre en France au XX siècle* (Paris: Éditions Belin, 2006).

24. Didier Eribon, *Michel Foucault* (Paris: Editions Flammarion, 1989), 310–11.

25. Daniel Defert, personal communication.

26. Eribon, *Michel Foucault*, 309.

27. Arpad Szakolczai, *Max Weber and Michel Foucault: Parallel Life-Works* (London: Routledge, 1998), chap. 9.

28. Eribon, *Foucault*, 336.

29. Ibid., 338.

30. Foucault, *Hermeneutics of the Subject*, 15.

31. The term comes up first as a problem to reflect on, as a possible concept whose genealogy would be worth exploring, in relation to Foucault's journalistic foray in Iran.

32. A detailed account, both personal and conceptual of this period, can be found in Szakolczai, *Max Weber and Michel Foucault*, esp. chap. 10.

33. Hypothesis: in logic, the antecedent of a conditional statement.

34. Foucault, *Hermeneutics of the Subject*, 15.

35. Ibid., 16.

36. Ibid., 192.

37. Ibid., 183.

38. Ibid., 182.

39. Ibid.

40. Ibid., 183.

41. Michel Foucault, "Course Summary, 1981–82," in *Hermeneutics of the Subject*, 505.

42. Frédéric Gros, afterword to *Hermeneutics of the Subject*, 507–10.

43. Foucault, *Hermeneutics of the Subject*, 184.

44. Ibid., 185.

CHAPTER FOUR

1. Frédéric Gros, "La parrhesia chex Foucault (1982–1984)," in *Foucault: le courage de la vérité*, ed. Frédéric Gros (Paris: PUF, 2002).

2. Thanks to Gaymon Bennett, Tobias Rees, Stephen Collier, Colin Koopman, Marilyn Seid, and Arpad Szakolczai for their comments and aid.

3. Gros, "La parrhesia chex Foucault (1982–1984)," 166.

4. Michel Foucault, "Le philosophe masqué," *DE*, vol. 4.

5. Michel Foucault, "Entretiens avec Michel Foucault" [Interviews with Michel Foucault], *DE* 4:84.

6. For an excellent and, to me, convincing development of these themes, see Mathieu Potte-Bonneville, *Michel Foucault: l'inquiétude de l'histoire* (Paris: Presses Universitaire de France, 2004).

7. For the troubles and limits of the venue, see Paul Rabinow, "Foucault's Untimely Struggle," *Theory, Culture and Society* 26, no. 6 (2009): 25–44.

8. Michel Foucault, *Foucault Live* (New York: Semiotext[e], 1989), 305.

9. Michel Foucault, *Le Gouvernement de soi et des autres, 1982–83* (Paris: Gallimard, 2008), 5.

10. Foucault discusses equipment, *paraskeuê*, at length in the 1981–82 lectures; see Foucault, *Hermeneutics of the Subject.*

11. Ibid., 5.

12. Ibid., 6.

13. Ibid., 5.

14. Ibid.

15. Michel Foucault, *La Courage de la vérité* (Paris: Seuil, 2009), 4.

16. Foucault, *Le Gouvernement de soi et des autres*, 5.

17. Foucault, *Courage*, 8.

18. In *The Order of Things* he began with the Renaissance.

19. Szakolczai, *Max Weber and Michael Foucault*, 58.

20. Foucault, *DE* 4:670.

21. Ibid., 598.

22. Foucault, *Remarks on Marx.*

23. Ibid., 42.

24. Ibid., 27.

25. Michel Foucault, "L'Intellectuel," *DE* 4:598.

26. Ibid., 749.

27. See the back cover of Foucault's *History of Sexuality*, vols. 2 and 3.

28. Foucault, "L'Intellectuel," 749.

29. Foucault, *Le Gouvernement de soi et des autres*, 322.

30. Ibid., 220.

31. Ibid., 286.

32. Ibid., 135.

33. Ibid., 326.

34. Nietzsche, *On the Genealogy of Morals,* 597.

PART TWO: IN SEARCH OF A CONTEMPORARY ANTHROPOLOGY

1. Roland Barthes and Richard Howard, *The Rustle of Language* (New York: Farrar, Straus and Giroux, 1987), 367.

2. Cited in Giorgio Agamben, *What Is Contemporary?* trans. Maxime Rovere (Paris: Rivages Poche, 2008), 8.

3. Geoffrey Harpham, *Shadows of Ethics* (Durham, NC: Duke University Press, 1999), 26.

4. The best example of this approach is James Faubion, *Foucault in Athens: Toward an Anthropology of Ethics* (Cambridge: Cambridge University Press, 2011).

5. Harpham, *Shadows*, 37.

6. Ibid., 39.

7. Pierre Bourdieu, *Outline of a Theory of Practice,* trans. Richard Nice (Cambridge: Cambridge University Press, 1977).

8. John Dewey, *Essays in Experimental Logic,* ed. D. Micah Hester and Robert B. Talisse (Carbondale: Southern Illinois University Press, 2007), 36.

9. Paul Rabinow, *Making PCR: A Story of Biotechnology* (Chicago: University of Chicago Press, 1997); Paul Rabinow, *French DNA: Trouble in Purgatory* (Chicago: University of Chicago Press, 2002); Paul Rabinow and Talia Dan-Cohen, *A Machine to Make a Future: Biotech Chronicles* (Princeton, NJ: Princeton University Press, 2004).

10. Paul Rabinow and Gaymon Bennett, *Designing for Human Practices: An Experiment with Synthetic Biology* (Chicago: University of Chicago Press, forthcoming).

11. Paul Rabinow et al., *Designs for an Anthropology of the Contemporary* (Durham, NC: Duke University Press, 2008).

12. Gerhard Richter, letter to Jean-Christophe Ammann, February 1973, in *The Daily Practice of Painting,* ed. Hans-Ulrich Obrist, trans. David Brittt (London: Thames and Hudson, 1995), 81.

CHAPTER FIVE

1. Tom Burke, *Dewey's New Logic: A Reply to Russell* (Chicago: University of Chicago Press, 1998), 157.

2. On the "social," see Jacques Donzelot, *The Policing of Families,* trans. Robert Hurley (New York: Pantheon Books, 1979); Paul Rabinow, *French Modern: Norms and Forms of the Social Environment* (Chicago: University of Chicago Press, 1989).

3. Rebecca Lemov, *World as Laboratory: Experiments with Mice, Mazes, and Men* (New York: Hill and Wang, 2005); Luke Lassiter, *The Chicago Guide to Collaborative Ethnography* (Chicago: University of Chicago Press, 2005).

4. Max Weber, "Objectivity in Social Science and Social Policy," in *The Methodology of the Social Sciences* (New York: Free Press, 1949), 50.

5. Susan Sontag, "Anthropologist as Hero," in *Against Interpretation and Other Essays* (New York: Picador, 1966).

6. Rabinow et al., *Designs for an Anthropology of the Contemporary.*

7. Reinhart Koselleck, *Futures Past: On the Semantics of Historical Time,* trans. Keith Tribe (New York: Columbia University Press, 2004); Ian Hacking, *The Social Construction of What?* (Cambridge, MA: Har-

vard University Press, 1999); Steven Shapin, *A Social History of Truth: Civility and Science in Seventeenth-Century England* (Chicago: University of Chicago Press, 1994); Peter Galison, *The Disunity of the Sciences: Boundaries, Contexts, and Power* (Palo Alto, CA: Stanford University Press, 1996); Georges Canguilhem, *Knowledge of Life*, trans. Stefano Geroulanos and Daniela Ginsburg (New York: Fordham University Press, 2008); Gaston Bachelard, *The New Scientific Spirit*, trans. Arthur Goldhammer (Boston: Beacon Press, 1984).

8. On these terms, see www.bios-technika.net.

9. Hans Wingler, *The Bauhaus: Weimar, Dassau, Berlin, Chicago*, 2nd ed. (Cambridge, MA: MIT Press, 1976); T. J. Clark, *Farewell to an Idea: Episodes from a History of Modernism* (New Haven, CT: Yale University Press, 1999).

10. Gilles Deleuze and Felix Guattari, *What Is Philosophy?* trans. Hugh Tomlinson and Graham Burchell (New York: Columbia University Press, 1994), 12.

11. "L'Abécédaire de Gilles Deleuze," http://en.wikipedia.org/wiki/Gilles_Deleuze.

12. Deleuze and Guattari, *What Is Philosophy*, 10. (Translation was modified.)

13. John Dewey, "The Control of Ideas by Facts," in *Essays in Experimental Logic* (Mineola, NY: Dover Publications, 2004).

14. For a full systematic formal theory of these elements, see Manuel DeLanda, *Intensive Science and Virtual Philosophy* (London: Continuum Books, 2002).

15. Hacking, *Social Construction of What*.

16. A classic, if idiosyncratic, presentation of the Western tradition is Martin Heidegger's *What Is a Thing?* (Washington, DC: Gateway Editions, 1968).

17. Manuel DeLanda, *A New Philosophy of Society: Assemblage Theory and Social Complexity* (New York: Continuum Books, 2006), 10.

18. Ibid., 11.

19. Ibid.

20. For a discussion of Deleuze's technical vocabulary, see DeLanda, *Intensive Science*, 15–16.

21. The domain of those capacities is the virtual.

22. John Dewey, *The Essential Dewey: Ethics, Logic, Psychology*, ed. Larry Hickman and Thomas M. Alexander (Bloomington: Indiana University Press, 1998), 178.

CHAPTER SIX

1. More detail can be found Rabinow, *French Modern*, chap. 1.

2. Steven Shapin, personal communication.

3. The term "interpretive analytics" was coined by Hubert L. Dreyfus and Paul Rabinow in their book *Michel Foucault: Beyond Structuralism and Hermeneutics* (Chicago: University of Chicago Press, 1982). Although it has gained no currency, it still seems like the most accurate term. If one does not believe the object is the "social" or "society," then it is hard to see how the "social sciences" can be the correct name of the activity under consideration. If one of the primary objects being problematized is "the human," then it is hard to see how the "human sciences" can be appropriate. Discussions on the vagaries of the term "science" have encumbered more than three centuries of thought. The other alternative is "anthropology." Not all objects and concepts of interpretive analytics, however, are directly *anthropos* centered.

4. Coined by student Adrian McIntyre

5. Michel Foucault, *The Essential Foucault*, ed. Paul Rabinow and Nikolas Rose (New York: New Press, 2003), 23.

6. See http://anthropos-lab.net/.

7. *MSN Encarta*, s.v. "Ramification," http://encarta.msn.com/encnet/features/dictionary/DictionaryResults.aspx?lextype=3&search=Ramification.

8. DeLanda, *New Philosophy of Society*, 11.

CHAPTER SEVEN

1. John Dewey, *The Middle Works, 1899–1924*, ed. Jo Ann Boydston (Carbondale: Southern Illinois University Press, 1980), 326.

2. Dewey, *Essays in Experimental Logic*, 8.

3. Thanks go to Gaymon Bennett, James Faubion, Christopher Kelty, Michael Meranze, Stephen Collier, and Marilyn Rabinow. For the background, see www.anthropos-lab.net "documents" and "On the Assembly of Things."

4. Rabinow and Dan-Cohen, *Machine to Make a Future*.

5. Berkeley Human Practices Laboratory, www.synberc.org.

6. Rabinow, *French DNA*.

7. Rabinow, *French Modern*.

8. Albert Hirschman, *Exit, Voice, and Loyalty: Responses to Decline in Firms, Organizations, and States* (Cambridge, MA: Harvard University Press, 1970).

9. Pierre Bourdieu, *Homo academicus* (Paris: Les Editions de Minuit, 1984); Luc Boltanski and Eve Chiapello, *Le Nouvel esprit du capitalisme* (Paris: Editions Gallimard, 1999).

10. Sydney Brenner, "Genomics: The End of the Beginning," *Science* 24 (March 2000): 2173.

11. See Paul Rabinow, *Reflections on Fieldwork in Morocco* (Berkeley and Los Angeles: University of California Press, 2007); Paul Rabinow, *Symbolic Domination: Cultural Form and Historical Change in Morocco* (Chicago: University of Chicago Press, 1974).

12. Niklas Luhmann, "Familiarity, Confidence, Trust: Problems and Alternatives," in *Trust: Making and Breaking Cooperative Relations*, ed. Diego Gambetta (New York: Blackwell, 1988). Luhmann identifies symbols performing these functions as religious or at least having had a religious origin; he seems to flirt with a functionalist evolutionary approach in which religion is historically paramount and temporally prior. In humanity's early days, the symbolic work of making a dangerous, largely unknown, and uncontrollable universe familiar was handled through the magic of symbols. At times, Luhmann seems to back away from such an epochal or evolutionary approach. Slightly later, however, he returns to the epochal framing, arguing that in "modernity" technology has functionally replaced religion. As I have argued elsewhere, Luhmann's Germanic epochal thinking, if taken literally, undermines his systems approach, turning it into a realist sociology, a position Luhmann at times distances himself from, turning it into one way of giving form.

13. Max Weber, "Science as a Vocation," in *From Max Weber: Essays in Sociology*, ed. Hans Gerth and C. Wright Mills (New York: Oxford University Press, 1946), 139.

14. Luhmann, "Familiarity, Confidence, Trust," 3.

15. Ibid., 5.

16. Ibid., 4.

17. John Dewey, *Reconstruction in Philosophy* (Boston: Beacon Press, 1948), xxvii.

18. Ibid., xxxvii–xxxviii.

CHAPTER EIGHT

1. Weber, "Science as a Vocation," 143.

2. The "last man" is sketched by Nietzsche in *Thus Spake Zarathustra* (Cambridge: Cambridge University Press, 2006), pt. 1, no. 5, 9–10.

3. Weber, "Science as a Vocation," 143.

4. For example, Theodor Adorno et al., *The Positivist Dispute in German Sociology*, trans. Glyn Adey and David Frisby (New York: Harper and Row, 1976).

5. Gyorgy Markus, "Why Is There No Hermeneutics of the Natural Sciences?" *Science in Context* 1, no. 1 (March 1987): 5–51.

6. An attempt I undertook to situate the obligatory modernist irony of much of science studies writing as a genre, especially to pursue a countertrope to irony, never developed to the point of publication.

7. Markus, "Why Is There No Hermeneutics," 27.

8. Shapin, *Social History of Truth*.

9. See: Paul Rabinow and Nikolas Rose, "Biopower Today," *Biosocieties* 1, no. 2 (2006): 195–217.

10. Weber, "Science as a Vocation," 156.

11. Markus, "Why Is There No Hermeneutics," 13.

12. Ibid., 24.

13. Ibid., 20.

14. Ibid., 15.

15. There is a vast literature on modernism in the arts. Of the many important books, one of particular interest is T. J. Clark's *Farewell to an Idea: Episodes from a History of Modernism* (New Haven, CT: Yale University Press, 1999).

16. Steven Shapin, *The Scientific Life: A Moral History of a Late Modern Vocation* (Chicago: University of Chicago Press, 2008). Shapin has noted how small these research communities were and continue to be numerically, a key fact in the establishment of familiarity, trust, and confidence. These paraveridictional practices supplement and to a degree underpin the genre of the writing that authorizes modern science. One finds here one of the micropractices, beyond the discursive, that an anthropologist has access to in a way that the practitioners of discursive analysis alone lack the tools to observe.

CHAPTER NINE

1. Weber, *Methodology of the Social Sciences*, 68.

2. Agamben, *What Is Contemporary*, 7.

3. Roland Barthes, *The Preparation of the Novel: Lecture Courses and Seminars at the Collège de France, 1978–1979 and 1979–1980* (New York: Columbia University Press, 2010), 408.

4. Agamben, *What Is Contemporary*, 19.

5. Ibid., 32–33.

6. Ibid., 32.

7. Ibid., 38.

8. Hal Foster, "Questionnaire on 'The Contemporary,'" *October* (Fall 2009): 3.

9. Helen Molesworth, response, *October* (Fall 2009): 112.

10. Ibid., 113.

11. Johanna Burton, response, *October* (Fall 2009): 22.

12. Alexander Alberro, response, *October* (Fall 2009): 57.

13. Vered Maimon, response, *October* (Fall 2009): 76.

14. Miwon Kwon, response, *October* (Fall 2009): 14.

15. Yves Michaud, *L'Art à l'état gazeux: Essai sur le triomphe de l'esthétique* (Paris: Editions Stock, 2003).

16. Another approach to these changes is Clark's *Farewell to an Idea*.

17. Michaud, *L'Art à l'état gazeux*, 14.

18. Ibid., 53.

19. Burton, response, 24.

20. Michel Foucault, "L'imagination du XIXe siècle," *DE* 4:112. This was originally a piece in the September 30, 1980, edition of *Corriere della sere*.

21. Ibid.

22. Ibid., 114.

23. Ibid., 112.

24. Ibid., 113.

25. Ibid., 115.

CONCLUSION

1. *MSN Encarta*, s.v. "Sacrifice," http://encarta.msn.com/encnet/features/dictionary/DictionaryResults.aspx?lextype=3&search=sacrifice.

2. Ibid., s.v. "Parameter," http://encarta.msn.com/encnet/features/dictionary/DictionaryResults.aspx?lextype=3&search=parameter.

3. Dewey, *Reconstruction in Philosophy*, xvii.

4. The full version of these terms can be found at www.bios-technika.net.

5. Weber, "Science as a Vocation," 156.

6. See W. G. Sebald, *On the Natural History of Destruction,* trans. Anthea Bell (New York: Random House, 2003).

7. Michel Foucault, "Des Travaux," *DE* 4:366.

8. Weber, "Science as a Vocation," 156.

Bibliography

Adorno, Theodor, et al. *The Positivist Dispute in German Sociology.* Translated by Glyn Adey and David Frisby. New York: Harper and Row, 1976.

Agamben, Giorgio. *What Is Contemporary?* Translated by Maxime Rovere. Paris: Rivages Poche, 2008.

Arendt, Hannah. "Bertolt Brecht." In *Men in Dark Times.* New York: Harcourt, Brace and World, 1968.

Bachelard, Gaston. *The New Scientific Spirit.* Translated by Arthur Goldhammer. Boston: Beacon Press, 1984.

Barthes, Roland. *Camera Lucida: Reflections on Photography.* Translated by Richard Howard. New York: Hill and Wang, 1981.

———. *La Chambre Claire, notes sur la photographie.* Paris: Cahiers du Cinéma, Éditions Gallimard et Seuil, 1980.

———. *Mythologies.* Paris: Éditions du Seuil, 1957. Translated as *Mythologies* (New York: Hill and Wang, 1972).

———. *The Preparation of the Novel: Lecture Courses at the Collège de France, 1978–1979 and 1979–1980.* New York: Columbia University Press, 2010.

Barthes, Roland, and Richard Howard. *The Rustle of Language.* New York: Farrar, Straus and Giroux, 1987.

Benjamin, Walter. *Theses on the Philosophy of History.* http://www.efn .org/~dredmond/Theses_on_History.html.

Blumenberg, Hans. *The Legitimacy of the Modern Age.* Cambridge, MA: MIT Press, 1983.

Boltanski, Luc, and Eve Chiapello. *Le Nouvel espirit du capitalisme.* Paris: Editions Gallimard, 1999.

Bourdieu, Pierre. *Esquisse d'une théorie de la pratique précédés de trois études d'ethnologie Kabyle* (Geneva: Librairie Droz, 1975). Translated as *Outline of a Theory of Practice* (Cambridge: Cambridge University Press, 1977).

———. *Homo academicus.* Paris: Les Editions de Minuit, 1984.

———. *Meditations Pasclaiennes.* Paris: Editions du Seuil, 1997.

———. *Outline of a Theory of Practice.* Translated by Richard Nice. Cambridge: Cambridge University Press, 1977.

———. *Un Art Moyen* (Paris: Les Éditions du Minuit, 1965). Translated as *Photography: A Middle Brow Art* (Cambridge: Polity Press, 1990).

Brecht, Bertolt. *Stories of Mr. Keuner.* San Francisco: City Lights Books, 2001.

Brenner, Sydney. "Genomics: The End of the Beginning." *Science* 24 (March 2000).

Burke, Tom. *Dewey's New Logic: A Reply to Russell.* Chicago: University of Chicago Press, 1998.

Canguilhem, Georges. *Knowledge of Life.* Translated by Stefano Geroulanos and Daniela Ginsburg. New York: Fordham University Press, 2008.

Ceccatty, René de. *L'accompagnement.* Paris: Éditions Gallimard, 1994.

Chalmers, Martin. Afterword. *Stories of Mr. Keuner*, by Bertolt Brecht. San Francisco: City Lights Books, 2001.

Char, René. *Selected Poems.* Edited by Mary Ann Caws and Tina Jolas. New York: New Directions Books, 1992.

Clark, T. J. *Farewell to an Idea: Episodes from a History of Modernism.* New Haven, CT: Yale University Press, 1999.

DeLanda, Manuel. *Intensive Science and Virtual Philosophy.* London: Continuum Books, 2002.

———. *A New Philosophy of Society: Assemblage Theory and Social Complexity.* New York: Continuum Books, 2006.

Deleuze, Gilles. "Contrôle et devenir." In *Pourparlers.* Paris: Les Editions de Minuit, 1997.

Deleuze, Gilles, and Felix Guattari. *What Is Philosophy?* Translated by Hugh Tomlinson and Graham Burchell. New York: Columbia University Press, 1994.

Dewey, John. *Essays in Experimental Logic*. Mineola, NY: Dover Publications, 2004.

———. *The Essential Dewey: Ethics, Logic, Psychology*. Edited by Larry Hickman and Thomas M. Alexander. Bloomington: Indiana University Press, 1998.

———. *The Middle Works, 1899–1924*. Edited by Jo Ann Boydston. Carbondale: Southern Illinois University Press, 1980.

———. *Reconstruction in Philosophy*. Boston: Beacon Press, 1948.

Donzelot, Jacques. *The Policing of Families*. Translated by Robert Hurley. New York: Pantheon Books, 1979.

Duvignaud, Jean. *Change at Shebika: Report from a North African Village*. New York: Pantheon Books, 1970.

Dreyfus, Hubert L., and Paul Rabinow. *Michel Foucault: Beyond Structuralism and Hermeneutics*. Chicago: University of Chicago Press, 1982.

Eribon, Didier. *Michel Foucault*. Paris: Editions Flammarion, 1989.

Faubion, James. *Foucault in Athens: Toward an Anthropology of Ethics*. Cambridge: Cambridge University Press, 2011.

Foster, Hal. "Questionnaire on 'The Contemporary.'" *October* (Fall 2009).

Foucault, Michel. "Des Travaux." *Dits et écrits*. Vol. 4. Paris: Gallimard, 1994.

———. "Entretiens avec Michel Foucault." *Dits et écrits*. Vol. 4. Paris: Gallimard, 1994.

———. *The Essential Foucault*. Edited by Paul Rabinow and Nikolas Rose. New York: New Press, 2003.

———. "Est-il donc important de penser?" Interview with D. Eribon. *Liberation* 15 (May 1981): 21. *Dits et écrits*. Vol. 4. Paris: Gallimard, 1994.

———. *Foucault Live*. New York: Semiotext(e), 1989.

———. "Friendship as a Way of Life." In *The Essential Works of Foucault, 1954–1984*. Vol. 1, *Ethics: Subjectivity and Truth*. Edited by Paul Rabinow. New York: New Press, 1997.

———. *The Hermeneutics of the Subject: Lectures at the Collège de France, 1981–1982*. Translated by Graham Burchell. New York: Palgrave Macmillan, 2005.

———. *The History of Sexuality*. New York: Pantheon Books, 1978.

———. "La poussière et le nuage." In *Dits et écrits*. Vol. 4. Paris: Gallimard, 1994.

————. *Le Courage de la vérité.* Paris: Seuil, 2009.

————. *Le Gouvernement de soi et des autres, 1982–83.* Paris: Gallimard, 2008.

————. "Le philosophe masqué." *Dits et écrits.* Vol. 4. Paris: Gallimard, 1994.

————. "L'imagination du XIXᵉ siècle." *Dits et écrits.* Vol. 4. Paris: Gallimard, 1994.

————. "L'Intellectuel." *Dits et écrits.* Vol. 4. Paris: Gallimard, 1994.

————. "Table Ronde du 20 Mai 1978." *Dits et écrits.* Vol. 4. Paris: Gallimard, 1994.

————. *The Order of Things: An Archaeology of the Human Sciences.* New York: Vintage Books, 1994.

————. "Politics and Ethics: An Interview." In *The Foucault Reader.* Edited by Paul Rabinow. New York: Pantheon Books, 1984.

————. *Remarks on Marx: Conversations with Duccio Trombadori.* Translated by James Goldstein and James Cascaito. New York: Semiotext(e), 1991.

————. *Society Must Be Defended: Lectures at the College de France, 1975–76.* Translated by David Macey. New York: Picador, 2003.

————. "Truth and Power." In *Power/Knowledge: Selected Interviews and Other Writings, 1972-1977.* New York: Pantheon Books, 1981.

————. "What Is Enlightenment?" In *The Foucault Reader.* Edited by Paul Rabinow. New York: Pantheon Books, 1984.

Galison, Peter. *The Disunity of the Sciences: Boundaries, Contexts, and Power.* Palo Alto, CA: Stanford University Press, 1996.

Geertz, Clifford. *The Interpretation of Cultures.* New York: Basic Books, 1973.

————. Preface. *Language and Art in the Navajo Universe*, by Gary Witherspoon. Ann Arbor: University of Michigan Press, 1977.

————. "Suq; The Bazaar Economy in Sefrou." In *Meaning and Order in Morocco: Three Essays in Cultural Analysis*, by Clifford Geertz, Hildred Geertz, and Lawrence Rosen. Cambridge: Cambridge University Press, 1979.

Gros, Frédéric. "La parrhesia chex Foucault (1982–1984)." In *Foucault: le courage de la vérité.* Edited by Frédéric Gros. Paris: PUF, 2002.

Guibert, Hervé. *À l'ami qui ne m'a pas sauvé la vie.* Paris: Éditions Gallimard, 1990.

Hacking, Ian. *The Social Construction of What?* Cambridge, MA: Harvard University Press, 1999.

Harpham, Geoffrey. *Shadows of Ethics.* Durham, NC: Duke University Press, 1999.

Heidegger, Martin. *What Is a Thing?* Washington, DC: Gateway Editions, 1968.

———. The Word of Nietzsche: God Is Dead." In *The Question concerning Technology and Other Essays.* Translated by William Lovitt. New York: Harper and Row, 1977.

Herskovits, Melville. *Cultural Anthropology.* New York: Random House, 1955.

———. *Man and His Works.* New York: Alfred Knopf, 1947.

Hirschman, Albert. *Exit, Voice, and Loyalty: Responses to Decline in Firms, Organizations, and States.* Cambridge, MA: Harvard University Press, 1970.

Koselleck, Reinhart. *Futures Past: On the Semantics of Historical Time.* Translated by Keith Tribe. New York: Columbia University Press, 2004.

Kroeber, Alfred, and Clyde Kluckhohn. "Culture: A Critical Review of Concepts and Definitions." *Papers of the Peabody Museum of American Anthropology and Ethnology* 47, no. 1 (1953).

Lassiter, Luke. *The Chicago Guide to Collaborative Ethnography.* Chicago: University of Chicago Press, 2005.

Lemov, Rebecca. *World as Laboratory: Experiments with Mice, Mazes, and Men.* New York: Hill and Wang, 2005.

Luhmann, Niklas. "Familiarity, Confidence, Trust: Problems and Alternatives." In *Trust: Making and Breaking Cooperative Relations.* Edited by Diego Gambetta. New York: Blackwell, 1988.

Macé, Marielle. *Le Temps de l'Essai: Histoire d'un genre en France au XX siècle.* Paris Editions Belin, 2006.

Markus, Gyorgy. "Why Is There No Hermeneutics of the Natural Sciences?" *Science in Context* 1, no. 1 (March 1987).

Michaud, Yves. *L'Art à l'état gazeux. Essai sur le triomphe de l'esthétique.* Paris: Editions Stock, 2003.

Nietzsche, Friedrich. *On the Genealogy of Morals,* in *Basic Writings of Nietzsche.* Edited by Walter Kaufmann. New York: Random House, 1968.

———. "On the Uses and Disadvantages of History for Life." In

Untimely Meditations. Translated by R. J. Hollingdale. Cambridge: Cambridge University Press, 1983.

———. *Thus Spake Zarathustra*. Cambridge: Cambridge University Press, 2006.

Potte-Bonnevile, Mathieu. *Michel Foucault: l'inquiétude de l'histoire*. Paris: Presses Universitaire de France, 2004.

Rabinow, Paul. "Foucault's Untimely Struggle." *Theory, Culture and Society* 26, no.6 (2009).

———. *French DNA: Trouble in Purgatory*. Chicago: University of Chicago Press, 2002.

———. *French Modern: Norms and Forms of the Social Environment*. Chicago: University of Chicago Press, 1989.

———. *Making PCR: A Story of Biotechnology*. Chicago: University of Chicago Press, 1997.

———. *Reflections on Fieldwork in Morocco*. Berkeley and Los Angeles: University of California Press, 2007.

———. *Symbolic Domination: Cultural Form and Historical Change in Morocco*. Chicago: University of Chicago Press, 1974.

Rabinow, Paul, and Gaymon Bennett. *Designing for Human Practices: An Experiment with Synthetic Biology*. Chicago: University of Chicago Press, forthcoming.

Rabinow, Paul, and Talia Dan-Cohen. *A Machine to Make a Future: Biotech Chronicles*. Princeton, NJ: Princeton University Press, 2004.

Rabinow, Paul, George E. Marcus, James Faubion, and Tobias Rees. *Designs for an Anthropology of the Contemporary*. Durham, NC: Duke University Press, 2008.

Rabinow, Paul, and Nikolas Rose. "Biopower Today," *Biosocieties* 1, no. 2 (2006).

Richter, Gerhard. Letter to Jean-Christophe Ammann, February 1973. In *The Daily Practice of Painting*. Edited by Hans-Ulrich Obrist, translated by David Britt. London: Thames and Hudson, 1995.

Sebald, W. G. *On the Natural History of Destruction*. Translated by Anthea Bell. New York: Random House, 2003.

Shapin, Steven. *The Scientific Life: A Moral History of a Late Modern Vocation*. Chicago: University of Chicago Press, 1999.

———. *A Social History of Truth: Civility and Science in Seventeenth-Century England*. Chicago: University of Chicago Press, 1994.

Slyomovics, Susan. *The Performance of Human Rights in Morocco*. Bloomington: Indiana University Press, 2005.

Sontag, Susan. "Anthropologist as Hero." In *Against Interpretation and Other Essays*. New York: Picador, 1966.

Starobinski, Jean. *Le remède est dans le mal*. Paris: Gallimard, 1989.

Stocking, George "Anthropology as *Kulturkampf*: Science and Politics in the Career of Franz Boas." In *The Uses of Anthropology*. Edited by Walter Goldschmidt. Arlington, VA: American Anthropology Association, 1979.

———. *Race, Culture and Evolution*. New York: Free Press, 1968.

———. *The Shaping of American Anthropology 1883-1911: A Franz Boas Reader*. New York: Basic Books, 1974.

Szakolczai, Arpad. *Max Weber and Michel Foucault: Parallel Life-Works*. London: Routledge, 1998.

Weber, Max. "Objectivity in Social Science and Social Policy." In *The Methodology of the Social Sciences*. New York: Free Press, 1949.

———. "Science as a Vocation." In *From Max Weber: Essays in Sociology*. Edited by Hans Gerth and C. Wright Mills. New York: Oxford University Press, 1946.

Wingler, Hans. *The Bauhaus: Weimar, Dassau, Berlin, Chicago*. 2nd ed. Cambridge, MA: MIT Press, 1976.

Index of Subjects

Index of Names and Titles

Printed in Great Britain
by Amazon

43240085R00140